MW00438695

As I read Living with Integrity, I had these thoughts:

First, this is a legitimate call to men, specifically, to take up their God-given, distinct roles. Second, This is a handbook, a very practical companion and guide. You can engage it in small or large bites. Third, Living with Integrity affirms that we are designed for a beautiful, integrated life. Under the Lordship of Christ, every part of who we are and what we do can synchronize into a seamless whole.

I'm so glad my friend, Dennis Borg, has reflected on his experiences to write this volume. His life is indeed one of faithfulness, learning and investing in others. You will be blessed by the pages that follow.

John Beckett
Chairman, The Beckett Companies
Author of Loving Monday and Mastering Monday

Dennis shows us the postures and practices of living with integrity in our families, our workplaces, and our personal lives. Built on decades of conversation and coaching, this book is a gift to all who read it. Through stories, wisdom, and clear points of application, it will equip and inspire many to live with integrity!

Peter Greer
President and CEO of Hope International Author of Mission Drift, 40/40, and The Spiritual Danger of Doing Good.

Typically men in business like books that are practical; having material which can be put to work. This is what you get in Living with Integrity. Dennis addresses the whole of life, looking at integrity in its various parts: husband, father, sexuality, work, retirement and more. Like a master technician, he disassembles a man's life, so you can better see how the parts relate to the whole. After reading chapter 1, "The Heart of Integrity" one can read the remaining chapters in any order (another feature impatient professionals will like) and go immediately to the chapter that will be most helpful. And every chapter will put you on the hook by asking personal questions that tie instruction to application.

Most of all, I would recommend this book because the man who wrote it lives what he writes - a life of integrity! And just as important, this book grows out of years of spending time with business men: praying with them, counseling them, teaching them how work is ministry. You will find other books on the topic but none as integrated. Read it and re-read it, and I promise you will find an abundance of practical help."

Jeff Bowen
President of Incoming & Scanning
OPEX Corporation

If you're looking for a Biblically-inspired guide on how to live as a Christian man in a world full of demands on your time, energy and abilities, Living with Integrity is an accessible and insightful read. Dennis Borg's practical focus provides a wealth of insights on how you might better glorify the Lord with an integrated life, from the halls of power to your living room.

D. Michael Lindsay, PhD
President, Gordon College
Author of Faith in the Halls of Power and View from the Top

As a former NHL goaltender, folks often ask me how I could focus on the puck, given the mask's protective bars only centimeters from my eyes. The reality is that I became conditioned to not even noticing the bars. All I saw was what I needed to see: the play in front of me. In Dennis Borg's book, Living with Integrity: A handbook for Business and Professional Men, we learn how to see what we really need to see.

The best coaches I played for were very in tune with their players and able to motivate them to success. Borg, after years of working with men, is this kind of coach. Not only does he realize our weaknesses, but he is also gifted in motivating us to exceed mundane routine, to seek and gain heights only attained by trusting the Lord. For example, Living with Integrity goes beyond encouraging us toward better communication, by supplying the nuts and bolts of great communicating in the context of every relationship.

As men, we all have an enlarged head plastered to the walls of our imagination; an image of the man we would like to be. Borg points out the downfalls we all face; and then, gives the wherewithal to overcome, rather than simply struggle with them. He readies us to face all that competes with becoming men of character, men of integrity, men of God.

Bob Froese, PhD
Pastor and Counselor
Former Philadelphia Flyer Goaltender

LIVING
with
INTEGRITY

A Handbook for Business
and Professional Men

Dennis R. Borg

integbks

This book is dedicated to

CHARLOTTE

My Loving Wife

Best Friend

and

Constant Source
of
Encouragement

Wisdom
is knowing the right path to take...

Integrity
is taking it

(Source Unknown)

TABLE OF CONTENTS

Acknowledgments

Any book is rarely the product of just one person, including this one. While I am responsible for the contents and shortcomings of the book you hold in your hands, many others have helped to give it whatever strengths it possesses. Because my memory is not what it used to be, and being fearful of omitting someone, I will not mention individuals by name.

That said, I want to first thank the members of my Integrity Ministries board, both past and present, who encouraged me to write the book in the first place; and who have been both encouraging and patient during the years it has taken to get it on paper.

Then, I want to thank those who have read parts, or all of the manuscript (you know who you are). You have given me valuable feedback; which I feel has greatly improved the usefulness of the book.

I also want to thank the many business and professional men I have had the privilege of working with for the past 26 years as part of our ministry. Much of what I have learned about a business professional's world, has come from group discussions and private conversations with you. I hope the book accurately reflects the issues and challenges you face each day; and that you find it helpful in your Christian walk.

Last, but certainly not least, I want to thank Jesus Christ my Lord; without whom there would be no Integrity Ministries, or this book. During the early, crucial writing period, He would wake me up at 4:30 a.m. each day, without an alarm to disturb my wife, so that I could write while my mind was still fresh. This book is ultimately about Him, and for His glory.

Introduction

The book you hold in your hand is about Christian integrity, especially as it applies to the life of a business and professional man. In it, we will examine what that looks like, using the example of Jesus and the teaching of Scripture as our model. We will also address the challenge of how one can develop more integrity, and apply it to various areas of life in practical ways.

Why a book specifically for business and professional men? Because, if you are one of them, you have both influence and responsibility for the lives of others, to an extent the average working man does not. This adds up to more demands on your time and more stress in your life. On the other hand, your position also provides you with more opportunity to make a difference for Christ and his kingdom. And living with integrity is the key to making this happen.

I am aware that women who are in business and the professions have similar challenges, and there are parts of this book that could probably benefit them. But my gender, and lack of experience with the additional challenges they face, preclude me from being able to address their unique issues with any confidence. I'll leave that for some feminine author to address.

Integrity is a rather broad and vague term, so you'll need to know how it's being used in this book. The Latin root for integrity means "whole" or "complete." It carries the idea of something *undivided*, with various parts coming together to form a single unit, such as when electronics experts speak of integrated circuits. Integrity can also refer to the *soundness* of a constructed object able to withstand stress, like a bridge or a piece of furniture. Scientifically, when a hypothesis is being tested and is found to have *consistency* between what was anticipated and what actually takes place, the results are said to have integrity. Interestingly, the word is also used to describe ancient pieces of sculpture that have no hidden internal cracks or "filler" that would identify them as counterfeit, thus conveying the idea of *genuineness*.

While all of the above uses of integrity deal with physical phenomena, it's evident that they apply in the personal realm as well. Here, it also has various shades of meaning. When we describe a man as having integrity, we typically mean that he exhibits high moral character, an important trait we'll be addressing. But, in a broader sense, as used throughout this book, integrity envisions a man whose life is integrated, whole, someone who operates from a solid inner core—a man whose attitudes and behavior are consistent and predictable, regardless of the setting. We will attempt to present a profile of someone whose values and convictions are a reflection of his Christian character.

Looking at this specifically through the lens of Christian faith, a man of integrity is one whose motives and commitments flow out of his identity as a follower of Jesus Christ, one who is the same person whether you find him at home, in church, on the golf course, or working in his place of business. The Bible calls this "wholeheartedness," a single-minded quality that enables a man to resist temptations and pursue a godly lifestyle.

One man who exhibited a lifetime of integrity was Billy Graham. While dealing with fame and finances and travel away from home, his reputation was unscathed. Whether in the company of heads of state or TV talk show hosts, he was always single-minded in his mission to share and live the gospel. It's little wonder that he was one of the most highly respected men of his day.

Most of us men have a tendency to divide our activities into compartments. Then, we live in one compartment at a time, taking on the persona that fits whatever we're doing, and whoever we're with. In our managerial or professional role, we're doing business as usual. When at home, we put on our husband and father hats. At church, we make sure our language and attitudes appear holy. And while coaching our kid's sports team, we may forget that we're *not* Vince Lombardi or Joe Torre. At times, one persona carries over into another area, which can create problems: like when we bark orders at our children as if they were employees, or become hard-nosed, no-holds-barred members of our church board.

Generally speaking, we are mostly comfortable with our various compartments, responding to the different demands of each, because it's easier that way. Let's face it—integrating the various parts of our life into a consistent whole is difficult. It takes insight, honesty, self-awareness, and, most of all, the willingness to undergo sometimes painful change. And yet, to live without that kind of integrity or wholeheartedness is to feel the constant pull of conflicting values, goals, motives, and desires. This instability is what the Bible calls being "double-minded," and leads to lives of pretending to be what we are not, especially in Christian circles.

For example, do you talk about sexual purity at church or with your family, but find yourself looking at pornography in your office or on the road? Or do you tell people that God is first in your life, yet find it easy to skip worship to play a round of golf? Do you claim that your family is a priority, but miss an important family gathering in order to nail down a contract or serve a client? This kind of duplicity tends to leave us feeling guilty, because we know in our heart of hearts that we're really not what we pretend to be.

This book has its origins in the relationships I've had with business and professional men over the past twenty-six years. During that time, I have sought to understand their lives and unique struggles, while attempting to help them find real Christian integrity in both the broad and narrow senses of that term. In his book, *If You Know Who You Are, You Will Know What to Do*, Ronald Greer makes this helpful distinction between the two: The broad sense he calls "personal integrity," living a life of wholeness and congruence. The narrow sense he refers to as "moral integrity," doing what's right because it's the right thing to do. Thus, integrity involves both character and the virtues that flow out of that character. That's what this book is about.

As a fellow struggler, who has spent a lifetime trying to integrate my own personal, professional, and spiritual lives, I feel like a partially blind guide trying to lead others. If I have gained any insight in this area at all, it has come from more sources than I can begin to name, but first and foremost from the Scriptures. A couple of key passages that come to mind in this regard are as follows:

> "The integrity of the upright guides them, but the unfaithful are destroyed by their duplicity." (Proverbs 11:3)

> "He whose walk is blameless and who does what is righteous, who speaks the truth from his heart . . . who does his neighbor no wrong . . . who keeps his oath even when it hurts . . . He who does these things will never be shaken." (Psalm 15)

My goal and prayer, for both myself and the men I have been privileged to work with, is that we become as consistently Christian in every area of our lives as we can be. And this is also my goal and prayer for you, as you use this book.

As you can see, it is written in the form of a handbook. Each chapter deals with a different area of life and is broken up into subtopics. You can turn to any chapter and hopefully find help there, depending on your interests or concerns. If you choose this approach, I would recommend that you read chapter one, "The Heart of Integrity," before exploring other topics, as it is foundational for all that follows. On the other hand, if you are a read-it-straight-through kind of guy, I trust the book itself has enough internal integrity to keep you interested and moving to the end.

We have also placed questions at various points within each chapter to use as a means of reflecting on what you have just read, or for discussion purposes with other men. Our hope is that the book can also be a resource for a group study.

The ideas throughout are based on my understanding of what the Scriptures teach, and I will note references to encourage you to further explore them for yourself. Unless otherwise indicated, all Biblical quotes are from the New International Version. (The italics used to emphasize a word or phrase are mine.) I will also recommend other books after each chapter, for those of you who want to read more on a particular subject.

If you are *not* a Christian and have picked up this book, either out of curiosity or because you are spiritually searching, my hope is that you will come away with a better understanding of what practical Christianity looks like and, further, that you might give serious consideration to becoming a follower of Jesus yourself. I guarantee it's a decision you'll never regret.

"A leader with integrity has one self, at home and at work, with family and with colleagues. He or she has a unifying set of values that guide choices of action regardless of the situation."

—James Kouzes and Barry Posner

Chapter One: The Heart of Integrity

He was unusual. One could even call him unique. And because he was different, he was often misunderstood, even by those closest to him. He had a way of speaking that amazed some people and infuriated others. But when he spoke, people listened. And where he went, people followed. Love him or hate him, they couldn't leave him alone.

He had an uncanny ability with people of all ages; children were especially attracted to him, and he to them. Social status was no barrier either. Rich or poor, educated or not, powerful or socially outcast, it made no difference. He was comfortable with everyone, and most were comfortable with him.

A kind and gracious man, he was also highly principled and truthful to a fault—qualities that earned him both friends and enemies. He was what the world would call, "his own man," unconcerned about what others thought of *him*, far more interested in what he thought of *them*.

Very focused, he always knew where he was going, what he was doing, and why. Never deviating from his goals, he was undistracted from his mission in life. And he did unusual things, things that left those who witnessed them stunned . . . sometimes even afraid.

His moral integrity was impeccable. No scandal was ever attached to his name, no indiscretion whispered about him. When his enemies set out to discredit and destroy him, they could only do so with lies.

And he was extremely comfortable with who he was. He never second-guessed himself. He possessed this inner compass that gave him a sense of direction in any situation he faced. It is safe to say that he was the most perfectly integrated man who ever walked the earth. His name was Jesus. There has never been anyone like him, nor will there ever be. And, for us Christian men, he is our model of integrity.

Christ at the Center

If Jesus is our model, then he needs to be at the center of our thinking and living. And yet, as business and professional men, we are easily distracted by the many demands on our attention: wives and children, home and car maintenance, various commitments at church and in the community. Then, of course, there's work, work, and more work. And when we're not at work, we are often talking to people at work, or thinking about and planning our work. So how are we supposed to keep Christ at the center of our lives and thoughts? It isn't easy. In fact, given our naturally sinful nature, it's impossible . . . without divine help. And thank God, he provides that for us.

One of the most encouraging Biblical verses in this regard is 2 Peter 1:3, which reads, "His divine power has given us *everything we need* for life and godliness through our knowledge of him who called us by his own glory and goodness." Everything we need—wow! And this from the pen of Peter, who had his own struggles understanding and following Jesus. Notice that this power comes "through our knowledge of him who called us." In other words, *knowing* Jesus is the key to *living* like Jesus.

The old saying, "You are known by the company you keep," is true. And we are also *influenced* by the company we keep, which is why parents try to monitor who their children hang around with. Our regular companions do rub off on us—look at any couple who've been married for a while. This is true spiritually as well. The primary way we grow to be *like* Jesus is by spending quality time *with* Jesus, the one we are trying to emulate. There's just no substitute for this.

Quiet Times for Busy Lives

When Jesus lived among us, he needed time to be alone with his heavenly Father and would often go off by himself to seek his presence. (Mark 1:35-39, 6:46) I am sure that this was one of the keys to his ability to live an impeccable life. So, if the Son of God needed these meetings with the Father, how much more do we?

Looking at our busy schedules, our first impulse is to say, "I don't have time for anything else." Yet, we tend to *make* time for the things we really *want* to do, don't we? If someone offers us tickets to a ball game or invites us to see the newest guy flick, somehow, we find time to go. Most of us probably spend too many hours surfing the web or "vegging out" in front of the TV, to use the "no time" excuse. After a long day at work, that's how we unwind. Doing any serious reading just seems like too much effort, and praying feels like fighting a losing battle with mental distractions. But, here's the rub: *there is no other way to grow spiritually.* With that in mind, here are some practical tips you may find helpful:

1. Change your sleep pattern. Most people find that morning is the best time to meet with the Lord. "But," you say, "I'm not a morning person." I wasn't either, but I learned that I could change. And I'm glad that I did. Getting up thirty minutes or an hour earlier requires going to bed sooner. The question is, what do you do with that last hour or so before you hit the sack? Is it more important than spending time with the Lord in the morning? That was the question I had to answer. "My body clock won't let me get to sleep earlier," you may protest. It will, if you set your alarm to get up earlier for a few days. The early morning hours are great for uninterrupted quiet time, undistracted by other commitments. I now look forward to them. Suggestion: Grab a cup of coffee before you grab your Bible.

2. Listen rather than read. Maybe you are an auditory learner—you remember more of what you hear than what you read. If so, you're in good company. The earliest Christians didn't own copies of the Bible. It was primarily an oral society, so they had parts of it read *to* them at their church gatherings. They *heard* it rather than *read* it. And that's a whole different experience, even for us visual learners. Several versions of the Bible are available in various electronic formats, and my favorites are those done by Max McLean, a professional actor and Biblically trained Christian. Rather than simply reading Scripture, Max stresses the words and phrases that should be emphasized, based on his serious study of the text. If you have a commute to work of any length, these would make for inspiring listening in your car, instead of the news or radio—a good way to begin your day.

3. Multi-task. Praying while you drive is another good use of time (Depending on where you drive, you may be doing this already, just to survive!). For several years, my job was a hundred miles from home, and I had a two-hour commute each way a couple of days a week. I found during that period that talking to God in the privacy of my car was a great use of time. I still do it every morning on my way to work, or going to an appointment, even though the drive is much shorter.

You can also listen to sermons or sing along with worship music as you drive. It really keeps you focused on the Lord.

Another way to multi-task is to combine prayer with exercise. This is helpful if you have trouble staying awake while praying (it happens to me). Some of my best conversations with God take place when I'm out power-walking. Surrounded by his handiwork also makes me feel closer to my Creator. A friend of mine, a seminary president, had a prayer list of students and faculty attached to the handlebars of his stationary bike. Every morning, he would pray while he pedaled. He's now with the Lord and can have those conversations face to face (without the bike).

4. Deal with distractions. Even first thing in the morning, you may find your mind distracted by all you have to do that day. This is normal, especially for business managers and professionals. There are two ways to deal with distractions. First, keep a pad nearby and write them down. Often, they keep intruding into our consciousness because we're afraid we'll forget something important. Putting it on paper can set your mind at ease. You might even do this the night before. Secondly, you may be anxious or stressed about a deadline or meeting on your agenda that day. Rather than fight those thoughts and feelings as distractions, make them the subject of your prayers. God is interested in the details of your life. What concerns you, concerns him, so talk to him about it (Phil. 4:6-7, 1 Peter 5:6-7) .

5. Ask the Lord to help you. He is more interested in meeting with you than you are in meeting with him. If you sincerely want to grow in your relationship with Christ, ask for his help. As a Christian man, you have the Holy Spirit in you, (Rom. 8:9-16) and two areas where the Spirit assists us is when we pray, (Rom. 8:26-27) and when we try to understand the Scripture. (John 16:13) After all, who better to help you understand the Bible than the one who inspired its writing? Who better to help you to talk to God than the Spirit of God himself? If you were to say to your wife, "Honey, I really want to spend more time with you; can you help me do that?" What do you think *her* response would be? The Lord loves you and wants to spend time with you, even more than she does. You can count on him to help.

6. Be real when you pray. One of the things I struggle with is keeping it real in my quiet time with God. Too often, when I pray, I find myself falling into a pattern: expressing the same things in the same way, hardly thinking about what I'm saying and fighting to keep my mind from wandering. This is true especially when praying for the same people or concerns day after day. If I talked this way to other people, it would sound like a recording. Of course, if I'm upset or really concerned about something, then my prayers become more heartfelt and real. Maybe you sometimes struggle with this as well.

To overcome praying by rote, it's good to ask ourselves, "What do I really want to say to God?" "What really concerns me today?" "If he were sitting right next to me, what would I talk to him about?" Throughout the day, when something comes into your mind that worries you, share it with him. If you are wrestling with a crucial decision, or going into an important meeting, or about to engage in a touchy conversation, ask for his guidance and help. When something good happens, take a minute to thank him. And when something bad happens, let him bear that burden with you. When you do or say something that is offensive to him (the Bible calls this sin), be quick to acknowledge it and ask for forgiveness. In other words, we need to treat God like our constant companion, because he *is*, even when we're not aware of it. (Psalm 139)

Jesus' Model Prayer

In more protracted prayer times, like in the morning, many people find that using the Lord's Prayer (Matt. 6:9-13) as an outline is helpful. After all, Jesus gave it to his followers as a model of how we should pray. He begins the prayer by addressing God as "Father in heaven"—very personal and intimate. We are encouraged to approach God the same way, as a perfect, loving parent. Then Jesus focuses on God's agenda: honoring his name, expanding his kingdom, doing his will. Our prayers typically focus more on *our* agenda, and we may never get around to what *he wants* us to do. Next, Jesus addresses our physical needs in one short sentence, something we tend to spend most of our prayers on. Finally, with much greater emphasis, he deals with our spiritual needs: forgiveness from God, forgiving others and handling temptation. We probably all could use more emphasis in our prayers on the spiritual side of our lives. Jesus' model would be a helpful one for you, either in the morning or at night.

When I look at the part of his prayer dealing with spiritual needs, two things in particular impress me. One is that we often don't address our sins quickly enough or specifically enough (at least, I don't). We're embarrassed to bring them up with God, like he doesn't know already! Or we get caught up in other things, and they get shoved to the back of our minds. But, like we do with offenses on the human level, if they aren't acknowledged, they create distance between us and our heavenly Father.

The second thing that strikes me is the idea of praying about our temptations. Confessing to God *after* we sin is essential, but *avoiding* the sin altogether is even better! Jesus is encouraging us to anticipate those situations where we are weak and vulnerable, and to seek God's help in addressing them, *before* they arise. If we do this, we'll be more alert spiritually, both before and during times of temptation, and we won't end up failing and having to confess later.

Notice also in the introductory verses to this model prayer that Jesus encourages us to keep our prayers short, to the point and oblivious to those who may happen to overhear us pray. (Matt. 6:5-8) Our prayers should be addressed to God alone, not for human consumption. Lengthy prayers don't impress him, and eloquent prayers tend to be motivated by a desire to impress others.

Here's a pattern you might want to consider for your prayer life: In the morning, start your day praising God for who he is, and thanking him for the night's rest and a new day to serve him. Then go over your schedule for the day with him, asking for his guidance and help. Pray the same for your family and friends. Throughout the day, say grace at your meals and pray short prayers for situations that arise, or for people that the Holy Spirit may bring to your mind. At night, before you turn in, spend a little time reviewing your day with God: thanking him for his provision and care, and confessing those thoughts, words and actions that were not pleasing to him. This way you can go to bed with a clear conscience and a pure heart. You'll probably even sleep better!

Questions for Personal Reflection or Group Discussion

1. What is the biggest struggle or obstacle you face when it comes to having a regular quiet time with the Lord?

2. Do any of the suggestions outlined above seem doable to you? Which ones?

3. What could you do tomorrow to begin changing your normal pattern in order to have that time?

Using the Bible as God Intended

One can't read the Bible without understanding that it is all about Jesus. The Old Testament looks forward to his coming and work of redemption. The gospels tell us what he taught, as well as how he lived, worked, died, and rose again. The Book of Acts records how the good news about him spread under the power of his Spirit. The Epistles are focused on understanding his ongoing work through the Spirit, and how we should act in response to him. The Book of Revelation looks forward to his return and future triumph over this world.

Like Jesus himself, the Bible is unique, unlike any other book you'll ever read. It is a book of books, written over several centuries by numerous authors in a variety of styles and three languages, yet it presents a single message of God's dealings with the human race. But it is more than a source of information, even important spiritual information. And it is more than simply inspirational. It is *inspired* by God himself. I have read many books in my lifetime, a few of them more than once. The Bible is the only book I read every day and have seriously studied for decades, yet I feel like I have barely scratched the surface of its depth. Paul wrote to Timothy, "All Scripture is God-breathed and is useful for teaching, rebuking, correcting, and training in righteousness so that the man of God may be thoroughly equipped for every good work." (2 Tim. 3:16) To paraphrase Paul's words, the Bible teaches us what we need to know about God and corrects our misunderstandings. And it trains us to live the way God wants us to live, while letting us know when we are out of line.

M. Robert Mulholland in his book, *Shaped by the Word*, points out that, because the Bible is unique, our approach to it needs to be different than other reading material we might encounter. When we pick up any other book, we control the outcome. We can choose to read it or not, read parts of it and ignore the rest, or agree with the ideas presented or reject them. But with the Bible, the situation is reversed. *It* has the authority. As God's inspired word, we can't afford to ignore it, pick and choose the parts we like, or disagree with its contents. It is *eternal* truth, applied to our hearts and lives by the Holy Spirit who inspired it. And it shapes us into the men God wants us to be . . . if we'll let him.

Scripture and Prayer Go Together

When you go to read your Bible, begin with prayer, asking God to show you what he would have you learn, asking him to help you be sensitive to what he may be saying directly to you. Don't be overly influenced by chapter and verse divisions when you read; they were added later for reference purposes, and sometimes interrupt the flow of thought. And in your quiet time, you don't need to read a whole chapter or chapters. Programs for reading through the Bible in a year are okay for getting an overview, but not real helpful for feeding the soul. Instead, read slowly and reflectively (even out loud, if you have trouble concentrating). Reread the same passage several times, noticing repeated words and key ideas. Pray over the passage, asking God what he would have you take from it: a new insight, a command to obey, a sin or habit to get rid of, a character trait to develop, an action to take, etc.

I personally like to begin my quiet time with one of the Psalms. It helps me to focus my thoughts on God. Since they speak *about* God or are directly addressed *to* God, they're good springboards for relating to him as I start my day. And when they capture my own feelings as I read, they become my personal prayers, expressed in better words than I could ever conjure up.

Don't Neglect the Old Testament

Another area of the Scripture I have come to appreciate is the wisdom literature of the Old Testament. The Book of Ecclesiastes wrestles with the basic issues of life (work, wealth, knowledge, family, death, etc.) and its ultimate meaning. The Proverbs are full of practical observations and principles for everyday living. Many Christians read them every day and find them to be an extremely helpful guide, especially for dealing with business matters. The Song of Songs deals with marital love, including its physical aspects in bold and unusual metaphors. And the book of Job, while lengthy and somewhat repetitious, gives us a perspective on human suffering that you won't find anywhere else.

Other parts of the Old Testament are valuable as well. Seeing God as the creator of all that exists reminds me that I am not God, only a creature made in his image. Reading how men in ancient times came to know God and how he worked in their lives (especially with leaders), gives me insight into what he expects from me. Observing how he dealt with Israel as a people in relation to the other nations around them provides me with a perspective on history, and how he may be working in our world today. The prophetic books at the end of the Old Testament show how Israel failed miserably to live up to her special relationship with God, and they force me look at myself, making sure I'm not guilty of the same kind of failure.

The New Testament: Jesus' Story

It's the New Testament that I try to focus on most. Reading something from the gospels every day keeps the life of Jesus before me. Seeing how he responded to various situations and people; being inspired by his character, commitment and compassion; listening to his amazing teaching and realizing that his life is the model for mine, both humbles and motivates me to become more like him. And daily meditation on the Letters of the Apostles gives me specific principles and directions for my daily walk with Christ. You can develop your own pattern of reading, but *do read*, reflect and put the Scriptures into practice. "Be doers of the Word, not hearers only." (Jas. 1:22) There's just no substitute for this, if you are serious about being a follower of Jesus.

Another good practice when it comes to the Scriptures is to memorize. It's clear from the gospel record that Jesus did. He quoted from the Old Testament in many situations: while being tempted by Satan, while teaching, in private conversations, and even while dying on the cross. If the Son of God needed to have the Scriptures "hidden in his heart," (Ps. 119:11) who are we to think that it isn't necessary for us? I realize that, as adults, it isn't as easy to memorize as when we were younger, but it still can be done. It's just a matter of repetition. Most of us know the Lord's Prayer by memory simply because we have recited it so often.

When you come across a verse (or verses) that especially speak to you, write it on a 3 x 5 card and carry it around with you. Then, while you're shaving in the morning, or waiting at a stop light, or anytime you have a free minute or two, practice it until you can say it in your sleep. Practice where in the Bible it's found also, and review from time to time those passages you have already committed to memory. A couple of my friends decided to team up and memorize together. Every week, they would get together and listen to how well the other had done on the assigned verse. It had to be word-perfect, or a contribution was made to their lunch kitty. They would also challenge each other on any verse that had been memorized previously. This was "iron sharping iron," (Pr.27:17) and the friendly competition kept both of them on track. Maybe finding a memorization partner would work for you as well, even if it's one of your kids.

Other Helpful Practices

Besides daily prayer and Bible meditation, there are other spiritual disciplines (not done every day), which many have found helpful in their walk with the Lord. One of these is fasting: going without food for a set amount of time. A typical fast would be twenty-four hours (missing two consecutive meals) or thirty-six hours, which would involve skipping all three meals on the same day. Interestingly, Jesus assumed his disciples *would* fast, just not while he was with them. (Matt. 6:16-18, Luke 5:33-34) Some people I know do this one day a week, as part of their ongoing relationship with God. Others only fast on certain occasions, and some for much longer periods.

Fasting has a number of spiritual benefits. For one, it clears the system of foods that tend to dull our thinking (like carbs), helping us to concentrate as we read the Bible. Combined with prayer (the usual pattern we find in Scripture), it often increases our sensitivity to the presence and voice of God. Fasting also breaks our American obsession with food and tends to carry over into other areas of our lives that call for discipline. You may want to try fasting, especially when you desire to get closer to God or are struggling with a major problem or decision.

A couple of other disciplines I have found helpful, although I don't practice them often enough, are solitude and silence. We live in a hectic, noisy world—itself a major distraction. Getting away to a quiet place and waiting in God's presence can be truly refreshing from a spiritual perspective. I find it is easier to do this on vacation, when I'm free from the demands of my work and busy schedule. But there have also been times, especially when wrestling with a major life decision, that getting away by myself with God for a couple of days has helped me gain clarity. As we saw earlier, Jesus did this on more than one occasion, and encouraged his disciples to do the same. (Mark 6:30-32, 45-46) If you would like to know more about spiritual disciplines, pick up one of the books recommended in the suggested reading at the end of this chapter.

All of the practices we have discussed have but one goal in mind: to assist us in developing a deeper relationship with Christ, so that God, by his spirit, can make us more and more like Jesus in our daily activities and relationships. There is no merit system here. We don't get points for doing these things, any more than we get credit for spending time with our wives or kids. But if you want your relationship with him to grow (like any other relationship), there is no substitute for investing the time and effort to help make it happen. If you do, he'll meet you more than halfway.

Questions for Personal Reflection or Group Discussion

1. What is your normal pattern of Bible reading/study?

2. Which of the suggestions made above do you think might help you improve in this area?

3. Do you memorize Scripture? If not, find an accountability partner to help you get started (probably not your wife).

4. Have you ever tried fasting, solitude, and silence or any other spiritual discipline? What was your experience? If it wasn't positive, use one of the resources listed below, but don't give up.

You Can't Do It Alone

Another area that is essential for our spiritual growth is fellowship. We need other Christians, especially men, to encourage us and keep us accountable and sharp in our life with Christ. "Lone Ranger" Christianity is contrary to the teaching of Scripture. Yet, I have noticed that business and professional men often do not take the time to develop real Christian friendships. I understand that our vocations are demanding, and the stresses are often great. And, at the end of the day, we just want to retreat to our families, feeling guilty for not spending enough time with them as it is.

As a result, our relationships with other men often boil down to the guys we rub elbows with at work and maybe some of the men at church, typically on a rather casual basis. Then there are also the buddies we play golf or go fishing with on occasion. But having in-depth relationships tend to be rare. And yet, they are so important for our spiritual growth.

Two things I have found helpful in this regard. One is belonging to a small men's group. Even Jesus had the twelve. Many churches have such groups, and we have purposely made them the heart of Integrity Ministries, the organization I lead. When you get together with a group of six to twelve guys for a time of Bible study, prayer, and fellowship, a lot of positive things happen. The spirit of Christ in each of you helps you gain insight from one another on how to understand and apply the Scriptures to life. And there's support and encouragement from having others pray with you, and for you, over the struggles and problems you may be facing.

You also develop a sense of camaraderie and caring while discovering common interests that form the heart of real friendship. In a group of men, you can talk about things you wouldn't discuss if there were women present. I have found that meeting early in the morning, before work, is the best arrangement for most men, although other times may work best for you.

In addition to a small group, I would encourage you to find two or three other men you would like to go deeper with, men with whom you can share with on a more personal level than is possible in a larger group. They should be men who will hold your feet to the fire in areas of your life where you need extra motivation and support. These are "peer-mentoring" or accountability groups. Once you have prayerfully found the right guys, you'll need to be very *intentional* about meeting together. With your busy schedules, it will be easier to *talk about* getting together than actually *doing* it. My own group meets every other week over lunch, usually on the same day and at the same restaurant, to keep it simple and easy to remember.

Questions for Personal Reflection or Group Discussion

1. How many close relationships with men do you have in your life?

2. Do you belong to a small group for Bible study/prayer or accountability?

3. If you already do, what can your group do to make it more spiritually beneficial for each member?

4. If you don't have such a group, find one other guy to talk to, and pray together about starting one. If it's for accountability, make sure they are men with whom you would feel comfortable sharing your personal life. Confidentiality is absolutely essential.

Worship

Of course, weekly corporate worship is a given. There is nothing quite like the experience of being with our fellow believers, praising God, praying together, hearing God's word read and taught, giving back to him through our offering and taking communion. Worship is the one activity we will continue to do in heaven, so it should be our first priority while we're still here on earth. Yet, how often do we treat it casually, something that can easily be skipped in order to attend a pro football game or to take our kids to play soccer? We figure we can always go to church *next* Sunday. Maybe part of the problem is our use of the phrase "going to church." It makes it sound like just another meeting. Perhaps if we said "going to worship God" instead, it would impress on our minds its importance, and help us give it the priority it deserves.

Worship is more than just sitting with a congregation on Sunday morning. One can go through the motions of worship without really engaging. Worship is giving God the honor and glory that are his due. It requires focus and a right attitude. We need to approach God with a sense of humility and awe, gratitude and praise. (Heb. 12:28-29) It's all about *him*, not what *we* may or may not experience in the process. And this requires preparation on our part. I've found that I am easily distracted in worship by the people around me, by the activity up front and by my own wandering thoughts. And I remind myself that Satan will also try to distract me. He hates it when we worship God. So, I try to prepare for worship by getting to bed at a decent time on Saturday night, and also by getting up early enough to spend time in prayer and devotional reading before church, in order to get my mind and heart ready.

But worship isn't confined to church on Sunday. We can worship any time, any place. Driving in your car can be a worship experience listening to or (better) singing along with praise music, or simply praising and thanking God in prayer for his goodness to you. It can also be incorporated into your daily quiet time, as you praise God for who he is and thank him for all he has done and is doing, before bringing him your needs for the day. Using a hymnal or praise music book or your favorite electronic medium is also useful for this purpose. How or wherever you do it, be a man who worships God "in spirit and in truth," for, as Jesus reminds us, "they are the kind of worshippers the Father seeks." (John 4:23)

Questions for Personal Reflection or Group Discussion

1. How would you evaluate the quality of your worship? In church? Alone?

2. What obstacles interfere with meaningful worship for you?

3. Do you think that physical and mental preparation would help? What changes would you need to make to your normal Sunday or daily routines?

Service

An important part of a Christ-centered life is service. Nothing gets us out of our self-centered tendencies quicker than having to think about the needs of others, rather than just our own. This is so essential that Jesus emphasized it over and over with his disciples. (Mark 9:33-37; 10:35-45, Luke 22:24-27) But, in the end, Jesus had to model this for the twelve before they really got the message. As seen in the foot-washing incident recorded in John 13:1-17.

One of the things that strikes me about this account is the way John introduced it to his readers. He says, "Jesus knew that the Father had put all things under his power, and that he had come from God and was returning to God," and then he goes on to describe Jesus washing their feet. It seems clear John is telling us that, in spite of Jesus' overwhelming authority, he wasn't afraid to lower himself to a servant's status in order to teach an important lesson. With this example, his disciples finally got the message.

But I believe there's more here. I think it wasn't just *in spite of* his authority that Jesus was willing to do this, but also *because of* his authority. Jesus knew who he was or, more importantly, *whose* he was. He belonged to the Father. His life was oriented around pleasing the Father, *always* doing the Father's will. (John 6:38) He was secure in his Father's love. He knew his own authority and power, and had demonstrated it time and again. He didn't need to prove anything to anyone. So when it came to doing a menial task like foot-washing—no problem. He wasn't worried about preserving his dignity or ruining his reputation (like his disciples evidently were); he just served.

During a controversy over greatness in the kingdom, he had earlier told the twelve, "Even the son of man did not come to *be* served, but *to serve*, and to give his life as a ransom for many." (Mark 10:45) If he was willing to serve by laying down his life in a most painful, humiliating way, then washing their feet was not that big of a deal for him. And it shouldn't be for us either. No act of service should ever be beneath us if we are going to follow Christ and his stunning example. Using our God-given gifts for others is an important part of what the Christian life is all about.

Questions for Personal Reflection or Group Discussion

1. In what kind of service are you presently involved?

2. Is it inside the church, out in the community, or both?

3. Are there needs in either place for which you have a burden?

4. How has God gifted you to be able to respond to one of those needs?

5. Are there ministries or organizations addressing those needs with which you could get involved?

Don't be afraid to get in over your head. God often uses our inadequacies to stretch our faith. Give that some thought and prayer.

Who's in Charge?

All of the things discussed above have one overriding purpose: to deepen your relationship with the Lord and help you learn how to trust him in every area of your life. As stated earlier, all relationships are built on trust, and this includes our relationship with Jesus. The Christian life is a walk of faith. We come to know Christ by believing that he died for our sins, by trusting that his death alone is sufficient payment in the eyes of God, and by yielding to him as Lord and master in our lives. (1 Cor. 15:3, Eph. 2:8-9, Rom. 10:9-10, 12:1-2) We walk with Christ daily by trusting him to help us love people we don't even like, to provide insight into situations we don't understand, to give us words beyond our own, to enable us to engage in activities we would normally avoid, and to resist temptations we normally couldn't. This is our real purpose for living. And in the process of living this way, we'll learn why we were created in the first place.

God is looking for willing partners to help advance his kingdom here on earth, and he wants to use us for his glory. But he *can't* do this if he isn't in charge, and he *won't* do it without our consent. Plus, we can't accomplish anything significant for him *without having* him in charge, leading, and empowering us by his Spirit. (John 15:5) I know this isn't easy. As managers and professionals, we have a tendency to be self-sufficient and to resist giving up control. We like to be the one calling the shots. But with God, there is no other way. Jesus is Lord (i.e., master), and he wants to live out his life in this present world through you and me.

So, what it really comes down to is *surrender*. Will we acknowlededge Jesus' right to rule in our lives? He is both our creator and redeemer. (Col. 1:16, 1 Pet. 1:18-19) He gave everything for us. (Phil. 2:5-11) As a fair exchange, he expects us to give everything to him. (Rom. 12:1-2, 2 Cor. 5:14-15) He gave himself because he loved us, like no one else has ever loved us. And only a deep understanding of his love can motivate us to yield ourselvesto him completely. (Eph. 3:16-19) He could demand it from us, but love doesn't make demands. Rebels at heart, our stubborn, sinful natures tend to resist obedience. But love motivates like nothing else. Do we understand how much Jesus loves us? And do we grasp that even our surrender is ultimately for *our good*, as well as for *his glory*?

The Heart of the Matter

This brings us to the heart of the matter, which is a matter of the heart. More than anything else, God is interested in the focus of our hearts. Biblically, the heart is the center of spiritual life, the seat of our emotions, our desires, our priorities, our motives, and our will. Scripture often refers to the heart in discussing our relationship to God and to others. Faith itself must come from the heart. (Rom. 10:9-10) God examines and tests our hearts, (Ps. 139:1, Heb. 4:12) and is looking for hearts that are pure, sincere, and obedient. (Matt. 5:8, Heb. 10:22, Rom 1:9) He encourages us to have hearts that are tender and whole. (Ezek. 11:19, Ps. 51:17 & 86:11) Thus, we are urged to seek and love God with *all* our hearts, (Jer. 29:13, Matt. 22:37) and to give him heartfelt service. (1 Chr. 28:9, Eph. 6:6-7) It's not surprising then, that Solomon urges us, "Guard your heart," (Pr. 4:23) because "a man's heart reflects the man." (Pr. 27:19)

Bottom Line

The bottom line simply is this. Where is your heart? What motivates you? What's the most important thing in your life—your family, your career, your business, your possessions, your leisure activities, or the Lord? Until you have settled that issue, living with genuine Christian integrity is impossible. For when push comes to shove, we'll always fall back to where our heart is. As Jesus said, "Where your treasure is" (what you value most), "there your heart will be also." (Matt. 6:21)

Additional Resourses:

Charlie Dawes, *Simple Prayer: Learning to Speak to God with Ease.* InterVarsity Press, 2017.

Richard J. Foster, *The Celebration of Discipline.* HarperCollins, 2018

John Ortberg, *The Life You Always Wanted: Spiritual Disciplines for Ordinary People.* Zondervan, 2002.

Gordon T. Smith, *Essential Spirituality: Renewing your Christian faith through classic spiritual disciplines.* Thomas Nelson, 1994.

Donald S. Whitney, *Simplify Your Spiritual Life.* NavPress, 2003.

"Unless our love and care for our family is a high priority, we may find that we may gain the whole world and lose our own children."

—*Michael Green*

Chapter Two: Leading with Integrity at Home

The Bible clearly places responsibility for leadership in the home *primarily* on men. In fact, one of the requirements for leadership in the church is that a man is able to *manage* his own family well. (1 Tim.3:4 & 12) The underlying Greek word used here is translated in other places as "to direct," (1 Tim. 5;17) "to devote oneself to," (Tit. 3:8 & 14) and "to provide leadership or oversight to." (Rom. 12:8, 1 Thess. 5:12) Yet, it's interesting how many business and professional men drop the ball when it comes to leading at home. The demands of leadership and decision-making at work leave them tired at the end of the day, and happy to let their wives run things in the family. This is understandable to a degree. Wives and mothers (especially stay-at-home moms) tend to be more tuned in to what's going on in the family, and typically are very capable of running a household. But this doesn't excuse a lack of involvement and initiative on our part as men.

Taking Business Home

One of the things I have noticed is that men in positions of responsibility have a tendency to leave their work at the office (unless they are workaholics). And it's natural to want to escape the stresses of our jobs and retreat into the safe haven of home at night. The irony is, in the process, we ignore our God-given gifts of family leadership. And we also leave valuable management practices at the office, which could benefit our families at home. In this chapter, I would like to discuss some of these work skills, and how they might apply in your family. In next chapters, we will get into the specific roles of husband and father.

Getting Perspective

A problem many families face is one of being over-scheduled, over-stressed, and under-organized. We often lack both quality time together and a clear plan as to how to fix it. What these families need is leadership, using the experience, skills, and techniques we learned in the workplace. Complicating this are three factors:

1. We often feel more competent at work than at home. Maybe it's because we didn't have fathers who were good role models for us to follow. Or perhaps we're convinced that women are just innately better at parenting than we are. This isn't true. By nature, they may generally be more nurturing, especially when children are young. But recent studies have shown the important place fathers have in a child's life, and the devastating results when fathering is missing. It always amazes me how long it takes for modern researchers to catch up with what the Bible says, and what common sense has taught us for centuries.

2. Our culture encourages men to focus on work rather than home. For one thing, we get our identity and self-worth primarily from our career. For another, our primary role in the family is often seen as mostly being a financial provider. Our society is slowly changing in this area, as more women are combining careers with motherhood and fathers are taking a more active role at home. Some families are even experimenting with women as the providers and dads staying home. In most of these cases, it's because the wife is able to earn more, or because the husband is more interested in being a parent. But, as a family counselor, I have never seen this arrangement work out well in practice.

3. As men, we typically need some challenge and adventure in our lives, and most of the time we get this from our professions. If not, we try to manufacture it through sports, hobbies, or service projects on the weekends, or we experience it vicariously via TV, movies, or books that stir our sense of masculinity.

But what if we looked at our leadership role in the family as more than simply a duty? What if we saw it as a privilege, an adventure, and the biggest challenge of our lives? What if we realized that having a good marriage and raising responsible, God-fearing children would bring us the greatest satisfaction and rewards in the long run? Always keep in mind that you are dispensable at work. If you died tomorrow, it wouldn't take long for someone to step in and take your job, but your family could never really replace you and what you bring to their lives.

Questions for Personal Reflection or Group Discussion

1. How much responsibility for your home life falls on your wife, and how much on you? Give a percentage and think about (or discuss) why that is true.

2. Does the idea of using management principles at home strike a negative vibe with you? If so, why?

3. Of the three complicating factors listed above, which one hits the closest to home for you, and how could that change?

Our Calling

As Christian men, our calling is to be committed followers of Jesus Christ and to make disciples for Christ by our life and witness. (Matt. 28:19-20) It is also to provide leadership in the home as loving husbands and "hands on" fathers. (Eph. 5:29-33, 6:4) This involves both leading by example and by service. Leading by example is so important, because in everyday life "more is caught than taught." Leading by serving is the model Jesus gave us. (Mark 10:42-45, John 13:3-17) Interestingly, in recent years, the concept of servant leadership has even caught on in parts of the business community (More on this in Chapter Eight).

Servant Leadership at Home

What exactly is servant leadership? It is being willing to identify and meet the needs of others, and to sacrifice our own needs for those we lead. At the root of servant leadership is love—not primarily as an emotion, but a choice, an act of the will. It involves extending ourselves for others by seeking their highest good. (Phil. 2:4-8) And it's by serving that we gain, not lose, authority. This is true both in the workplace and (especially) in our homes. Being a servant leader does not mean giving up control or relinquishing the ability to determine the direction, values, and policies of our businesses, or our families. It is largely an attitude. It's wanting to see everyone succeed and doing whatever we can to help them, by offering assistance and encouragement.

Being a servant leader in your home means putting the needs of your wife and children ahead of your own agenda and needs, to help them become everything they are capable of becoming. It means providing leadership, *in partnership with your wife*, by sensitively taking the initiative to address the concerns and problems of the family in a caring, loving way. *Taking initiative is the key.* I don't believe that, as husbands and fathers, we need to have all the answers, or do all the decision-making by ourselves. But I am convinced we need to be quick to recognize situations requiring attention (just like at work) and to take the lead in working out a solution with our wives, even if they are the ones who are better at implementing it. Some men try to use power tactics to micro-manage their families, and it just doesn't work. They may gain temporary compliance, but their wives resent their attempts to exert control in areas where the wives are more competent. And their children eventually will either rebel in overt or subtle ways, or grow up lacking the confidence to make decisions on their own.

Questions for Personal Reflection or Group Discussion

1. What's your style of leadership at home? Your wife's?

2. Who generally takes the initiative in family plans, and why?

3. Do you see any advantages of servant leadership? If so, what are they?

Strategizing

As leaders at work, we constantly work on strategies to improve performance. Among other things, this involves knowing our purpose and core values and setting goals, priorities, and schedules for our organization. However, when it comes to our homes, we're often not nearly as intentional in these areas as we could be. Take purpose statements, for example. One question every organization has to answer is, "Why do we exist? What do we have to offer to our customers or clients that others don't have?" But how many families ask similar questions when it comes to their home life? Questions like, "What is our purpose as a family?" "Do we have an overall sense of who we are?" "What makes our family unique?" "How do we differ from other families we know?" If you don't have answers to these questions, you won't have a firm basis for making decisions, and you'll end up caving under the peer influence of other families around you. For instance, is your family time consumed with running kids to soccer practices and games because you really want this, or because several other families in your neighborhood are doing the same?

When it comes to core values, every organization or business has certain principles and characteristics that are fundamental to its culture. These are the guidelines by which it operates on a day-to-day basis. If they are spelled out and communicated on a regular basis, it keeps everyone who works there on the same page. With our families, it's also good to ask, "What are the principles and characteristics that are non-negotiable in our household?" For example, in my family growing up, church attendance was never questioned (which included twice on Sunday and also Wednesday evenings). My parents were first generation Christians and wanted their children to know Christ as well. Education was also highly valued by them (neither of whom finished high school), so we were encouraged to do well in school.

Your household has core values also, whether spoken or unspoken. It's good to examine what they are and decide if you would like to change or add to them. Then you can use them as a guide for evaluating decisions you make as a family.

Goals are also essential for success in any enterprise. It has been said that "he who aims at nothing, usually hits it." Thus, we ask ourselves and our leadership teams at work, "What do we want to accomplish over the next six months, a year, or two years?" Families also operate more effectively with stated and understood goals. "What do we want to accomplish as a family over the next six months, a year, or two years. etc.?" Maybe it's moving into a new home, or remodeling an existing one. Perhaps it's getting the kids through college with a minimum of debt, or saving for a truly memorable family trip. The point is this: just coasting along day to day, without planning and goals, will not accomplish what we want to see happen for our families.

Scheduling hours, meetings, appointments, and tasks are also part of workplace life. Households have schedules, too, both for the family as a whole and for its individual members. Healthy families schedule time to be together. Research has shown that eating dinner together as a family has many positive benefits over the long run. Instead of simply running with the herd that is chasing their kids from one activity or sporting event to another, stop and think about what it's doing to your family life, and especially your mealtimes. Prioritizing activities according to your family's core values, and being careful not to over-schedule, is really important, as is knowing each family member's schedule, so you can all be on the same page.

Having a master calendar in a prominent place (like the kitchen) is useful for this purpose. A good rule of thumb is that parents should not commit to any outside activity without first checking with their spouse, and children should not be involved in an activity outside the home without both parents being in agreement. This seems like common sense, but it's surprising how many family conflicts arise because independent decisions are made, or because there is a lack of communication about what's happening.

Questions for Personal Reflection or Group Discussion

1. Try to come up with a purpose statement for your family.

2. What are some of your family's values, even if unspoken? How about family goals?

3. Are you satisfied with the schedule your family has and the allotted times for each activity? Does it line up with your family values and goals?

4. If not, what changes would you like to see happen?

Set aside a time to talk about this with your wife and come up with a new plan together.

Finances

In the world of commerce, it's all about the bottom line. The simple fact is that organizations need money in order to stay in business. And families do too. Finances are a major area of tension and argument for many couples. Part of this revolves around *who* handles the family's funds and *how* they are being handled (often reflecting one's family of origin). Who brings home the money, along with each partner's perspective on how it should be spent, is also a contributing factor. For example, you may view money as something to be saved for security reasons, but your wife might see it as something to spend on things you both enjoy. You can see the potential struggles there. Here's where your knowledge of business can provide a viable model for your family's use as well. If you think of your marriage as a business partnership (at least financially), the following principles might be useful:

1. Each person has equal say in all financial decisions made.

2. Partners decide together who will handle the financial details (typically the one who is best at it, or who dislikes it the least).

3. Regardless of who handles the details, both partners should be fully informed concerning *all* significant financial transactions.

4. Budgets are necessary to keep track of income and spending, and should be drawn up with input from both partners. (It's amazing how

many couples have no real idea of how much money is coming in and where it goes).

5. Financial goals should be established together.

6. All borrowing, spending, saving, and investing decisions are made jointly.

7. Creating cash reserves and avoiding or minimizing debt should be a priority. It's common in our culture for families to live above their means and incur debt. The attitude has been "buy now, pay later" with the assumption that they'll *be able* to pay later. Then unexpected expenses occur, and tension levels rise in the home. If we can learn to live below our means and "save for a rainy day" as it were, we'll eliminate a lot of financial stress in the family.

8. Each partner draws a salary (allowance) for which they are not accountable to the other partner. Depending on one's income, it doesn't have to be a large amount, but it's freeing not to have to account to one's partner for every little personal expenditure each of you desires to make.

My wife and I have used this model in our own marriage and have found it to be very practical. If this is something that might work for you, take the initiative as the servant leader in your home to work it out with your spouse. Be sure to take your differences into account and be willing, as always, to compromise.

Questions for Personal Reflection or Group Discussion

1. Are you and your wife on the same page when it comes to family finances? Where are your differences, and are they creating tension?

2. Try to discover the roots of these differences together, and work out a compromise.

3. Does the business partnership model laid out above make sense to you? Why or why not?

Organization

Division of labor and delegation are common business practices. More is accomplished by many people using their varied skills than by one person with limited skills doing everything by him or herself. (Eccles. 4:9) This is important in the home as well, especially in marriages where both husband and wife are employed full time. It's a fact, even in cases of dual employment, that most wives end up doing the bulk of chores around the house. No one steps up to the plate, and they get tired of nagging their husbands and kids. So they suffer in silence and do it themselves, but they often resent it—and rightly so.

I want to encourage you, as a servant leader, to take the initiative to sit down with your wife and decide who will be responsible for what, making sure chores are evenly distributed. You should also decide together what can be delegated to your children, assuming they have the maturity, ability, and training necessary to do the assigned task. In the process, they will be learning valuable life skills, and will begin to understand that living in a family means *sharing responsibilities*. As with all areas of delegation, be sure to follow up and see if the child needs assistance or encouragement.

And don't forget to express gratitude and praise to both your wife and children. Performance reviews are a part of business life, and they work at home as well. Our wives and children need "atta boys" as much as our employees. People need to know how they are doing so they can take pride in a job well done, or else improve their performance. As the leader in the family, no one's approval is more important than yours. Kids get report cards at school to evaluate their progress. It's good for them to know how they are doing at home as well. This can cover anything from handling their household chores to how well they're treating their little sister.

It's always healthy for leaders to be evaluated, also. We all have room for improvement, and the best way to discover where it's needed most is to ask those we lead. In the graduate school where I taught, the students did an evaluation of the professors at the end of each course. While it did not always make for pleasant reading, I found it very helpful in improving my skills as a teacher. Several years ago, I read about a man who decided to ask his wife each month, "How am I doing as a husband?" and to ask his children, "How am I doing as a dad?" Once they realized he wanted honest answers, they gave him valuable feedback for areas to work on to improve his game. A pretty gutsy move on his part, but it paid big dividends. I dare you to try it!

Every organization needs policies and rules in order to function properly. Rules establish the parameters of behavior and are created for the safety and well-being of everyone concerned. Children respond to rules. It gives them security knowing what is expected of them and what to expect from others. If you worry that rules may be too confining, remember that your kids deal with rules from the time they get on the school bus until they get home again: bus rules, recess rules, lunchroom rules, classroom rules, etc. Your only concern should be if the rules are reasonable and fair, and that they apply equally (with a few exceptions) to everyone, including the parents.

In his book *Positive Parenting with a Plan*, Matthew Johnson says that the problem many families encounter in this area is due to either a lack of clearly stated rules (i.e., parents who make them up as they go along), or inconsistency in enforcing the rules they have. This inconsistency is generally the result of two factors: mood and energy. If we're in a bad mood, we come down too hard on our kids. If we don't have the energy, we let them get away with too much or we nag rather than taking action.

Another problem is parents who disagree about discipline in front of the children, setting themselves up for "divide and conquer" manipulation (I believe that's strategy number ten in The Kids' Handbook on How to Get Your Way). The bottom line is that families need to have rules, agreed upon by both parents, clearly articulated to the children (even in writing), and fairly and consistently enforced. The penalty for non-compliance also needs to be made clear in advance, so there is no question as to why the child is being disciplined. Dr. Johnson points out that a parent's primary responsibility is to prepare children for the real world of order, structure, and authority. Having to obey rules and respect authority at home is a key part of that preparation. He is also a big advocate of rewards for good behavior (part of the real world) and expressions of grace, which should be incorporated in our life as Christians.

Meetings are a crucial part of business, and while some of you may feel like there are too many meetings at work and too few productive ones, they *are* necessary to running an organization. Business meetings are necessary in families too. These should include parental meetings for discussing finances, planning, and goal-setting (perhaps monthly); problem-solving and decision-making (as needed); and especially for family scheduling (every week). Family meetings, which include the children, should be used to inform the children of decisions made, evaluate progress toward family goals, deal with problems involving the children, and celebrate important events and triumphs (good report cards, goals reached, etc.). Getting input from older children on issues involving them is also important. These meetings are best held as needed.

Questions for Personal Reflection or Group Discussion

1. How is labor divided in your household? Is it equal and fair?

2. Do you delegate to the children, or get tired of nagging and do it yourself? What do you think that teaches them?

3. Do you have a set group of policies and rules, and are they consistently enforced? How could you improve?

4. How often do you have parental or family meetings? Can you see their value and how might you implement them?

Spiritual Leadership

While spiritual leadership isn't exactly a transferrable business skill, I would be remiss if I didn't include it as part of your role as a leader in the family. In too many Christian homes, it is the wife who takes the lead spiritually. I realize some men feel intimidated by their wives in this area, because she may be more spiritually mature. Maybe she's been a Christian longer and/or has had more opportunities to grow in her spiritual life through women's classes at church, home Bible studies, or reading on her own. Or it could be that the demands of our work leave us so tired, it's just easier to let her lead, or both. All of which may be true, but it doesn't let us off the hook of assuming our God-given role as a spiritual leader in the home.

What does this look like? For starters, it means setting an example by making worship, prayer, and devotional reading a personal priority. Our children (or wives) should never wonder if church is a priority for us, or if prayer is an essential part of our lives, or if reading the Bible and other devotional literature is important to us. Nor should they ever question our Christian commitment when it comes to our everyday values and morals. This is especially crucial if we have sons, who look to us as role models (although daughters also see us as role models, albeit to a lesser degree).

Leadership also means initiating and encouraging involvement in church functions and ministries, perhaps even getting involved in a service project the whole family can do together. For example, my daughter, son-in-law, and their four teenage children served together at a local mission that provided a hot breakfast for the homeless on Saturday mornings. They found it very fulfilling, and it was a wonderful experience for my grandkids to be exposed to how the less fortunate live.

Even putting money in the offering plate each Sunday sends a message to our children about the importance of giving back to God part of what he has graciously given to us. As a boy, I remember once asking my dad why other families in our neighborhood seemed to have little "extras" that we didn't enjoy. He explained to me that, as a family, we were committed to tithing to the Lord's work and also supporting missions (a major emphasis in our church), which is where the extra money went. I recall that I didn't feel resentful about that at all, but rather proud of our family for doing that.

Saying grace at meals is a simple way to lead, either by praying yourself as the head of the family, or by calling on another family member to do it. Leading a family devotional time is also an option (we'll discuss this in more detail in the chapter on fathering). My point is that you don't have to be a spiritual giant in order to lead your family in this area. If your wife is the more mature believer at this point, draw on her as a resource and decision-making partner. And keep in mind, like in any area of leadership in business or elsewhere, you'll need to *grow* into the position. In fact, it will *force* you to grow spiritually, and that's a good thing.

Questions for Personal Reflection or Group Discussion

1. How much spiritual leadership are you providing for your family? In what areas do you need to improve?

2. How might talking with your wife about it and coming up with a mutual plan together be helpful?

3. Think about small ways that you can begin right now, and let your wife and children know what you are doing and why.

Going further: Study Deuteronomy 11:18-21; 1 Timothy 3:2-7; and Titus 1:6-9.

(Even though you may not be an overseer or elder in your church, you *do* have that function at home). Reflect on (or discuss) these passages and their application to your situation.

Bottom Line

No doubt there are other business skills that you could apply at home, but the important thing is providing the leadership your family needs, and which they are looking for in every area of your life together. In the end, effective leadership comes down to relationships, which is our topic in the chapters that follow.

Additional Resources:

Tom Hirschfield, *Business Dad: How Good Businessmen Can Make Great Fathers (and Vice Versa)*. Little-Brown, 1999.

Matthew A. Johnson, *Positive Parenting with a Plan (Grades K-12)*. Family Rules, 2001.

Patrick Lencioni, *The 3 Big Questions for a Frantic Family*. Jossey-Bass, 2008.

Rich Wagner, *The Expeditionary Man: The Adventure a Man Wants, the Leader His Family Needs.* Zondervan, 2008.

"When I as fourteen, my father was so ignorant I could barely stand to have him around. When I got to be twenty-one, I was astonished at how much he had learned in seven years."

—*Mark Twain*

Chapter Three: Fathering with Integrity

"The people brought children to Jesus, hoping he might touch them. The disciples shooed them off. But Jesus was irate and let them know it: 'Don't push these children away. Don't ever get between them and me. These children are at the very center of life in the kingdom. Mark this: Unless you accept God's kingdom in the simplicity of a child, you'll never get in.' Then gathering the children up in his arms, he laid his hands of blessing on them." (Mark 10:13-16, MSG)

Jesus, Our Example

Although Jesus never married or had children of his own, this incident from his life shows us how we ought to treat children—loving them and handling them with special care. As with everything else, he is our model for fatherhood as well.

Being a father is one of the most challenging responsibilities a man can assume. It taxes your intellectual abilities, your emotional endurance, and keeps you on your knees more than anything I know. Plus, Christian fathers have the added challenge of raising our children to know and love God, in a secular world that doesn't share our values. At the same time, however, few things have the potential to bring greater joy and fulfillment than parenting. I wouldn't trade the experience for anything.

On one occasion, when Jesus' disciples were having one of their "disputes" about who was going to be the greatest in his kingdom, he set a small child in the middle of them and told them that, unless they humbled themselves like this child, they weren't even going to *get in* the kingdom, let alone be in positions of authority. (Matt. 18:4) And thus began a series of lessons in humility, culminating at the cross. (Phil. 2:5-8)

What *we* learn from *our* children is often humbling also, but it is one of the joys and pains of parenting. On many occasions, I have remarked that my kids have taught me more than I ever taught them. Next to marriage, nothing rubs off our rough edges, teaches us humility, and requires self-sacrifice as much as being a parent.

It's also good to note that some of the strongest warnings Jesus issued concerned the mistreatment of children. He said if anyone caused these little ones to stumble, that person would be better off tossed in the sea with a millstone tied around his neck (Luke 17:2)—a pretty sobering picture for us who live in a society where child abuse is a major problem. Jesus took the treatment of children *very* seriously... and so should we.

God, the Perfect Father

A second reason Jesus is a model of fatherhood is reflected in his words to the disciples, "I and the Father are one," and "If you have seen me, you have seen the Father." In other words, Jesus is telling us that he is the perfect reflection of God the Father, who is the ultimate standard of fatherhood for us all. I am glad the Scriptures, in general, and Jesus, in particular, present God to us in fatherly terms. Many descriptions focus on God as creator and ruler of nations, or as lawgiver and judge. But picturing God as father is both authoritative and also more personal, loving, and approachable.

But seeing God as father can be a problem for some. I have learned, from both counseling and personal experience, that many people project their feelings toward their earthly dads onto their heavenly Father. If they had a father who was domineering, absent, abusive, or emotionally distant, they will tend to see God the same way. At the other extreme, if their father gave them whatever they wanted and treated them like they could do no wrong, they will often picture God as a permissive parent, pandering to their every wish.

My own father was exemplary in many ways. He was warm and approachable, spent time with my brothers and me, and taught us many life skills. One of the vivid memories I have from my childhood is playing catch with him in front of our house (Yes, I lived *Field of Dreams*). Best of all, he modeled for us what a good husband and a fine Christian man looked like. Although not real affectionate (thanks to his Scandinavian roots), we knew he loved us, and I'll always be grateful for him. But there was one area where I struggled with him as a father: he often corrected shortcomings, but rarely praised accomplishments. He wrongly thought that praising his children would make them egotistical, and he didn't want his sons to have a "big head." As a result, I grew up seeking recognition and feeling as if I would never gain his full approval.

Unfortunately, I projected those same feelings onto God, who (as I had been taught from my Sunday School days) was my heavenly Father. I lived with the fear that at the end of my life, standing before my Maker, I wouldn't hear, "Well done, good and faithful servant," but rather, "Sorry kid, not good enough." Wrestling through those feelings as a middle-aged adult, I sought the face of God through meditating on the Scriptures and prayer. And, thankfully, God met the need of my heart and changed my view of him and our relationship. I came to realize that God is the perfect Father, one who accepts me as I am and who desires the very best for me. Do I disappoint him at times? Absolutely. But I never question his grace and love.

If God is the perfect Father with a capital "F," and the very personification of fatherhood, then we need to look at him and his inspired Word for our own pattern of fathering. This is what we will attempt to do in this chapter.

Questions for Personal Reflection or Group Discussion

1. What do you think of the idea of Jesus as a model father figure?

2. What have you learned from your children, or what rough edges of your personality have they rubbed off?

3. What was your relationship with your father growing up, and how has that affected your relationship with God?

Parental Modeling

Since God is our model for parenting, let's start by examining what *we* model for *our* children. Many men work hard to do the *right things* with their offspring, but set a bad *example* by their lives. They don't recognize the truth in the old saying, "More is caught than taught." Several years ago, a TV ad showed a man outdoors playing with his young son, who was about three years old. They sat down under a tree where the father lit up a cigarette and set the rest of the pack down beside him. Just as the young boy reached for the pack of cigarettes, the picture froze, and an anti-smoking message flashed across the screen.

This ad vividly illustrates how closely we are watched by our children, especially fathers by their sons. We *are* their role models, whether we embrace that responsibility or not.

One of the struggles we have as dads is catching ourselves doing or saying things with our children that we resented our own fathers doing with us. We say to ourselves, "Oh no, I'm becoming my father!" and it's a scary thought. The reality is that we *do* often duplicate the mistakes of our parents, and need to come to terms with them. This means facing old, painful memories, and then letting them go. The Bible calls this forgiveness. It may be difficult to forgive our fathers (or mothers) for certain things done to us in our youth, but if we don't, we may well repeat it with our own children, or go to the opposite extreme, which can be equally damaging. God, who extends grace to us, expects and helps us to extend that same grace to our parents. None of us had perfect parents, and we won't be one either. Your children and mine will have to forgive us for our mistakes, as well. If you find forgiving especially difficult, I suggest you work it through with a good Christian counselor.

Modeling Love

"God is love." (1 John 4:8,16) More than anything else, our children need to feel loved. Being open and loving toward them will help them understand that their heavenly Father is also loving and approachable. As parents, we naturally love our children, but they don't always *feel* loved. The things we do for them every day, like putting a roof over their heads, food in their stomachs, and clothes on their backs, are pretty much seen by them as our parental duty, not as an expression of love. Ross Campbell, in his great book on parenting (see below), points out three things that convey love to our children in unmistakable terms: eye contact, physical affection, and individual attention.

Eye contact: Campbell says that, when our children speak to us, we need to turn off the TV we're watching, or set aside the project we're working on, and give them our undivided attention (our wives probably feel the same way). If our children are small, this means also getting down at their level. He observes that the only time some parents look their kids straight in the eye is when they are disciplining them—wrong message. Making eye contact while conversing with our children lets them know we are really listening. (James 1: 19) It also shows an interest in what they are saying and, thus, *interest in them*. More importantly, listening is an act of love. Think of how good it feels when someone you are talking to is fully attentive and how frustrating it is when they are distracted or looking around.

Affection: Most kids love to be touched. To give them hugs and kisses, to hold their hand, to snuggle with them, or set them on your lap makes them feel loved and secure. As mentioned earlier, my father was not particularly affectionate. But one of my vivid memories of him took place when I was about ten years old and had returned from a two-and-a-half-week vacation out west with my grandparents. My father came home from work that day, and we met in the dining room. He gave me this long bear hug, and I remember thinking while in his embrace, "He really does love me."

The fact that the memory is still fresh in my mind shows how important it was. Simple things like putting your arm around your child's shoulder, especially in public or in scary (for them) situations, or patting them on the head as you walk by them while they're playing, all send messages of love. And don't stop when they get to their teens. They may protest, like they're too old for that stuff, but secretly, they still need and want it. Just don't embarrass them in front of their friends, unless they are comfortable with you doing it. This need for affection is especially true with teenage daughters. If they don't feel loved by you, they will look for it in other places.

Individual attention: When you always do things or go places as a family or with your kids as a group, it doesn't make them feel particularly loved. They figure you *have to* include them because they're part of the family. But if you show them individual attention—whether it's playing a game, working on a project, or running errands together—he or she will feel like, "Wow, Dad wants to spend time *just with me.*"

This includes dating your children. One of the best ways to prepare your daughters for dating is to take her out yourself during her pre- or early adolescent years. You can use this time to teach her what to expect and insist on from the boys who might date her. You will also learn things on dates about your child's personality, interests, and challenges, which they might not express when the family is together. On an early lunch date with my son, I discovered that this normally quiet kid had a lot to say. This didn't come out in family gatherings, where his voice had to compete with his parents and more talkative older sister. But when he had me all to himself, it was a different story.

Breakfast or lunch dates on weekends work well (let them pick the restaurant). Also doing activities they enjoy—whether going to the movies or bowling or miniature golf, ice skating or fishing or attending a ball game—helps in bonding and creating shared memories with your children. And don't neglect attending their sporting events, concerts, or dance recitals. They want you to be there, as long as you don't embarrass them by being too vocal in your encouragement.

Questions for Personal Reflection or Group Discussion

1. What did your father (or mother) model for you growing up that you have found to be valuable or helpful? What are you trying to model for *your* children?

2. How are you doing in conveying love by eye contact, physical affection, and individual attention? Which area(s) do you need to work on?

3. Think about (or discuss) some specific ways to implement these in your relationship with your kids. How do you think they will react, at least at first?

Loving Discipline

Campbell also points out that, when we do these things and our children's *love tanks* are full, they are less likely to misbehave, because acting up is often their way of getting attention (negative attention is better than none at all). If they do feel loved, yet *still* need to be disciplined, they will tend to accept the discipline as another sign of our love for them. On the other hand, if they aren't feeling loved (love tanks running on empty), they'll probably interpret our discipline as just another indication that we don't really care about them that much.

Disciplining our children is one of the most difficult responsibilities we have as parents. I never understood my father saying, "This is going to hurt me more than you," until I had to discipline my own kids. No parent enjoys doing this, but it's a necessary part of loving them. See what the writer of Hebrews has to say:

"My son, do not despise the Lord's discipline and do not resent his rebuke, because *the Lord disciplines those he loves,* as a father the son he delights in . . . Our fathers disciplined us for a little while as they thought best; but God disciplines us *for our good,* that we may share in his holiness." (Heb. 12:7,10)

Did you catch that? "The Lord disciplines those he loves," and he "disciplines us for our good." That should always be our motivation as well. Neglecting this part of parenting isn't in the best interests of our children. And we shouldn't leave it up to our wives, for children respond to a man's voice quicker than to a woman's.

On the other hand, we need to be careful about coming on too strong, especially with young children, to whom we appear as giants! Harshness is out of place. Proverbs 15:1 tells us that "a harsh word stirs up anger," and Paul instructs fathers in Colossians 3:21, "Do not embitter your children, or they will become discouraged." Interestingly, the Book of Job cites an ostrich as a bad example of parenting: "She treats her young harshly, as if they were not hers . . . for God did not endow her with wisdom or give her a share of good sense." (Job 39:16-17) Hopefully, we have more wisdom and good sense than an ostrich!

Paul, who saw the Corinthian Christians as his spiritual children, (1 Cor. 4:14-15) wrote to them, "This is why I write these things when I am absent, that when I come I may not have to be *harsh in my use of authority*—the authority God gave me for building you up, not for tearing you down." (2 Cor. 10:13) As fathers, we too have a God-given authority in the lives of our children, and, like Paul, that authority is for building them up, not for tearing them down. No one can tear down a child's self-esteem easier than a parent, and one of the quickest ways to do this is by being harsh with them.

This means not disciplining them while we are angry, which is when we are most likely to do something harsh, or stupid. We'll either spank them too hard (spanking should always be a last resort), or we'll hand out ridiculous penalties like "You're grounded for a year" or "No

TV for the rest of your life." Those spur-of-the-moment disciplinary decisions can end up penalizing *you* as much as them (*Who* gets to stay home to make sure the "grounding" is enforced?). It's far better to give yourself time to cool down, and then come up with a rational idea for dealing with major infractions, by consulting with your wife.

And, as much as possible, it's also wise to anticipate potential problems and work out your responses in advance with her. Then communicate them to your children so they know what behavior you want from them and what they can expect if they fail to obey. Speaking in "we" terms also presents a united front to them, and avoids either you or your spouse being labeled "the bad guy."

Our disciplining of children, like God's discipline, should always be designed to correct bad behavior and develop good character. When we react in anger to their behavior, we end up punishing them to get even. Then the only lesson our children learn is, "Don't get dad mad." The reality is, when we are able to discipline calmly, we exude a sense of authority far more than when we "lose it" emotionally. Teaching them to respect and obey authority also prepares them for future relationships with teachers, bosses, civic authorities, and especially God.

One of the best examples of this I have witnessed was watching the wife of a professional hockey player I knew handle her four young boys. If one was misbehaving, she would call him over, get down at his level, look him in the eyes, calmly tell him what she expected from him, *and* the consequences for non-compliance. She made sure he was really listening and understood her, and then she sent him back to play. If he continued his misbehavior, she quietly got up, separated him from his brothers, and took him to his room to ponder his actions for a while. She talked softly, but carried a big stick (metaphorically speaking, not a hockey stick).

This is good parenting. She made sure her son understood her request and the consequences, giving him *one* chance to comply. If he disobeyed, she carried out her promise and he had no one to blame but himself. When we as parents give our children multiple chances to obey, we don't do them or ourselves any favors. They learn we don't really mean it the first time we speak, so they push our buttons until we get serious. By that time, we are frustrated and angry, probably reacting in ways we regret.

The best kind of discipline is one that either fits the infraction or teaches a life skill. For example, if a child is not getting along while playing with his or her siblings or friends, the most appropriate response would be to send them to their room to think about their behavior, as my friend did. Or if they do something to hurt or offend another person, a heartfelt apology is in order (a skill they'll need the rest of their lives). Also, a violated curfew without good reason may call for subtracting the amount of time they were late from their curfew the next time they go out (an hour home late this time, an hour home early next time). Be creative, but always keep the goal in mind: to teach and mold character, not to vent your spleen and punish (for more on discipline see Chapter Two).

Compassionate Grace

Another quality we learn from our heavenly Father is compassionate grace. One of the most beautiful descriptions of God as father is given to us by David in Psalm 103:

"The Lord is compassionate and gracious, slow to anger, abounding in love . . . He does not treat us as our sins deserve or repay us according to our iniquities . . . As a father has compassion on his children, so the Lord has compassion on those who fear him; for he knows how we are formed, he remembers that we are dust." (vss. 8, 10, 13, 14)

There's a time to discipline, and a time to forgive. Sometimes our children do things that may be destructive of property or hurtful to people, but it really isn't intentional. Young children *will* spill their milk; their coordination isn't that good (adults sometimes spill drinks too). Kids *will* break windows playing ball in the backyard; their athletic abilities are still developing. Adolescents *will* sometimes say things that are inappropriate; their social skills are not yet finely tuned. These are good opportunities to teach, not to discipline. And, as always, it's important not to embarrass them in front of others (especially their friends). Better to take them aside alone for a heart-to-heart talk. The point is to teach, not humiliate. Compassion is called for in these situations. We need to remember that they are immature (as we once were), and they're still learning life lessons.

At other times, there may be extensive damage done to property (like an accident with the family car), or to people's emotions (like saying something really hurtful). On those occasions, we may be ready to administer discipline, but find that our child is really upset and already truly remorseful for what they have done. This is a time to exhibit understanding. They don't need to be punished; they are already punishing themselves. Instead, they need for us to offer them compassion and grace. This will also help them understand the compassion and grace of their Father in heaven.

Rewards and Gifts

In addition to correcting bad behavior, it's also wise, as fathers, to reward good behavior. Here again, we are following the model of our heavenly Father who will reward each of us for whatever good we have done. (Matt. 16:27, Eph. 6:8, Rev. 22:12) This includes enduring persecution for Christ (Luke 6:23), doing good to our enemies (Luke

6:35), practicing spiritual disciplines (Matt. 6:1-18), and our labor for God's kingdom (1 Cor. 3:8, 14).

I have heard parents say you shouldn't *have* to reward good behavior; it ought to be the expected norm, not requiring rewards. It's true that some people go overboard in rewarding kids to the point where it could be considered a bribe. And, yes, children should learn to do the right thing for its own sake. But at the same time, good behavior needs to be encouraged, just as bad behavior needs to be discouraged. The best reward is praise and recognition (more on encouragement later). But there are times when tangible rewards are in order. For example, taking a child out for an ice cream sundae after helping you with yard work or to a special event for bringing home a good report card are ways of teaching them that extra effort has benefits. We get pay increases, promotions, or bonuses on the job for work well done; why shouldn't they have the same satisfaction?

Gifts are different than rewards. While rewards recognize good performance, gifts are, by nature, undeserved. Just like we extend grace at times to our repentant and remorseful children (as God does with us), so we also give gifts to them, simply because we love them. God is a giver. His greatest gift, of course, is the gift of his Son and the eternal life that we have through Christ (John 3:16, Rom.6:23, Eph. 2:8). And he also gives us his Holy Spirit (Luke 11:13), not to mention virtually everything else we value in life—including life itself.

Like God's gifts to us, gifts to our children should be *good gifts* that will benefit or enhance their lives. In my home growing up, about the only time we received gifts were at Christmas or on our birthdays; not unusual in those days. Anything beyond those occasions was a complete surprise. Because gifts were infrequent, they were special and appreciated. In many homes today, children are given too much, too often, to the point where it's expected and taken for granted. "What have you given me lately?" seems to be the resulting attitude. So, in our giving, we need to strike a balance between overdoing and withholding. Unexpected surprises from time to time (even little ones) can be expressions of love, and teach gratitude at the same time.

There may be times when big gifts are in order, like providing financial help to a child who is working hard to earn money for school or needed transportation, but again, we have to be careful not to do too much for them. Letting them struggle and develop a good work ethic by earning things for themselves is also part of parenting.

Beyond material gifts, and like our heavenly Father, the best gift we can give them is the gift of *ourselves*—our time, our attention, our energy. Shared activities and conversations will be remembered and cherished, long after material gifts are gone.

Questions for Personal Reflection or Group Discussion

1. Are you more of a discipliner or a punisher as a parent? Do you and your wife work together on this?

2. Is there anything in the Loving Discipline section that resonated with you? Any changes you would like to make in your own approach?

3. Have you shown compassionate grace with your children at times? What was their response?

4. What's the pattern of gift-giving and rewards like in your household? Is there anything you would like to do differently?

Favoritism

It is also important to be impartial with our children, whether we're showing love or disciplining them. One of the classic indicators of dysfunction in a family is the favored child, like Joseph in the Old

Testament. Usually this is the child who is the brightest, most talented, or best looking. He may also be the one who most lives up to the parents' expectations. Other siblings pick up on this favoritism and resent it. It's an easy trap to fall into as a parent, and one that needs to be avoided.

Our heavenly Father is impartial. In the Sermon on the Mount, Jesus instructs us to love even those who are treating us badly (Matt. 5:45,48). And Peter tells us that when we pray, we "call on a Father who judges each man's work impartially" (1 Pet. 1:17). We are told repeatedly in Scripture that God does not show favoritism in his dealings with people (Acts 10:34, Rom. 2:11, Eph. 6:9). Thus, James instructs us, "My brothers, as believers in our glorious Lord Jesus Christ, *don't show favoritism*" and "the wisdom that comes from heaven is . . . *impartial and sincere*" (James 2:1; 3:17). If being impartial is an attribute of God, and an important part of Christian living in general, it's so much more when dealing with our own children.

Protection

"Love always protects," Paul tells us, (1 Cor. 13:7) and since God *is* love, (1 John 4:16) we know that he also protects us, as his children (Ps. 32:7, 91:14, 2 Thess. 3:3). Having been created in God's image, it seems built into our DNA to be protectors of our children, and our society has many dangers from which our children need protecting. When I was young, many of these dangers were non-existent, or minimal at best. But they are here today, and need to be reckoned with. It isn't enough to respond to situations as they arise. As Christian fathers, we need to be proactive in anticipating issues, before they become problems. Let me share a few examples.

TV and movies have largely become a wasteland of un-Christian morals and values. Monitoring and limiting what our children watch on TV, or the movies they are allowed to attend, rent, or download is important. When my children were young, they were limited on how much TV they could watch, and their mother and I had the final vote on what they were viewing. As adults now, neither of them is addicted to the tube, if they have something better to do. It's also not a bad idea to watch things with them, and use what they are seeing as teaching moments. In this way, they learn to view things critically from a Christian perspective, instead of just passively absorbing the images, values, and ideas being portrayed.

Computer, tablet, and cell phone use also needs to be monitored. I would not recommend allowing a child to have Internet access or a TV in their own room. It provides too much temptation for viewing things they shouldn't without parental supervision. It also encourages isolation from the rest of the family. Having a family TV in a common living area where what is being watched has to be negotiated, as well as monitored, is not a bad thing on several levels. The same holds true for the computer. Cell phones certainly are useful, but they are also potential hazards with their Internet capacity. Their peers can too easily introduce them to information and images you wouldn't want them to be exposed to.

Pornography is prevalent in our society, especially on the Internet. It's just too easy to access (see chapter on Sexual Integrity). The average age for a boy to encounter porn is eleven years old, so you can't begin too early in warning him about its deadly effects. There is software that can be installed on electronic devices that can filter or monitor objectionable material. But they can be exposed by what their friends have access to, so you still need to have the conversation. It's good to begin by asking them if they have ever seen porn, and then take the conversation from there.

Sex: Of course, dealing with pornography takes us into the whole realm of sex in general. Yes, you need to have "the talk" with your sons (your wife is better at talking to your daughters). It's not the easiest discussion for most parents to have, but it will be a lot easier if you have raised your comfort level by discussing sexual things with your wife (see sex chapter again). There are materials written from a Christian perspective that you might have them read first, and then talk about later. Don't leave it up to the sex education program at school, which will have a secular viewpoint very different than your own. In fact, it would be good to learn what's being taught in school, so you can either correct the objectionable things with your child at home, or have them excused from the class altogether.

Drugs and alcohol are the other things from which we need to protect our children. This has been a problem in our society for a while, and kids are being introduced to it at an increasingly earlier age. It isn't just an intercity problem. In certain suburban areas, for example, heroin use among teens is an epidemic. Prescription painkillers are also highly addictive and have become popular street drugs, along with medications prescribed for ADHD (these drugs designed to slow down hyperactivity in patients actually work as "speed" for others). Don't depend on the public school's drug education program. Peer pressure often trumps classroom instruction. Warn your children of the dangers, and know their friends and their friends' reputations. Don't be fooled by clean-cut, popular teens. They are often the ones doing the most partying.

I have a friend who is a recovered alcoholic. His father and grandfather before him also had major drinking problems. When his son was approaching adolescence, he sat down with him for a heart-to-heart about the family history, including his own (he had quit when his son was very young). He told his son that he couldn't stop him from drinking, but given his background, it would be a dangerous thing for him to do. Fortunately, he had a very close relationship with his son, who took his advice seriously. To this day, I don't think the son has touched alcohol, even though he works in a stressful profession where his coworkers unwind that way.

Bullying is becoming a problem in our society today. It can be psychological, in the form of cruel texts, pictures, and emails circulated among other students; or actual physical intimidation. Learn as much as you can about this problem. There are books and articles you can find with a little research on the Internet. Some of these books are designed to be read by your children, who will probably be exposed to bullying at a fairly young age. They may not bring the subject up, so raise the question with them yourself, especially if your child seems unhappy or reluctant to go to school.

Friends are another area where our children may need protection. We are all influenced by the people we spend time with, but as adults, we're mature enough to pick our friends wisely. Our children lack that experience and may be drawn to kids who are a negative influence. As a teenager, I once dated a girl who had a troubled family life. She was a new Christian and a nice girl, but very needy. Tending to be a rescuer by nature, I was pulled into the emotional vortex of her dysfunctional family. This was affecting my school grades, so my father wisely stepped in and put a moratorium on the relationship until the end of the school year. At the time I was a bit upset, but he was right. Interestingly, when the semester was over and I was free to renew the relationship, I had lost interest and so had she, so we were able to part friends.

Questions for Personal Reflection or Group Discussion

1. Do you find yourself favoring one of your children, because of their abilities, common interests, or easy to get along with personality? Think about (or discuss) what you can do to change that.

2. What hedges of protection have you put around your children in the areas discussed above?

3. Which areas need to be strengthened?

Guidance

As Christian men, we often encounter things in our lives where we don't know what we should do, so we seek guidance from God or others. We can pray about the situation, search the Scriptures, or seek the counsel of godly people who may have more discernment than we do. It's comforting to know that our heavenly Father is one who desires to guide us and not leave us in the dark. (see Ps. 48:14, 73:24, Isa. 58:11, and John 16:13)

Part of our responsibility as fathers is also to provide guidance for our children. By definition, childhood means lacking the maturity needed to handle certain situations, and so, they often look to us for help. In order to provide the wisdom they seek, we first need to ask questions and listen carefully while they describe the situation they are facing. In other words, we try to put ourselves in their shoes. Then, instead of telling them what to do, it's good to lay out their options, plus the possible consequences of each, and then explore their thoughts and feelings. Finally, share with them what you would do under the circumstances, and why. This process also helps them learn how to think things through and make decisions for themselves later on in life. All of this, of course, takes time and assumes you are dealing with a child old enough to reason.

Approachability and Openness

All of what we have discussed so far will only be effective if we are approachable: if our children feel like we really care, and can talk to us about anything. Because God is loving and approachable, it's easy for us, as his children, to approach him in prayer. (Heb. 10:19-22) It should be this way for our children as well. Keep the communication lines open. Be available, even when it isn't convenient for you.

Looking back on my daughter's adolescent years, I recall having long conversations with her late into the night, when all I wanted to do was go to bed. But I realized it was important to stay engaged, and so I hung in there with her. She was also the one I had the most confrontations with (she's a lot like me), and I was determined on those occasions to keep talking until our differences were resolved. Was it tiring? Yes. But it paid big dividends in the long run. Many years later, she's now the mother of four adolescents herself, and not only do we still have good open dialogue between us, but she has the same pattern going with her own children.

Encouragement

The Lord is also an encourager, (2 Thess. 2:16, Heb. 12:5-6) and as followers of Christ, we need to heed his example. In Colossians 3:21, Paul warns fathers they shouldn't do things that discourage their children. And in 2 Timothy 4:2, he gives instructions on how to teach (or preach): "correct, rebuke, *and encourage*— with great patience and careful instruction." Since, as parents, one of our tasks is teaching our children, we ought to take these words to heart as we do so.

Children need encouragement. To be *en*couraged is to have courage put into you, while being *dis*couraged is to have courage taken away. Children (like all of us) often need to be encouraged in dealing with the problems or obstacles they face. They need a mature, positive perspective, one that only an adult can give them. Sometimes they may lack self-confidence and need to be encouraged to try things they may be reluctant to tackle on their own.

In middle school, my son excelled at discus throwing in his physical education class. When he reached high school, I tried to encourage him to go out for the track team and compete in field events. He didn't think he was good enough, and hadn't thrown a discus for a couple of years. So, I bought him one and we went out to the middle school playing field so he could practice, with me retrieving his throws. He got his confidence back, made the track team, and I got to watch him compete and win many field events (discus, shot put, and javelin). I felt comfortable pushing him because I knew he could succeed. One of my regrets was not pressing him a little harder in other areas as well, and I think he now wishes I had done that too.

There is a fine line here between encouragement and pushing *too* hard. Our children should be to encouraged to take certain risks, and we need to be prepared to catch them if they fail. But I have watched parents pressure their children so hard to live up to *their* expectations, that it became all about the parent, instead of what was good for the child. Even if the child was successful, they often grew up resenting the parent, and lost interest in the very thing at which they were being pushed to excel. This would include not just sports, but academics, music, art, etc. Know what your child is capable of, and then set realistic expectations and be their biggest *positive* cheerleader.

Questions for Personal Reflection or Group Discussion

1.How are you doing with the task of guiding your children? Is this an area where you can improve?

2. How open and approachable are you? Do you spend enough time with them at home to have a comfortable relationship? How approachable are you? Ask *them* sometime.

3. In what ways do you encourage your children? Do you find yourself pushing them too hard in certain areas

Teaching

Along with guidance and encouragement in the face of life's challenges, we also have the task of teaching our children those things that will prepare them for adulthood. Of course, the most important thing we can teach them is to know, love, and serve the Lord. Modeling this in our own lives is the most effective way to do this. Telling them without living it would make us hypocrites. A family devotional time, beginning when they are very young, is a good practice, although it's wise to keep it brief and not preach. Helping them understand the truth of Scriptures and applying it to situations applicable for them is the goal. There are many Christian books geared to various age levels that can assist you in this area. Praying with them regularly and encouraging them to talk to God about everything in their lives is also essential.

Personally, I was never very successful in pulling off group devotions in my family, but found that reading to my children at bedtime and praying with them one on one worked better for us. Bedtime is also a good time to ask about their day, the positive and the negative things they experienced. When they are tired, their guard is down and they are more likely to share their feelings. I have often felt that, when a child won't settle down and go to sleep, it's either because they are excited about something coming up the next day, or they are troubled by something that happened that day. Giving them a chance to voice what's bothering them and then praying with them about it both helps them go to sleep peacefully and gives them a model for future use.

It's also good to take advantage of what they may be learning in Sunday School, Youth Group, or from the Sunday sermon. Ask them what it was about and what they took away from the lesson or sermon. This can help you know what your children are learning in church, and hopefully stimulate further discussion at home that will reinforce their learning or enable you to correct any misconceptions they may have.

Teachable Moments: Even more important than formal teaching, from you or others, are those situations where lessons can be taught within the context of everyday living. For instance, if your son or another child exhibits bad behavior during a Little League game, it gives you an opportunity to speak to him about the importance of good sportsmanship. Or if your daughter is being treated badly by one of her friends, you can use that situation to talk about forgiveness versus retaliation. If a family pet dies, it's a good time to discuss the meaning of death and grief, along with the hope Christians have in the face of life's difficulties.

In Deuteronomy 6:7, Moses instructed the Israelites concerning God's commandments, "Impress them on your children. Talk about them when you sit at home and when you walk along the road, when you lie down and when you get up." In other words, *all of life* provides these teachable moments, especially in regard to our faith. It also helps our children to see that Christianity is not simply something to believe, or confined to church settings, but also a relationship with God that is lived out in practical ways every day.

Teaching Responsibility: One of the most important lessons we can teach our children is that every privilege has a corresponding responsibility. For example, when our teenagers wanted the privilege of using the family car, my wife and I made them pay for their share of the added insurance and the gas they used. When our daughter wanted her own phone, we told her she could have it, as long as she paid for the use of it. When they went to college, we agreed to pay for their tuition, room, and board, but they were responsible for everything else: books, lab fees, clothes, transportation, etc.

Our approach may seem rather tough by today's standards, where many kids tend to be handed everything, but we were teaching them three important lessons: (1) It costs money to have the things they take for granted; (2) If they are willing to work for it, they can have those things; and (3) They will appreciate what they have to labor for, far more than if it's just been given to them. Although my children weren't too happy about our approach at the time, both of them thanked us later on, and both have a good work ethic today (more on finances below).

Doing their share of home maintenance is another area of responsibility children need to learn simple things like: picking up after themselves, putting things back where they found them, rinsing and placing dirty dishes in the dishwasher, making their beds, depositing dirty clothes in the clothes basket, etc. Is it easier to do it yourself, rather than try to get them to do these things? Yes. But the goal of parenting is to raise responsible, mature adults. Not making them take the responsibility will train them to expect that someone else will do it for them. You will also be doing their future wives or husbands a big favor.

Being responsible includes remembering what's required of them outside the house, like doing homework or taking things to school. When my son was young, he rushed out the door to school one day and left his lunch behind. Since the school was only a few blocks away, I dropped it off on my way to work. Forgetting his lunch then occurred several more times, with me dutifully taking it to him. Then the light in my head went on (sometimes I'm a little slow on the uptake). I was being trained to be his delivery boy! That night I sat him down and told him that, the next time he forgot his lunch, he'd go hungry. It only happened once after that, and he learned his lesson—that boy always did love to eat (I wonder where he got that from . . .).

A final area, and probably the most crucial one, is taking ownership of one's words and actions. Children need to know that they are responsible for the things they say and do, especially when it involves, and may hurt, other people. It's too easy to rationalize or try to put the blame on somebody else for one's behavior. This is also good spiritual training, for we all need to face ourselves and acknowledge our sins and failures before God so we can receive his grace.

Taking responsibility for their feelings is also important. No one can make us feel angry or jealous or sad. These emotions are from our own perceptions and expectations. It's good for them to understand early on that they can't control other people's actions, but they are responsible for their own reactions in those situations. Responding to an unkind word, or dealing with the disappointment of not making the team, or not being asked to the prom are a part of life. Helping them deal with these issues and process their feelings is yet another element of good parenting.

Teaching Financial Management: One of the things I have observed, as a counselor, is how frequently parents neglect to teach their children about finances. This is something they will have to handle for the rest of their lives, and yet so little is said about it in many homes except maybe, "Do you think money grows on trees?" The kids' thinking is, "Yes," if parents simply hand it to them whenever they want it. Besides requiring children to earn some of it (see above), teaching them what to do with the money they earn is part of our responsibility as parents.

Rather than just providing money as needed, consider giving them an allowance instead (depending on their age, of course). As they get older, and before they are old enough to get a job, you may want to pay them for certain household chores like cutting the lawn. Let them experience the satisfaction of earning money for themselves. Along with providing an allowance, teach them the joy of giving a certain amount away (a tithe, for instance), and the advantage of saving a certain amount for future wants or needs.

Giving is such an essential part of being a Christian. By nature, we all tend to be takers, looking out for number one. Yet we know that Jesus taught us to live lives of self-denial, to consider others rather than just ourselves. Certainly, giving back part of our income as a gesture of gratitude and worship is part of it. So, training our children to give to the Lord's work, and to those less fortunate, is good Christian parenting.

When I was a child, my parents always gave us money to drop in the offering plate during Sunday School, a part of Christian education in those days. And when I received my fifty-cents-a-week allowance, I made my first pledge to missions during our church's missionary conference, a nickel a week (you could actually buy things with a nickel back then). That teaching and modeling began a pattern of giving that has remained with me to this day, and for which I am truly grateful. It is, indeed, "more blessed to give than to receive." (Acts 20:35)

Teaching our children the value of saving is also really important. Having to save up to buy a larger item they desire will increase their enjoyment of it once they own it. This will also tend to eliminate impulsive buying. After saving for a while, they may have second thoughts about how they want to spend it. When they are older, and are earning more money, help them open a savings account at a local bank. With money in the bank not earmarked for any particular item, they'll have funds available for future opportunities or emergencies. My father, who lived through the Great Depression, taught my brothers and me the value of regular saving, and this has eliminated a lot of stress from our lives as adults. You can do the same for your children.

We live in a society of instant gratification. Credit cards enable us to buy now and pay later, which encourages impulse spending and produces a lot of debt. So many live under heavy loads of credit card indebtedness at exorbitantly high interest rates. Warn your teenage and young adult children about credit cards. Help them understand that, every time they use one, they are taking out a high interest loan, unless they pay it off completely at the end of each month.

Questions for Personal Reflection or Group Discussion

1.What approach do you use in teaching your children spiritual things, or do you leave it to the church to do that?

2. Do you tend to do for your kids what they should be learning to do for themselves? Think about (or discuss) ways to change this pattern in your home (your wife needs to be in sync with this).

3. Are you teaching your children how to handle money? Are you also a good model for them in this area?

Granting Independence

One of the trickiest parts of parenting is how to balance freedom and control. We don't want to lose control of our children for the sake of their safety and well-being. At the same time, we want them to grow up to be independent adults, who can make good decisions and take care of themselves. The rub is *we can't have it both ways*. This tension is particularly felt during the teen years, when they are pushing for more freedom, and involved in activities out of our sight. The first time my daughter took the family car out by herself, I remember thinking, "What have I done?" Up until then, whenever she needed to go someplace, her mother or I would take her, and so we knew where she was. But now she could be anywhere!

Independence is also a privilege that comes with a corresponding responsibility. As they grow up, it's good to give them more and more freedom as they demonstrate the ability to handle it. For instance, if they ask to go to a friend's house and promise to be home at a certain time, let them. If they don't come home when promised, or were not where they said they would be, then they lose that freedom for a while. Of course, it's always good to know what kind of friends they are hanging with, and if the parents are responsible and at home to supervise. Getting the parents' phone number and checking to make sure they got there is also a smart idea.

During the teen years, it's important to know the parents of their friends and to communicate with them. Adolescents share information with each other on how to put things over on their parents, so it's good for the parents to work together as well. For instance, one parent shared with me how their teen (with no license) went for a joy ride in one of the family cars while the parents were out for the evening. They smartly checked the odometer before they left and rechecked it when they got back home, learning exactly how many miles their child had driven.

Of course, my wife and I figured our child would *never* do something like that! But, as a precaution, we did an odometer check one night when we went out. Sure enough, our daughter had pulled the same stunt. Now you're probably thinking, why not simply take the keys to the other car with us? We could have done that, but we wouldn't have learned how sneaky she was. And besides, informing her that we knew what she did, without telling her *how*, gave her the impression that we were psychic. Anytime you can get a leg up as a parent, take it!

Adolescence and young adulthood are also times when children are learning to think for themselves and deciding what values and beliefs they are going to embrace. This can be disconcerting for Christian parents, especially if they seem to be moving in a direction away from our faith. Here's where good, open communication is an extra bonus. If they know that we are open to discuss these things, even if they don't agree with us, it will be helpful. Sometimes, out of fear, we may be tempted to preach to them, but this isn't productive. We'll simply come across as defensive, rather than confident in our convictions. Since our faith is "more caught than taught" with our children, sharing our views with them in a loving, respectful way will send a message as important as our words. It also helps to have credibility by making sure *we* really understand our Christian faith and *why* we believe what we do. They'll lose respect for us if we don't. Besides regular study of the Bible, numerous books are available to assist in this area.

To have genuine maturity in their faith, young people need to struggle with what they believe, and come to their own conclusions. Then their convictions are really *their own*, not just something passed down to them from their parents. So, give them time, keep loving them and providing a good example of Christian manhood, and don't stop praying for them. It may take a while, but I often see prodigal children come back, after they've had a taste of the world and found that it's not all that it's cracked up to be.

Choosing Colleges

One of the biggest decisions your adolescent will have to make involves their future occupation and how to prepare for it. There's a lot of societal push to send our children to college, but not every child is college material. And there are too many out-of-work college graduates with large school loans to repay. Your child may be a "hands-on" person who would do better in a craft or trade. In our rapidly changing world, there will always be a need for those who know how to deal with the world of technology. Jobs in the mechanical field and the building trades will always be needed as well. They can earn a good living and will probably have more satisfaction from their work than they would sitting behind a desk.

Because of the cost of higher education today, one of the wisest moves parents can make is sending their child to a community college for the first couple of years and/or having them take some courses online. This not only saves a bundle of money, but keeps them at home longer to mature, before taking on the new freedom they'll enjoy at a school away from home. Too many students never make it past their freshman year because they thought college was party time on their parents' dime. Those first years in college are also times when students change majors, after learning that the field of study they were interested in isn't so interesting after all. They also may find that academics isn't for them, and pursue a trade instead.

When my son graduated from high school, he wasn't sure he wanted to go to college, and so we investigated a school that focused on the building trades (his real interest). He did finally decide to attend a Christian college where he majored in business and met his wife. During the summers, he made good money working construction jobs, and upon graduation, he took a job with a home-building company. His hands-on skills and business degree, plus experience with that company, prepared him to operate his own construction and remodeling business today.

All of this to say, it's important to know your child's interests and abilities before investing in their education. My daughter knew she wanted to be a nurse like her mother while she was still in high school. She got her nursing degree and did graduate work in health-care administration, and has been in the nursing field at several levels ever since. With both of my children, I am thankful that they are in fields where their skills will always be needed. If your child is uncertain about what they would like to do for a living, getting help from a vocational counselor would be a worthwhile expenditure before investing tens of thousands in their education.

Think "Christian" when looking at colleges for your child. Too many parents are overly impressed with schools that have a reputation for academic excellence, like the Ivy League colleges; or with large state universities that have outstanding athletic programs. Unfortunately, most of these schools are extremely secular, and even have an anti-Christian bias. Some of the things that take place on these campuses, in the name of education, would make a Christian parent's hair curl. At a time when your child is forming his or her worldview, this kind of environment could be deadly to their faith.

There are many fine colleges and universities that teach from a Christian perspective and can help strengthen your child's faith, not destroy it. If the purpose of higher education is to teach a student to think and to prepare for a life's vocation, it's better to have them do it in a Christian setting, if possible. Many young people meet their future mates in college as well, and a Christian school increases their chances of finding one who shares their faith and values.

Of course, your child may be interested in pursuing a field of study not offered at a Christian school. In that case, it's wise to take the time to check out various secular options. Some schools, while not Christian, have a strong Christian presence on campus with many faith-based organizations. Others have good churches nearby with effective ministries to college students. The state university that I attended my first two years had an active InterVarsity group and my home church within walking distance of the campus. Both helped to keep me spiritually grounded. Although I was rushed by a fraternity, I didn't need one in order to have a social life.

Keep in mind that college life is much different today than when you were in school, so it's good to educate yourself about various colleges, many of which have reputations for being "party schools." You may be footing the bill for their education, so you should have the final say as to where they will go. They'll often choose a school that has a nice campus, or a reputation as a fun place, or where several of their friends are planning to attend. Your more mature perspective ought to prevail. After doing your homework, it would be helpful to offer two or three choices (that meet your approval) from which your child can select. Also think about schools within a couple of hours' drive from your home. This way, they can get away from campus frequently and you can also make regular trips to see them at school. Both of my kids were within two hours of home while in college, and it was much easier to stay connected with them as a result.

Questions for Personal Reflection or Group Discussion

1. How much independence do your children have? Do you and your wife have a plan for easing them into it gradually? What is it?

2. Do you assume that your children will go to college, or have you considered other options based on their abilities and interests?

3. What do you think of sending them to community college for the first two years? Will you let them totally choose the school they attend, or will you have major input? Consider the advantage of having them (and you) graduate with little or no debt.

Emptying the Nest (or Not)

For some parents, the thought of having their child leave home is a difficult one to contemplate. Our children are a part of our everyday lives for so long, it's hard to imagine not having them around. Going away to college is the first step for many, and it's a major adjustment for parents when the first one leaves the nest—the family circle is broken. And when the last one leaves, the nest really feels empty for a while, and there will be a sense of loss and sadness. But if your marriage is good, it won't take long for you to adjust to *your* new freedom. It's like being newly married all over again.

It's helpful to prepare your children for going out on their own. From the time my children were small, my wife and I used to tell them two things: "When you go to college . . ." and "When you're out of college and on your own, you can . . ." This is seed-planting. As a result, both of them assumed they would go to college, which they did (although, as indicated earlier, we were open to other options), and both assumed that, after college, it was time to leave home, which they also did.

But what if they return to the nest? In recent years, this has become more common, as young people have been unable to land a job that pays them enough to live on their own. Or, they may be between jobs and need to circle back home temporarily. The question is, how do you parent an adult child living under your roof, especially one who has already experienced independence? The answer is . . . *you negotiate*, while remembering that you have the upper hand. It's your house, and there are certain values and standards you live by, as well as expenses you incur. Having grown up with you, they should be well aware of what those standards are. Household rules are negotiable, Biblical standards are not.

They may need to understand that there are certain expectations now that they are adults. Things like, you are not running a cleaning and laundry service for them, nor is your wife a short order cook. They need to take care of their own personal needs. They also should be contributing to household expenses, like groceries and utilities, all of which will increase with another adult in the house.

I once counseled a middle-aged couple who wanted to know how to launch an adult son who had never left home and a daughter who had circled back with a child after her divorce. Both children were gainfully employed. When I asked who cooked their meals, did their laundry, and cleaned their rooms, the wife indicated that it had fallen on her. They also weren't helping with household expenses. From where I sat, this was a no-brainer. These kids had simply taken advantage of a good deal—for them! I encouraged the parents to start charging rent and putting the responsibility for meals, laundry, and cleaning back on them, while still maintaining the family rules. It didn't take long for both of their children to move out on their own.

I understand that, for some ethnic groups, staying at home until marriage is part of the family tradition. If you are comfortable with that, fine. But research has shown that the best preparation for marriage is to live on your own. That way you learn both personal and financial responsibility *before* getting married. If young men, especially, are used to their mothers doing everything for them, they will expect their wives to pick up where Mom left off. I have seen this often in couples with whom I have worked.

Parenting Children Out of the Nest

Once your children have left home and are on their own, your relationship with them will change dramatically. Although you will always have a parent's instincts of love and concern, and a desire to protect your children, they no longer need to be parented. This will be a major adjustment for your wife, in particular, especially if being a mother has been her major role in life. Thus, working on your marriage is so important during the child-rearing years. When couples neglect their marriage and allow family life to revolve around the children, they often find there's nothing left when the children are gone. The result is frequently and sadly, divorce.

With independent adult children, you aren't in the position to give them advice any longer, unless they ask for it or grant you permission to give it. Some of the decisions they make will require you to bite your tongue at times, but it's *their* life now. And you had many years to influence them while they were growing up. If you did a good job as a parent, and they respect you for it, you will probably find that most of what you taught and modeled for them will stick. As was true when they were younger, the important thing is to keep your communication with them open and encouraging. They should know you are always there for them, but not going to interfere in their lives.

Married children present an additional challenge for you and your wife. Now you have to share them with a husband or wife, who takes your place as the most important person in their lives. In addition, your child has taken on a set of in-laws, who will want their share of time and attention, as well as holiday family gatherings. This requires major adjustments on your part; not only of scheduled time together, but also in attitude and expectations.

One of the best things you can do is to develop a relationship with your new son or daughter-in-law early on, even before the wedding. Spend time one-on-one with him or her, if possible. Let them feel comfortable with you, and vice versa. They are likely to be a bit intimidated by you at first and desire your approval, so it's important for you to take the initiative to reach out to them. If possible, also get to know your son or daughter's in-laws. This will help things to run more smoothly when it comes to making wedding plans, and negotiating holidays, birthdays, and other special occasions afterward the wedding. For my wife and myself, having good relations with our children's in-laws has made things so much more pleasant, as we have been able to compromise or share special occasions together with them.

The Joy of Fatherhood

At different stages in my children's lives, I had different feelings about myself as a father. When they were young, I thought I was doing a pretty good job. During the teen years, I felt like a total failure. While they were in college, I began to feel a little better. And now, many years and many prayers later, I am truly proud of the adults they have become, by God's grace, and largely *in spite of* me. One conclusion I have come to is that you can't really evaluate yourself as a parent until you see *your* kids with *their* kids. Thank God, mine are good parents— in many ways better than I was—and I am truly grateful.

Questions for Personal Reflection or Group Discussion

1. Are you in the empty nest phase, and how is it going for you? Are you investing the extra time in your relationship with your wife?

2. If you are not in that phase yet, have you and your wife developed a game plan for that time?

3. If your children are fully launched singles or married, what are you doing to maintain a good relationship with them?

4. A piece of advice—don't wait for them to call you or invite you to do things. They are probably wrapped up in their own careers, families, etc., and probably don't think that much about you. Don't be hurt. You take the initiative. It's worth it.

Going Further: Read and reflect on (or discuss) the following passages of Scripture—Hebrews 12:7-11, Ephesians 6:4, and Colossians 3:21—and how they might apply to your own parenting as a father.

Bottom Line

Being a father is an awesome privilege as well as a responsibility. When my children were small, I was told by older people, "Enjoy them while they're young because they grow up fast." At that time, I thought they couldn't grow up fast enough! But now that our children are grown and our grandchildren are rapidly reaching maturity, I understand what they meant. These years are precious, so make sure that you don't miss them by being too busy with your work, recreation, and other responsibilities. You'll never regret the time you spend with your children, but you *will* have regrets if you fail to spend it.

Additional Resources:

Ross Campbell, *Relational Parenting.* Moody Press (2000)

Carey Casey, *Championship Fathering.* Tyndale House (2009)

Kenneth and Jeffrey Gangel, *Fathering Like the Father*. Baker Books (2003)

Matthew Johnson, *Positive Parenting with a Plan*. Family Rules (2001)

Frank Martin, *The Kid-Friendly Dad*. InterVarsity Press (1994)

Meg Meeker, *Boys Should Be Boys: 7 Secrets to Raising Healthy Sons*. Ballantine Books (2009)

Meg Meeker, *Strong Fathers, Strong Daughters: 10 Secrets Every Father Should Know*. Ballantine Books (2007)

Jim Newheiser & Elyse Fitzpatrick, *You Never Stop Being a Parent: Thriving in Relationship with your Adult Children*. P&R Publishing (2010)

Robert Wolgemuth, *Daddy @ Work: Loving Your Family, Loving Your Job, Being Your Best in Both Worlds*. Zondervan Publishing (1999)

"A good marriage is not a contract between two persons, but a sacred covenant between three. Too often Christ is never invited to the wedding and finds no room in the home."

—Donald T. Kauffman

Chapter Four: Integrity in Marriage

Marriage is the most intimate, intense, and demanding of all relationships. It can be both frustrating and fulfilling at the same time. It's frustrating because we can't always have our own way. It's also fulfilling because we can't have our own way - which is a good thing! It forces us out of a self-centered lifestyle and into a world where it's *not all about us.* Gary Thomas states it well as the thesis of his book, *Sacred Marriage.* He poses the question, "What if God designed marriage to make us holy more than to make us happy?" (p. 13) We *can* have happy marriages, of course, but this is both a gift from God and the result of working at it. I am convinced that marriage isn't as much a matter of finding the right person, but doing the right things with the person we've found. In this chapter, we'll explore some of those things together.

The Foundation

Marriage is God's idea. From the beginning, God recognized that "it is not good for man to be alone," (Gen. 2:18) so he created woman to be man's companion in life. At the end of this creation account, we are given the foundation for marriage in a single verse of such immense importance that both Jesus and Paul quote it in their discussions on this topic. (Matt. 19:5, Eph. 5:31) That verse is Genesis 2:24:

"For this reason a man will *leave* his father and mother and be *united* to his wife, and they will become *one flesh*."

This verse lays three foundation stones for a healthy marriage. *First*, we have to *leave* our family of origin. The underlying Hebrew word has the root meaning of "to be torn away from." Depending on the home in which we were raised, shifting our loyalty from parents to spouse may not be an easy transition. A man may be overly dependent on his parents, or they (especially mothers) may not be ready to let go of him. In my experience as a counselor, one's primary commitment has to be to a marriage partner in order for the marriage to work (this is true for the woman as well).

The *second* foundation stone is being *united* to our wives— another strong Hebrew word root meaning "to be joined together." A healthy marriage requires total commitment. Your relationship with your wife has to take priority, over your parents, your siblings, your friends, your business partners, and even your children. This will be a difficult adjustment if you grew up in a family where the children came first. Unfortunately, in these families, it's often the case that when the parents' marriage isn't very good; they focus on the children instead of on each other. Many of these marriages end when the last child leaves home, or just unhappily plod on out of a sense of duty.

The importance of marital commitment is reflected in our traditional wedding vows, where couples promise to forsake all others and to be there for each other, "for better, for worse; for richer, for poorer; in sickness and in health" until death. Those vows are a covenant, not a contract. Society views marriage as a *legal* arrangement with reciprocal responsibilities. But the church, following Scripture, has always seen it as a *covenant* between two people, where each makes binding promises, *regardless* of the other's response. In other words, you promised to love your wife under any circumstance, whether she reciprocates or not.

And when each partner takes their promise seriously, you have the potential for a good and fulfilling marriage. Studies of couples in long-term marriages have shown over and over again that one of the keys to their success is that divorce isn't part of their vocabulary. These couples are determined to keep their vows and work through their differences (which we all have) no matter what. Bailing out of the marriage just isn't an option for them.

The *third* foundation stone for marriage is becoming *one flesh*. While this phrase has sexual overtones to it, it is far more than simply the physical consummation of a marriage union. It involves a deep emotional and spiritual bonding between husband and wife—the most intimate relationship possible between two persons. I never *really* understood what "one flesh" meant until my first wife died. And other widowed people I talk to report the same experience: it's like having part of your heart ripped out. You feel like half a person.

This special bond in marriage can only happen when we make other loyalties secondary, and totally commit to our wives. When this takes place, it must be protected and maintained, not taken for granted. Forget the fairy-tale endings where couples effortlessly live "happily ever after." While Hollywood creates those happy endings for their movies, most Hollywood couples fail to pull it off in real life. A good marriage doesn't just happen; it has to be worked at every day.

Love

So what kind of work is needed to make your marriage what it ought to be? To begin with, the Scriptures command us to love our wives "as Christ loved the church and gave himself up for her." (Eph. 5:25) Clearly, the love Paul writes about here is far more than the romantic impulses that brought you together in the first place. It is a love modeled after Christ's sacrificial death on the cross, a love that gives without expecting a return. While Jesus never married during his time on earth, his love for the church (his bride) is the model we are given for our marriages.

Paul gives us a detailed picture of this love in 1 Corinthians 13 where he writes, "Love is patient, love is kind. It does not envy, it does not boast, it is not proud. It is not rude, it is not self-seeking, it is not easily angered, it keeps no records of wrongs . . . it always protects, always trusts, always hopes always perseveres." (vs. 4–7) This is the daily challenge: to step out of our me-first mindset and respond to the people around us in love, *especially* our wives. Are we patient, kind, and humble toward them, or are we proud, selfish, impatient, or insensitive? Do we keep a score of offenses, or do we let them go? Are we protective, trusting, and persevering with a confident hope for our future together? These are good questions to ask ourselves.

Respect

Related to love is respect. While Ephesians 5:33 stresses a wife's need to respect her husband, 1 Peter 3:7 instructs men to "be *considerate* as you live with your wives, and treat them with *respect* as the weaker partner and heirs with you of the gracious gift of life." Consideration and respect are so important in the way we treat our wives. The word "considerate" translates a Greek word with a root meaning of "to know or understand." Clearly then, being considerate (or thoughtful) involves really *knowing* our wives well enough to discern what they might need, or would appreciate from us, in any given situation. This involves being sensitive to her needs; something at which most of us are not particularly adept, but it's what we're commanded to do.

Jesus is our model when it comes to respect as well. You can't read the gospels without seeing that people responded to him because he accepted them and respected them for who they were. It didn't matter if they were wealthy noblemen or poor beggars, a hated tax collector like Matthew, or a political zealot like Simon. He sat down with both a Jewish religious leader and an outcast Samaritan woman, and addressed each of them at their level of need. For our purposes, it is especially important to see how Jesus treated women, particularly those of questionable morals and low social standing. Someone has observed that the reason women were attracted to Jesus is because he was probably the first man they had ever met who didn't try to selfishly *use* them, but one who treated them with respect instead.

Attention

Being sensitive to our wives' needs requires paying attention, like we do when at work or watching a football game. It means really listening when she's talking to you, instead of giving her half an ear while your mind is somewhere else. Since the male brain is wired to focus on one thing at a time, it will take some effort on your part to pull this off.

It's good to keep in mind that women communicate differently than men. They tend to use more words, filling in background details of whatever or whoever they are talking about. For example, if a woman is sharing a story about another person with a friend, she will tell her that person's marital status, how many children she has and the ages of each, what they had for lunch during their conversation, etc. Because women are generally more relational than men, these details are important.

But as men, who usually like to get quickly to the point, it feels like we're going down rabbit trails or listening to stories with no point at all. And so we either zone out completely, or we wander around the thickets of our minds trying to pick up the scent again. But in fairness to our wives, they probably feel the same way when we're describing the golf game we played, the fish we landed, or the glories of some new technical toy we just purchased. It may be simply a difference in interests, as well as style.

But there's more to attentiveness than really listening when she's speaking. It also involves being observant when she's not. How much to do you know about your wife? Do you know her favorite colors, foods, TV programs, reading materials? Do you know who her best friends are? Are you aware of what excites or pleases her, what stresses or worries her, what irritates or hurts her? Do you understand what's really important to her and what's not? As a counselor, I am always amazed at what people (particularly men) *don't know* about the partners they've been married to for years!

Perhaps the most important thing to know about your wife is what makes her feel loved. Gary Chapman's book, *Five Love Languages*, is especially helpful here. Chapman identifies five ways people tend to express and receive love: words of affirmation, quality time, receiving gifts, acts of service, and physical touch. He points out that how we show love is also the way we prefer to receive it. For example, I can give my wife words of affirmation or physical affection (my love languages), but while she may appreciate it, that isn't what really "floats her boat." However, if I take care of needed chores around the house, or spend quality time with her (her languages), then she really feels loved. Learn your wife's love language, and use it!

Acceptance

Acceptance is another way of showing love and respect. Again, your wife is different than you. Besides obvious physical differences, she comes from a different family background, has a different temperament and personality, as well as different needs, strengths, weaknesses, interests, and ways of doing things than you do. One of the reasons you married her is because of those differences; opposites *do* attract and complement each another. But all personality traits have both positive and negative poles. We marry the positive side and learn to tolerate the negative. For example, being stubborn is a negative trait. But stubbornness has a positive side called loyalty, and who wouldn't want that in a partner? In other words, your wife's differences can be either a source of irritation, or a source or growth and pleasure, depending on whether or not you accept her as she is.

I have found that couples who struggle in their marriages are generally focused on the negatives in each other while overlooking the good things. On the other hand, those whose marriages are going well emphasize the positives, without being blind to the negative side. The difference is *where you focus*. I once heard an interview with a man who decided to reflect on all the things he liked about his wife while he's driving home from work each night. He said that, by the time he got home, he could hardly wait to see her! Some might call that the "power of positive thinking," but I would call it "the power of appreciative thinking."

Affirmation

Affirmation is yet another way we demonstrate love. This involves acknowledging your partner's worth on a regular basis. You may love her deeply, but do you express it? Don't take for granted that she knows—she also needs to *hear* it. And not only hear that she is loved, but that she is *valued*. Point out the qualities you appreciate in her: her patience with you and the kids, her organizational skills that enable your home to run smoothly, her efforts at keeping herself and the family healthy and fit, or whatever is true in your marriage. Let her know you are grateful for her kindness or gentleness, her gracious hospitality, or her willingness to support you even when she doesn't agree with you. Tell her that you are aware of the personal sacrifices she makes for the well-being of the rest of the family.

A practical suggestion—make a list of the things you appreciate about her. Writing them down will tend to fix them in your mind. Review and add to your list from time to time. Then, when she does something on your list, you'll be more aware of it, and you can take the opportunity to express that to her. This will also help to keep you from taking her for granted, and stay focused on the positive.

Compliments also go a long way toward lubricating a marriage. They have to be genuine, of course, not forced. When was the last time you told her that you liked her cooking, or that she really looks nice, or smells good, or decorates the house tastefully, or is a good mother, etc.? You get the picture. We get so used to living with our mate's positive qualities that we don't even think about them.

Sensitivity

As mentioned earlier, being sensitive to our wives' needs is crucial in expressing love. Paul also tells us in Ephesians 5 to love our wives "as we love ourselves." He goes on to say that we give special attention to our bodies, feeding and caring for them, and we should give our wives in the same consideration (vs. 28, 29). Think about what this means in practical terms. If she's hungry, you should be just as concerned as if your stomach was growling. If she's tired after chasing kids all day, or had a rough day on her job, you need to provide a way for her to rest, even if you'd like to kick back and relax yourself. If she longs for more sleep, you need to find a way for her to get it, just as if your own body was crying for extra zzz's.

This will require self-sacrifice on your part, which brings us back to Ephesians 5:25: "Husbands love your wives as Christ loved the church and *gave himself* for her." How often does she set aside her agenda or needs to accommodate you? You need to do the same for her, whether she does it or not (Paul's command here is to *you*, the husband, *not* to your wife).

Questions for Personal Reflection or Group Discussion

1. How are you doing at loving your wife as described above? Where do you need to show improvement?

2. How much respect does she get from you?

3. How much attention? Think of how you might be more attentive.

4. Have you accepted your wife for the different person she is from you? When was the last time you expressed it? Look for new ways to affirm her as a person.

5. How sensitive do you think you are to her needs? Would she agree? In what areas do you feel you need to be more sensitive?

Needs, Wants, and Expectations

We all go into marriage with certain expectations of how it's going to be; or more specifically, how *she's* going to be. Those expectations are based on a combination of our wants and needs (not to mention fantasies), along with the model we brought into the marriage from our childhood. We all have certain basic needs—to be loved, accepted, valued, etc.—and our wives have those same needs as well.

In addition to our needs, we also have certain wants, those things we would like our wives to do for us that don't really fall into the *need* category. Things such as cooking a hot meal for us every night, always being available and willing to make love whenever we're in the mood, sharing our enthusiasm for the local sports teams, or not dragging us to shopping or to social events where we don't know anybody.

Sometimes we get our wants and needs confused, feeling that what we *want* is actually something we *need*. It's good to recognize the difference. Expecting our wives to meet certain needs associated with marriage is normal and fair. Expecting her to meet *all* of our needs is not. And thinking that she should meet all of our *wants* is totally unrealistic. No woman is capable of that, any more than you could meet all of her wants and needs.

Whatever desires she may meet over and above your basic needs should be considered a bonus. For example, most wives are not their husband's golfing buddy, but if she's always there for you when you are going through hard times, you are blessed. She may not be interested in discussing business or politics with you, but if you can tell stories, laugh together, and share your feelings with her, count yourself fortunate. Your spouse may not a "neat as a pin" housekeeper, but if she provides a warm and welcoming atmosphere in your home, that's an extra dividend.

Having said that, the question which remains in light of Ephesians 5 is, how well are *you* meeting *her* needs? And how many of *her* wants do you satisfy? Marriage is like a dance. Each partner responds to the movements of the other. Sensitivity to my wife's needs and trying to satisfy her desires makes her more inclined to do the same for me. On the other hand, if I am insensitive to her needs or not tuned in to her desires I could easily meet, she will tend to shut down, creating distance between us.

I'm not suggesting that we approach this part of marriage with a quid-pro-quo attitude (i.e., I'll be nice to her so she'll be nice to me). That's manipulation, and a set-up for frustration on both sides. But satisfying her basic needs *is* important.

William Harley, in his book *His Needs, Her Needs*, identifies five primary needs of men and women. For men, they are sexual fulfillment, recreational companionship, an attractive wife, a peaceful and quiet home, and admiration. Women's primary needs, on the other hand, are affection, conversation, honesty and openness, financial support, and family commitment. As both a husband and a counselor, I have found Harley's observations to be pretty much on target.

One need he doesn't specifically discuss is the need for trust. Every relationship we have is built on trust: teacher–student, doctor–patient, merchant–customer, parent–child, husband–wife, and especially our relationship with God. Without trust, there is no relationship of any value. In a marriage where trust is missing, one is unable to give himself or herself totally to the relationship. Emotional intimacy is withheld for fear of being hurt. To build trust in your marriage, you have to be consistent and reliable on a daily basis. You need to always be where you say you'll be and do what you say you'll do. Openness, honesty, total commitment, and predictability are the keys.

When needs go unmet, frustration and disappointment follow. And where you find frustration and disappointment, there will be either anger and conflict, or bitterness and emotional withdrawal. Either way, it's deadly to a good marriage. This is probably the biggest source of conflict I see in marriages. In practical terms, the bottom line is this: understand your wife's needs and do whatever you can to meet them.

You also need to communicate *your* needs to your marriage partner. You can't expect her to meet your needs if you're not sharing them. She's not any more of a mind- reader than you are. And yet, mind-reading is often a problem between couples, especially those who have been married for a while. Men, in particular, commonly complain that their wives expect them to be mind-readers. Have you noticed that if you anticipate your wife's need and meet it, you get all sorts of credit? But if she has to *ask* you to do something for her, *even if you do it willingly*, you get practically no points at all! I have even had women, without embarrassment, admit to me that this is true.

After quite a bit of head-scratching and investigation, I think I've figured out why this happens. Our brains just work differently. The male brain is very focused. Basically, we have one-track minds. Women's brains are much more diffused. They take in everything around them, and can multitask more easily than men. Thus, when we come home from work and walk right past the trash bag sitting by the back door, because we're preoccupied with something else, it drives them crazy! And frankly, when I've tried to explain this brain difference to my female clients, many of them don't buy it. They think I'm just making excuses for their husbands.

But I believe there's also another reason we get more credit when we can anticipate her wants and needs. It's because she doesn't like to nag. And, more importantly, it makes her feel like you *really* love her, if you can sense what she needs in advance. The moral of this discussion is, when you are with her, pay attention! And because *she* may be distracted by the many things filling her mind, it would be helpful to let her know what *you* need or desire from her as well.

Questions for Personal Reflection or Group Discussion

1. What were your expectations going into marriage? Have they been met? How have they changed?

2. Make a list of your wife's actual needs. How many are you able to meet? In which area could you use improvement?

3. Are there wants she has expressed that you could also meet? Think about (or discuss) specific ways you could do this. Then make a plan.

4. Which of *your* needs or wants are not being met that you feel your wife should be meeting? Have you discussed them with her? Why, or why not?

Communication

Good communication is important in any relationship, but particularly in marriage. Without it, couples struggle in virtually every area of their lives together. We need to understand what our partner is thinking, planning, feeling, wanting, or needing. If we don't, we will inevitably find ourselves enmeshed in conflict. Here are some suggestions for improving communication with your wife:

1. Daily Talk Time: When our lives get busy, the opportunity for having real conversations with our spouse decreases. Interaction gets reduced to sharing snippets of information necessary to keep the family running on schedule. Yet, nothing is more important to a good marriage than staying connected; quick texts and brief phone messages are not enough. Build into your schedule a daily, face-to-face twenty- to thirty-minute conversation with your partner, preferably at the end of the day, before both of you are too tired to concentrate. Of the hundreds of couples who have come to me for counseling, not one has had a regular talk time as part of their marriage. But couples with good marriages do.

There are several benefits to building this into your marriage. For one thing, it lets you know what each other's day has been like. If you have a bad day, it provides an opportunity to get it off your chest so that it doesn't spoil your evening together. It also clues you in regarding your wife's frame of mind, so that if she is tired or stressed out from the challenges of her day, you can provide her with a little extra TLC that evening. Also, just sharing what goes on in one another's lives while you are apart helps build more understanding and intimacy into your relationship. In addition, it reduces tension and heads off conflict by letting you deal with small misunderstandings between you, or hurts as they arise, rather than having them build up over several days and then exploding.

2. Timing and Setting: When and where to have an effective conversation are important considerations. If you have children around, you may need to train them to leave you alone for a while after dinner, while the two of you talk over a cup of coffee (my parents' pattern). Or you may have to retreat to the privacy of your bedroom to keep from being interrupted. If you are empty-nesters, having a good talk-time together over dinner would seem the most natural way.

For most couples, the ideal time is after dinner. There's something about a meal that both relaxes and energizes you. Plus, meals and talking just seem to go together. If you wait until late in the evening, when you are both tired and your concentration level is down, you are less likely to have a good conversation. If you have pre-school children, you may have to wait until they are in bed. In that case, make sure they get to bed early. Also, having your talk time at the same time every day (as much as possible) will make it a regular part of your routine. Good marriages are largely made up of good habits and routines. If you make a habit of daily conversations together, I think you'll enjoy the benefits, and your wife will also.

3. Undivided Attention: To really engage in conversation, you need to give each other more than half an ear. This means getting away from the computer, turning off the TV, putting down the newspaper or smart phone, and ignoring incoming calls while you talk. How often have you been focused on watching a ballgame on TV or engrossed in reading when your wife has said something to you? You nodded your head and replied, "Uh-huh." Then she went out the door, leaving you wondering what she just said and where she's going, or worse, what you just agreed to. Because men do have one-track minds, we need to be sure we are tracking with her while she's talking (also read the previous section on Attention).

4. Listening: Probably the most crucial element in any conversation with your wife is *really listening* to her. Some people are better at listening than others, but it is a skill that *can* be learned. It does take more energy than talking, especially if you struggle with attention deficit. Listening also tells her you are interested in what she is saying and, indirectly, that you genuinely care about her. It is ultimately *an act of love*. True listening takes place on three levels.

First, we need to listen with our ears. This involves not only hearing the words, but deciphering the meaning behind those words. It may require giving feedback or asking questions, to make sure we understand what our wives are telling us. When we're not on the same page, it leads to misunderstanding; and I'm sure, as you have probably experienced, this can result in an argument.

Second, it's important to listen with our eyes. Eye contact is so crucial. It's been said that "the eyes are the windows of the soul," and there's a lot of truth in that. Eye contact is especially an expression of interest and love, which encourages the other person to open up and share. Watching her body language is also important. It often conveys the real meaning of what she's saying. Pay attention to the look in her eyes (particularly if she's teary), the expression on her face, and the position of her body. These are all things that counselors learn to do, and it helps immensely to understand what's going on inside of a person.

Third, it's essential to listen with our hearts. This means tuning in to the emotions behind her words. We generally live at the level of our emotions, our words and body language often reflecting what we feel. And since men are not as good at either understanding or communicating feelings, this will require special effort on your part. If you're not sure what she's feeling, ask. Or better yet, try putting yourself in her shoes when she's sharing an experience, and suggest what she might be feeling: "Boy, that must have been scary," or "I'll bet that made you nervous," or "That would have made me really angry," etc. If you touch the right emotion, she'll feel like you truly do understand. And even if you don't hit it right, she'll know that you *are trying* to understand what she's feeling. Either way, you'll be expressing love and concern.

5. Listening to Signals: It's important to keep in mind the difference between men and women when it comes to the signals we give, like nodding and saying "uh-huh," to let the other know we are paying attention. Women generally do this to convey attention, while men typically do this only when we agree with what the other person is saying. In other words, just because she is nodding, doesn't mean she agrees with you. You'll need to check that out to be sure.

6. Interruptions: Men are more likely than women to interrupt when the other person is talking. I struggle with this myself. This can be very irritating to your wife, especially if she is trying to get an important point across, or share a sensitive situation with you. One of the reasons we tend to do this is we're afraid we'll forget an important point *we* want to make, or maybe because she has touched a nerve by something that was said. And if you have attention deficit problems, it will be particularly challenging for you to sit on your tongue. Remember what James 1:19 tells us: "Be quick to listen, slow to speak, slow to get angry." It's worth it.

7. Give Sympathy, Not Solutions: As men, we tend to be problem-solvers. This is what most of our jobs demand all day. Thus, when our wife is sharing a problem or something that upsets her, we want to jump right in and "fix it"—big mistake. What she really wants is affirmation and understanding. Let her know you understand her feelings and can see her point of view. If she wants your opinion, she'll ask for it.

Or if you really feel like you can be of help, *after* she has vented and you have shown proper concern, you might *ask* her if she'd like your perspective on the situation. (Caution: Don't try to help her see the other person's point of view. That may be a good strategy at times for a counselor, but not for a husband. She'll think you are taking the other person's side, and it'll be all downhill after that.)

8. Respond First, Comment Second: There have been times, when my wife was expressing her thoughts about something, I disagreed and replied with contrary ideas of my own. This created tension between us, which was confusing to me. I thought that I was simply expressing my point of view, the way she had just expressed hers! But I learned that she felt like I had run over her ideas without giving them, *or her,* proper consideration. This is another area where men and women differ. In the course of a conversation, women will tend to respond to what the other person said *before* making comments of their own. We men, on the other hand, tend to simply throw in our own opinions, without responding first (like we do with other guys).

But our wives feel like they haven't been heard. Or worse, if we disagree, and state our opinion without first affirming hers, it feels like we are dismissing or invalidating her thoughts. This, of course, can lead to an argument rather than a productive discussion. Affirming what she says first, doesn't mean you need to agree. It just lets her know she has been heard. And it gives you the opportunity to explore her ideas with her, making sure you understand, and then affirming the parts you agree with, *before* offering your own opinion.

Questions for Personal Reflection or Group Discussion

1. How would you rate your communication with your wife?

2. How many times a week do you have uninterrupted one-on-one conversations with her?

3. How would you rate yourself as a listener? What do you think you need to do in order to improve in this area?

4. What would be a good time and place for a daily talk time with her?

Handling Conflict

Some conflict is inevitable in marriage. A wise person once said, "If you never have any disagreements with your spouse, one of you is unnecessary." As mentioned earlier, we do tend to marry people whose differences complement our own, and at times those differences can create tension between us. Although most couples don't enjoy conflict, avoiding it doesn't always work, especially if there are negative feelings involved. Sometimes issues arise over and over again, but never get resolved. After a while, you stop talking about them, because you just don't want to endure the frustration and pain of another go-round. But that creates separation.

And not dealing with problems also pushes them underground, where they will fester and resurface in some other part of your relationship, not uncommonly in your sex life. So it's good to find a way to work these things through. But how? Let me make a few suggestions.

1. Time and Place: Many marital arguments take place at night, and in the bedroom. This is because we're tired and our guard is down. Thus, we tend to say things and react to what is being said in ways that we wouldn't at other times. So if you need to have a sensitive conversation with your wife, put it off until morning, or wait until after you've had a good meal and both are feeling more relaxed and open. Also, find a private place where you can hash it out. If you can do it amicably, it's all right to disagree with each other in front of the kids. That's where they will learn how to settle differences—by watching you do it effectively.

2. Strive for Understanding: Most arguments between couples occur as a result of misunderstandings. One of the lines from a well-known prayer by Francis of Assisi is,

"O Divine Master, grant that I may not so much seek . . . to be understood, as to understand." This is a good perspective for us to have with our wives. If you are more interested in understanding *her*, than in getting her to understand *you*, you'll be way ahead of the game.

One way to achieve understanding is by going deeper. If you think you know what her point of view is, reflect it back to her in your own words. If she confirms that you *do* understand her perspective, ask her *why* she feels the way she does, or *why* this issue is so important to her. Then let her explain. Once you're sure that you understand where she's coming from, share the reasoning behind your point of view with her. Since you have heard her out, she should also be willing to listen to you.

3. Attack the Problem Together: Always remember you are life partners. You're on the same side. Avoid being competitors who need to win an argument. With this in mind, once you come to a point of mutual understanding, put your heads together and attack the problem as a team, setting aside your personal agendas, in order to come to a "meeting of the minds."

4. Always Aim For a Win-Win Solution: Keep in mind that any solution to a conflict of ideas or desires that is less than a win-win is always a lose-lose proposition. You may win an argument because your partner caved in, but you'll have lost something in the relationship in the process. And the relationship is far more important than whatever you were arguing about. Personally, I'm more comfortable staying engaged in a conversation when there's disagreement, than my wife is. And she will sometimes acquiesce to my point of view. I then walk away feeling that I convinced her by the brilliance of my argument. But if, upon further reflection, I go back and ask if we really are on the same page, I often find that she didn't agree at all. She just gave in to "keep the peace." At that point, it's necessary to for us to open the discussion again; because if she isn't happy, I know that, ultimately, I won't be either.

5. Check Your Motives: If we are honest with ourselves, I think we'll find that most of our disagreements happen because we're not getting *our* way. By nature, we all tend to look out for number one. We want what *we* want. And when we're not getting it, we find ourselves in conflict. James 4:1- 2 describes this so well: "What causes fights and quarrels among you? Don't they come from your desires that battle within you?" There are times in marriage when we need to set aside our agenda, our desires, and even (at times) our needs for the sake of our wives. We do this out of the self-sacrificing kind of love Paul described for husbands in Ephesians 5:25-33.

Forgiveness

One of the most important habits you can develop in your marriage is the habit of forgiving one another. New Testament writings that address relationships in the church also apply to our marriages (your wife is your sister-in-Christ as well as your marriage partner). One of the most instructive passages in this regard is Colossians 3:12-14:

> "Therefore, as God's chosen people, holy and dearly loved, clothe yourselves with compassion, kindness, humility, gentleness and patience. Bear with each other and forgive whatever grievances you may have against one another. Forgive as the lord forgave you. And over all these virtues put on love, which binds them all together in perfect unity."

Every couple ought to have these verses posted on their refrigerator. What a great recipe for a good marriage! But notice the middle section in particular. First, he says "bear with each other." Marriage involves a lot of simply bearing with or putting up with one another. We all have habits and mannerisms that bother our partners, and there are things they do that annoy us. We might mention it to them from time to time, and they may or may not change. If they don't, we have a choice. Do we let it irritate us so that it becomes a bone of contention between us, or do we accept that it's probably not going to change, and simply overlook it? Love puts up with it.

On the other hand, things happen that require forgiveness, which is why Paul adds "and forgive whatever grievances you may have against one another." There are times when we feel unfairly treated or spoken to. We might try to overlook it, but it just keeps eating at us. What then? This calls for forgiveness, which is simply *letting it go*. That's not the same as overlooking things. When we forgive, we are fully aware that we have been hurt, and it may be necessary to talk to our partner about it, especially if it is a pattern or an incident we don't want to repeat. If she apologizes, it's easier to forgive her. But even if she doesn't, we still need to forgive for *our* own sake. The alternative is to carry it around, letting it eat away at our insides, and creating a wedge between us. It's just not worth it.

Some people feel like forgiveness is letting the other person off the hook, but it really isn't. You're *not* saying that it didn't hurt, or didn't matter, or that the other person wasn't responsible for your pain. What you *are* saying is that you are not going to judge her (we're really not in a position to do that—that's God's job), or punish her, or try to get even in some way. You *choose* to let it go, to forgive her. Not because she deserves it (forgiveness is never deserved; it's an act of grace), but you offer it to her as a gift. Which takes us back to our Colossians 3 passage: we forgive because the Lord forgave us. It's good to humbly remember our own failures and God's grace to us. And the time will no doubt come when you'll need her to forgive you also.

Learn to say "I'm sorry" and "I forgive you." Those two sentences are among the hardest ones for us to say, because they require that we eat our pride. But, for the health of our marriages, they also may be the most important ones we can utter. Leaving them unsaid breeds hurt and distance, while expressing them provides healing and closeness.

Questions for Personal Reflection or Group Discussion

1. What issues in your marriage most often lead to disagreements or conflict?

2. Are you able to resolve them? What's your approach?

3. Are any of the above suggestions for handling conflict helpful for you? Which ones?

4. When was the last time you had to apologize to your wife? Was it difficult to do, and why do you think that it was? How was it received?

Romance

Romantic love is secondary to unconditional, self-sacrificing love. It isn't adequate to build a marriage on, but it's not unimportant. The Bible may emphasize the former, but romance is not ignored - the Old Testament Song of Songs is one of the most romantic pieces of literature ever written. Some marriages lack romance, and those couples seem okay with that. But my suspicion is that they have settled for humdrum, and would secretly enjoy a little sizzle in their relationship. In fact, one of the reasons people get involved in extramarital affairs is that someone comes along who stirs up those dying embers of romance in their souls.

Interestingly, we knew how to romance our wives when we were courting—that's how we won her heart. But after the honeymoon is over and we settle into our jobs, housekeeping, and parenting, it tends to fall through the cracks. It's true that we'll never have the same level of romance after marriage that we had before. Everything was new and exciting then, we had more time for each other, and there were fewer outside commitments to distract us. But the romantic part of our relationship doesn't have to die altogether . . . *if we choose to keep it alive.*

Like anything important in life, romance takes commitment, time, and planning. First, you have to *want* it in your marriage and be determined to make it happen. Then, you have to *arrange time* for it. Part of the reason that romance was alive during your courtship was because of the amount of time you spent seeing each other, talking on the phone, and thinking about the other person when you were apart. You also planned your dates together, as well as giving cards, gifts, and romantic gestures that expressed your love for her. It's not too late to start doing those things again. Here are some suggestions:

1. Date her frequently. When was the last time you took your wife on a *real* date, just the two of you (going out with another couple doesn't count; your attention is on them, instead of on each other)? Many couples stop dating after they get married for any number of reasons: They're too busy keeping up with the kids' schedules of games and practices, music or dance lessons, and youth group activities, or their own extracurricular schedules. It's too hard to find a good babysitter. They're too tired after working all week, etc. All of these things may be a challenge, but we do manage to make arrangements for the things we *really* want to do, don't we?

The advantages of dating your wife are many. For one thing, it gets you away from the distractions of home—TV, computer, kids, neighbors, pets, etc.—so you can focus on each other without interruption. You're able to engage in conversations that may last for hours, which can also lead into deeper discussions than the surface things we say to each other on the fly. More importantly, dating brings back memories of your courting years, and it helps you to remember that you are a *couple*, not just parents. You were a couple before the children came along, and hopefully you will still be a couple after they leave home. Parenting is temporary; marriage is (or should be) for life.

Dating doesn't have to be expensive. Walking around the local shopping mall or taking a stroll in a park, and stopping for pie and coffee on the way home, is a date, because you are doing it alone together. Let me share a couple of things about dating that worked in my marriage, and may work for you. When our kids were school-aged, money was a bit tight, but my hours were flexible. So we would often go out for extended lunch dates. We didn't need to hire a sitter (the school was doing that for us), and we found that we could get a good meal at a nice restaurant for a lot less at noon than we would pay for in the same establishment at night.

Another thing we did for a while was play, "Guess where we're going on a date?" To take the pressure off either of us having to plan the dates all the time, we would take turns. One week I would plan a date, make the arrangements, and tell her what time to be ready and how to dress. She wouldn't know where we were going or what we were doing until we got there. It might be dinner, a movie, bowling, roller skating, miniature golf, or whatever, but part of the fun was the surprise. The next week she would do the same for me.

Many couples want to date, but don't seem able to squeeze it into their schedules. With that approach, dating gets *squeezed out* most of the time. To be consistent with *any* activity, I really have to make it *part* of my schedule. So, when the kids got older, my wife and I designated Friday as date night. Other things would come up on occasion; then we'd have to change our date to another night that week. But designating a "date night" kept it on our schedule and made it a priority. Every week may not work for you, but I would recommend you do it at least every other week to keep the romance alive.

2. Give tokens of love. Don't neglect the little things you did when you were dating, like bringing her flowers. Most women love flowers. It doesn't have to be a dozen roses or a special occasion. Pick up a single rose or a small bunch of her *favorite* flowers (learn what that is) on your way home from work. When you're waiting in line at your local drug store, grab her favorite candy bar. Bring her the milk shake of the season from Chick-fil-A, or offer to pick up a pizza for dinner if you know she's had a hectic day. Besides appreciating the gesture, little things like this let her know that you think about her, even when you aren't together.

3. Send messages of love. During the day, call her just to ask how she's doing. Leave a message on her voice mail, or send a text simply telling her you love her. More lengthy love notes via email, regular mail, or just left on her vanity are even more effective. And don't forget cards. Hallmark has cards for lovers that express a number of sentiments better than you or I could probably put into words. Don't wait for a birthday or anniversary to send one. Surprise her with it when she picks up the mail on an ordinary day.

One way you can use cards effectively is when you go out of town for a few days on business. Pick up a handful of suitable cards, including the "Missing you" ones. Put one under her pillow the day you leave, so she'll get it that night. Drop another in the mail so she'll get it the next day. Then send one each day from your destination so she'll keep receiving them every day. This takes just a little bit of planning and effort, but she's worth it, isn't she? (Tip: If you're not a particularly thoughtful guy, or your mind tends to be filled with work problems or other responsibilities, mark your calendar with reminders to pick up flowers, a card, etc.) Keep the goal in mind: to let her know how much you love her.

4. Show her affection. This is one of your wife's primary needs, and unfortunately, too many men only warm up physically when they are in the mood for sex. That's foreplay, not affection. She needs to have you hold her hand, give her hugs and kisses, or cuddle with her while you're watching TV, without feeling like she's being manipulated into the bedroom. Affection is as important to her as sex is to you. Is sexual intimacy important? Absolutely! And we'll deal with that in the next chapter.

You may not be an especially touchy-feely guy. Maybe the family you grew up in wasn't especially demonstrative, so this doesn't come naturally to you. My family wasn't either. But I learned to be more affectionate, *and* comfortable with it. It just took doing it frequently. Start with giving her a full body hug and a real kiss, rather than a quick peck on the cheek before going to work. The same thing when you get home. Let her know that your intentions are simply affection, not anything more (and make sure those *are* your intentions!).

5. Follow the first-four-minute rule. It has been shown that the first four minutes at the start of a day set the tone between you two for the rest of the day. And the first four minutes when you return home at night also set the tone for the evening. In other words, if you "get up on the wrong side of the bed," or you come home grouchy and distracted after a hard day at work, it probably won't help the romantic feelings between you. So focus on starting and ending your day with warmth and affection. It will keep the embers burning in the furnace of her heart, and in yours.

Questions for Personal Reflection or Group Discussion

1. On a scale of 1 to 10, how would you rate the romantic temperature in your marriage? How do you think your wife would rate it?

2. What romantic things did you do when you were dating her? When did you *stop* doing them? Do you think she would like you to do them again?

3. Make a list of romantic gestures you would like to add to your marriage, and put them as reminders in your datebook.

4. Incorporate a regular date night into your schedule (with her input, of course).

Prayer and Marriage

And last, but most important, make prayer a part of your marriage, and make your marriage a part of your prayers. Pray *for* your wife in your quiet time each morning and when you think of her throughout the day; not just during difficult times, but for her everyday challenges with you and the kids and extended family and work etc. Praying for her regularly is a good way to keep her on your mind and to keep your heart warm toward her. And thank God for her every day, even spelling out the specific things for which you are thankful.

Pray for *yourself* in relation to your wife. Ask God to help you be more sensitive to her needs and to show you how to meet those needs. Ask him to teach you how to love her better, in ways that are most meaningful to her, and especially with the self-sacrificing love commanded in Ephesians 5 that we referred to earlier.

Finally, pray *with* her. This is part of spiritual leadership in the home. Prayer may be a very private thing for you, something that's hard for you to share with anyone else, even your wife. When you share your heart with God, it makes you very vulnerable, and that may be uncomfortable. But praying together can be very bonding, which is something God desires in your marriage. Start small with a slightly extended grace at meals (if it's just the two of you). Or pray a short prayer together in bed when you turn in each night, or before you leave the house in the morning.

During our normal weekly routine, my wife and I have our own personal quiet times with the Lord in the morning. That seems to work best with our widely differing schedules. But on vacation without a schedule, and being empty-nesters to boot, we like to have our quiet time together. We read the Scriptures aloud and discuss what we are reading. Then we take turns praying for our family and friends and the activities of the day. I love to hear her pray! It lets me see into her heart. And, when she prays for me, it makes me feel so much closer to her.

So, when you pray *with* your wife, be sure to also pray *for* her during your prayer. It'll let her know where *your* heart is at, and that will be much appreciated. And don't forget to thank God for her, and to tell him just how much she means to you. (Caution: Don't preach . . . pray!) There may be things in her life that you would like to see God change. That's between her and her Lord. Even in your private prayers for her, focus on *your* need for change, not hers. We all have our own spiritual baggage to get rid of, without worrying about our partner's stuff.

But do incorporate prayer into your daily life as a couple. A well-known saying goes, "Prayer changes things." In reality, God changes things, but prayer puts us in a position for him to do so. Mostly he changes *us*, and in the process, you will find that your marriage can change for the better, too.

Questions for Personal Reflection or Group Discussion

1. How often do you pray for your wife? With her?

2. What keeps you from doing so on a regular basis? Feeling that she's more spiritual? That your prayer life is personal and shouldn't be shared? Too busy and distracted?

3. Think about the obstacles, and how to remove them. Get her involved in the process.

Going Further: Read and reflect on (or discuss) the following Scriptures and their specific application to your marriage: Ephesians 5:25-33, Colossians 3:12-14, 1 Peter 3:7, and 1 Corinthians 13:4-7.

Additional Resources:

General Books

Emerson Eggrichs. *Love & Respect.* Thomas Nelson, 2004.

Willard F. Harley. *Fall in Love, Stay in Love.* Revell, 2001.

Gary Thomas. *Sacred Marriage.* Zondervan, 2000.

Paul David Tripp. *What Did You Expect?* Crossway, 2010.

Specific Issues

David and Claudia Arp. *The Second Half of Marriage.* Zondervan, 1998.

David and Claudia Arp. et al. *Empty Nesting: Reinventing Your Marriage When the Kids Leave Home.* Jossey-Bass, 2001.

Jack & Judy Balswick. *The Dual-Earner Marriage.* Revell, 1995.

Willard F. Harley. *He Wins, She Wins: Learning the Art of Marital Negotiation.* Revell, 2013.

Les & Leslie Parrott. *Love Talk: Speak Each Other's Language Like You Never Have Before.* Zondervan, 2004.

Les & Leslie Parrott. *Your Time-Starved Marriage: How to Stay Connected at the Speed of Life.* Zondervan, 2006.

Charles & Virginia Sell. *Spiritual Intimacy for Couples.* Crossway, 2001.

"Sex is not merely a physical expression of love or a significant relational encounter with another human being. And certainly, it is far more than an outlet for physical needs that cannot be met in any other way. It is, by its very nature and God's design, intricately bound up with marriage; for it completes the other elements that form a marriage."

- Dennis P. Hollinger

Chapter Five: Sexual Integrity

Sexuality is one area that especially calls for integrity on the part of Christian men. Clearly, we live in a sex-obsessed culture. Whether one considers movies, TV, the Internet, advertising, magazines, or books, we can't get away from it. Most of the social issues of our day revolve around sexual desire and activity: pornography, homosexuality, abortions, sexually transmitted diseases, sex trafficking, date rape, children born out of wedlock, sexual abuse, sexual addictions, marriage-destroying affairs, etc. The list goes on and on.

Yet, if you read the social histories of ancient civilizations, or the Biblical record, you'll find (to quote Solomon), "There is nothing new under the sun." Fallen humanity has always struggled with sex, in every culture and period of history. So, the challenge for us today is not a new one. Our Christian forefathers faced this as well. Granted, contemporary society is more openly sensuous and permissive than many previous generations, and our multimedia world makes it impossible to avoid sexual temptation. But this doesn't excuse us from living godly lives. If anything, sexual purity ought to be one of the things that makes us stand out as Christians in the world.

Is this really possible? Yes, but it's not easy. And it's certainly not done in our own strength. We're all vulnerable here. Here's some good news from Scripture: "His divine power has given us *everything we need* for life and godliness through our knowledge of him who called us by his own glory and goodness." (2 Pet. 1:3) This passage is saying that God's grace and power gives us *all the resources necessary* to live sexually pure lives, through our *relationship* with Jesus Christ. More on this later.

The Foundation

Like marriage, sex is God's idea. He created us male and female, and commanded us to populate the earth. (Genesis 1:27-28) Obviously, there's only one way to do this: by having sex and babies! To top it off, God made sex extremely pleasurable, something he didn't need to do. He could have made sexual intercourse about as exciting as shaking hands, but he didn't. It's clear that sex is something God intended for us to enjoy and want to repeat over and over again.

In addition, sex was designed by God to bond us to our partners. It's part of the relational glue that helps to hold a marriage together. Genesis 2:24 refers to this union as becoming "one flesh." The permanence of this marital bonding is emphasized by Jesus in Matthew 19:4-6, and its sexual element is stressed by Paul in 1 Corinthians 6:16. Interestingly, neuroscientists have found that, during sexual activity, certain chemicals are released in the brain, which produce a connecting bond between the persons involved. We truly are "fearfully and wonderfully made." (Ps. 139:14) And it's all part of our creator's beautiful plan for marital union.

Unfortunately, humans have taken God's good gift of sex and made it something ugly and perverted. Under the influence of sin, it has become an activity to be used and abused for our own selfish pleasure, rather than a wonderful expression of committed, mutual love between a husband and wife. As Christian men, the Bible calls us to redeem this area of our lives and to restore our sexuality to the place God intended in the beginning. Thus, Paul eloquently writes in Eph. 4:17-24:

> "You must no longer live as the Gentiles *(i.e. heathen)* do, in the futility of their thinking . . . Having lost all sensitivity, they have given themselves over to sensuality so as to indulge in every kind of impurity, with a continual lust for more. You, however, did not come to know Christ that way . . . You were taught, with regard to your former way of life, to put off your old self, which is being corrupted by its deceitful desires; to be made new in the attitude of your minds; and to put on the new self; created to be like God in true righteousness and holiness."

In 1 Corinthians 6:18-20, Paul adds this:

> "Flee from sexual immorality. All other sins a man commits are outside his body. But he who sins sexually sins against his own body. Do you not know that your body is a temple of the Holy Spirit, who is in you, whom you have received from God? You are not your own; you were bought at a price. Therefore honor God with your body."

On the positive side, marital intimacy is discussed by Paul in First Corinthians 7:1-5. There he points out how important it is that both husband and wife meet each other's sexual needs, warning them to be sure they "do not deprive each other." In the pages that follow, we will be looking at how to meet your wife's sexual needs. We'll also examine what sexual purity looks like both inside and outside of marriage, and how to handle the sexual temptations that are common to all men.

Questions for Personal Reflection or Group Discussion

1. Do you think it's more difficult for a Christian to deal with the sexual obsession of our society today than it was in past generations? Why or why not?

2. Do you think that this lack of sexual morality causes Christians to become numb to its seriousness? Or to lower our own standards?

3. As a Christian, do you tend to see sex as a good gift from God, or more as an area of personal struggle?

Sexual Integrity in Marriage

After thirty-five years of marriage, a husband and wife went for counseling. When asked what the problem was, the wife went into a tirade, listing every problem they ever had over the years they had been married. On and on and on she went: neglect, lack of intimacy, emptiness, loneliness, feeling unloved and unlovable - an entire laundry list of unmet needs that she had endured.

Finally, after allowing her to continue for a sufficient length of time, the therapist got up, walked around his desk, and after asking the wife to stand, he embraced and kissed her long and passionately as her husband watched, with raised eyebrows. The woman shut up and quietly sat down as though in a daze.

The therapist turned to the husband and said, "This is what your wife needs at least three times a week. Do you think you can make it happen?"

"Well, I can drop her off here on Mondays and Wednesdays, but on Fridays, I go fishing." (source unknown)

As a counselor, I have never tried that technique (nor could I pull it off without losing both my license and my wife), but this joke does illustrate the importance of physical affection in the marital relationship. The writer of Hebrews says, "Marriage should be honored by all, and the marriage bed kept pure." (Heb. 13:4a) Notice he is saying the marriage bed *is pure*—keep it that way! Despite the way our culture has degraded it, there is nothing sorted or dirty about sex, *within the context of marriage*. It is, in fact, *still* a beautiful thing, when treated the way God intended.

Understanding Your Differences

Is there a *Christian way* to engage in sexual activities with your wife? I believe so. To begin with, it starts with your sexual desires. For the most part, men are more interested in sexual intercourse than women (there are exceptions). This largely has to do with the difference in our testosterone levels (we have ten times as much as they do). Consequently, there will be times when you express interest and she could care less. How do you react? By getting your nose bent out of shape? Reminding her of her marital duty? Guilting her into satisfying your desires? Or do you, as a Christian man, exercise patience and self-control (two fruits of the spirit), and put her needs ahead of your own?

Understanding how her perspective on sex differs from yours is crucial. For most women, affection is a greater need than sexual intercourse. She wants to be held and hugged, snuggled and kissed.

She needs to be romanced (see the previous chapter). She doesn't think much about sex during the day, unless her hormones are talking to her. This means that, when you hop into bed, you may have sex on your mind, but she probably has sleep on hers. So expecting her to be ready when you suddenly "put the move on her" is very unrealistic. Now, if she is *never* interested in sex, don't get angry with her. There could be issues from her past, or problems in your relationship involved here; and exploring them, especially with a counselor, may be in order.

I once counseled a couple where the husband's complaint was that his wife wanted to have sex *every* night. You're probably thinking that guy had it made, but he found that sex-on-demand can get old real fast. When I spoke to the wife in a private session about this issue, she explained that it really wasn't sex that interested her. She said, "I want it because it's the only time I have his undivided attention." Wow!

As a Christian husband trying to be sensitive to your wife's needs, make sure she is getting all the attention, as well as the affection, for which she longs. And when you are in the mood for sexual intimacy, let her know *ahead of time* what's on your mind. Even a call or text in the middle of the day would be helpful, so that she can get on the same page with you and prepare herself physically and mentally for love-making. Like the National Guard, you may be "Always ready, Always there," but she isn't.

Planning for Intimacy

Women need to prepare for sexual activity. They need to make sure the kids are safely tucked away, out of sight and out of earshot. They need to get other things off their multi-focused minds so they can concentrate on the moment. Where men build to an adrenaline high, women need to relax and go with the flow, if they're going to get maximum enjoyment from the experience.

Like with dating, it's also good to *plan* for intimate times together. Set aside a time or two (or more) every week for this purpose. Waiting until you can squeeze it into your schedule, and hoping that both of you are in the mood at the same time, is a recipe for limited engagement. Lovemaking is too important to leave to chance. Putting it on each of your calendars creates time for it (if it's on the family calendar, use a code word). This doesn't mean you *have to* engage in sex at those scheduled times. If you both are too tired or stressed out to really enjoy it, you might want to just snuggle and talk. That's also good for your marriage. And planning specific times doesn't exclude spontaneous lovemaking. If it's not on the schedule and you're both in the mood, by all means, go for it!

Sometimes couples complain to me that their sex life is lacking because one partner likes to stay up late while the other is an early-to-bed, early-to-rise person. That's an easy fix. If you are the night owl, go to bed when your partner does and enjoy some intimacy before she goes to sleep. But you *don't have to stay* in bed, if you're not tired. Another solution is to change your sleep pattern to adjust to your partner's. A few early morning risings and you'll be ready to go to bed sooner after that. I was able to change my sleep pattern that way.

It's important also to make your bedroom a sacred space. Teach your children to respect your privacy when the bedroom door is closed: to knock first and wait for permission to enter. And your kids *should not* be sleeping with you, except on rare occasions if they are very young and frightened by a nightmare or thunder storm. And heated discussions should also be held elsewhere. Too many marital arguments take place at night in the bedroom. This changes the atmosphere of the room from one of restful sleep or intimate lovemaking into a relational war zone. Hopefully, you'll avoid heated conversations altogether, but certainly *don't* have them in the bedroom.

Sexual intimacy is also too important not to require some preparation on your part. You may be game to engage in it whatever the circumstances, but your wife would probably appreciate a little forethought on your part. Some soft, romantic music, candles strategically placed (in front of a mirror doubles the effect), and perhaps a little scent sprayed on the sheets can help create a conducive atmosphere for making love. Lilac, I have read, seems to be a good scent for increasing sexual desire. So is pumpkin pie, but I don't think you want your bedroom smelling like a kitchen. A shower, a shave (if a scruffy beard bothers her), mouthwash, and a bit of cologne can also be helpful.

Making Love versus Having Sex

Now that the stage has been set, what about sexual activity itself? Is there a way to engage in sex that is different for us as Christians, or are we like anyone else when it comes to "a roll in the hay"? I believe, as Christ-honoring men, we can't just do as the world around us does. First of all, there is a difference between "having sex" and "making love." Some men never grasp this difference. Having sex is focused on the *physical act* and the personal pleasure derived from it. It is mostly concerned with oneself, i.e., "What am I getting from it?" Making love, on the other hand, is focused on the *person* you are having intercourse with, and is an expression of affection and the bond between you two. Its concern is, "How can I give her pleasure, and express the deep love I have for her through this intimate physical contact?"

When sexual intimacy is approached in this way, it is deeply satisfying and fulfilling. It is even a spiritual experience when we express it the way God intended in the first place. There have been times during the afterglow of lovemaking that I have had the urge to worship, and have quietly thanked God for his good gift of sex and for the partner he has given me to share my life with.

With this perspective in mind, I feel that face-to-face intercourse is the most natural and gratifying approach. I know sex manuals will describe or show you all sorts of positions that are possible (although many are far from comfortable). But when you are not facing your partner, the focus tends to be on the physical pleasure, instead of on her as a person. Face-to-face lovemaking allows you to look into each other's eyes, to kiss, to whisper words of love, to truly make her the object of your affection. It also is most intensely pleasurable, when done right.

Secondly, you should never engage in a form of sexual pleasuring that your partner is uncomfortable with. It will tend to turn her off rather than on. I once counseled a couple where the husband was *only* interested in oral sex. He kept pressuring his wife (who did not like it) to the point where she lost interest in any kind of sex at all! He thus ended up, as they say, "shooting himself in the foot" (or someplace else). Not a wise move on his part. Again, as Christian men, our first concern should be to *love* our wives, not to try to manipulate them into serving our desires.

Thirdly, approach lovemaking with your bride slowly and gently. Because we are more quickly and easily aroused, we may become impatient to get to the "good stuff" and short-change her on foreplay. For many women, foreplay *is* the "good stuff." It also takes time for her to become aroused to the point where she is adequately lubricated for easy entry. Some have compared the differences in arousal time to a crockpot and a microwave. It doesn't really require hours for her to heat up, but there is a significant time gap. Take your time: move slowly, go with the flow, and enjoy the warm-up. You will find that delayed gratification will enhance the experience for you as well.

Gentleness is also extremely important. In the words of a well-known country song, "Darling . . . you want a man with a slow hand; you want a lover with an easy touch." There's a lot of truth there. Again, as men, we need to control our adrenaline when sexually aroused. In that state of mind, it's easy to forget that a slow and easy touch is much more soothing and titillating than a Swedish massage (although you might begin with a gentle back massage, if she likes it, and then move to a more sensuous touch). There may be times when passion takes over both of you and things become more physically energetic, but most wives are not interested in what is called, "rough sex."

Gentleness is a fruit of the spirit, (Gal. 5:23) and it applies in the bedroom also. In Peter's first letter, addressing Christian men regarding their relations with their wives, he writes, "Husbands, in the same way be considerate as you live with your wives, and treat them with respect as the weaker partner." (1 Pet. 3:7) The Greek word translated "live with" has strong sexual overtones, and "weaker partner" refers to physical weakness or vulnerability. Our wives are typically weaker physically than we are, and when they are opening themselves up to be sexually penetrated, it places them in a very vulnerable position. Thus, it is vital that we, as Christian men, "be considerate" and "treat them with respect" sexually, as well as in other areas of our married life together. Here are a few words of caution:

First, don't assume you know what will sexually arouse your wife every time. What works one night may not be effective the next. It's her body; let her guide you. She knows what feels good and what doesn't, where she's physically sensitive and where she isn't, at any given time on any given day.

Second, it's not your responsibility to bring her to an orgasm. Some women are more orgasmic than others. On the other hand, there are women who never get there, but don't really care. It's the closeness and affection they enjoy. A lot also depends on *their* frame of mind (as we have indicated). For your part, make sure that you are not *interfering* with her ability to get maximum enjoyment by failing to be sensitive to her needs in this area. Technique is not the most important thing, but it's not unimportant.

Third, don't just hop out of bed or roll over and go to sleep when you're finished. Just as it takes her longer to become aroused, it takes her longer to come down as well. Hold her, talk to her, and enjoy the afterglow together. You should feel emotionally closer at this point. You don't want to spoil the moment.

Fourth, be sure to communicate with her regarding what works for you sexually. She can't read your mind, any more than you can read hers. Many Christian couples can talk about almost anything but this. Although our culture is very open about sex, talking about it may still be a struggle for you, depending on how the subject was handled in your family or the Christian circles you grew up in. At the end of this chapter are a few good books for you to read further on this subject. If you choose to read one or more of them, I would recommend that you read them out loud together with your wife. Not only will you find the content helpful, but it will enable both of you to become more comfortable talking about sex and opening up dialogue concerning your personal love life.

A Closing Word on Marital Sex

A healthy, fulfilling love life is ultimately the frosting on the cake of a good marriage. There is a strong correlation between communication, conflict resolution, and a couple's sex life. If you can't discuss things, especially feelings, you won't be able to work through your differences. And if you can't work through differences, they will fester into resentment and create distance. So resolve any unfinished business between you two. If you have offended her, set aside your pride and learn to say, "I'm sorry. Please forgive me." More so than men, women need to feel good about their relationship with their spouses, before they can really give of themselves sexually. In other words, if she doesn't *feel* loved, she's not going to feel like *making* love. First things first.

Questions for Personal Reflection or Group Discussion

1. Have you given much thought to the difference in sexual interest between you and your wife (assuming there is)? How has this affected your relationship? Are you able to discuss it with her calmly, and not while you're in bed?

2. Does planning and even scheduling sex seem strange to you? Do you have a better plan for ensuring adequate frequency?

3. What did you think of the author's discussion of making love versus having sex? How might having that perspective improve intimacy in your marriage?

Going Further: Read and reflect on (or discuss) 1 Corinthians 7:2-6, Colossians 3:12, and 1 Peter 3:7. What would sexual intimacy with your wife look like if you consciously put these passages into practice?

Sexual Integrity Outside of Marriage

Dave was a highly successful man. As the head of a national enterprise, he enjoyed tremendous wealth and power. A war hero and handsome, he was the kind of man that women noticed. Dave had a beautiful wife named Abby and several good-looking children. And on top of all that, he was a man who loved and served the Lord. Life was good. Dave's next door neighbor was Hugh, a friend who also worked for him, and one of his most trusted men. Hugh had a wife named Beth, who was also very beautiful.

One warm spring day, Hugh was out of town on an extended business trip. Dave was also supposed to make that trip, but elected to stay home and relax—a fatal choice. While enjoying the evening breezes on the upper deck of his mansion, he happened to catch a glimpse of Beth sun-bathing next door. From his vantage point, he was able to look over the privacy fence into his neighbor's yard. And look he did. Instead of turning away, as his conscience was telling him to do, he continued to gaze and to lust.

The rest of the story is predictable. Dave arranged a meeting with Beth, seduced her, and an evening of mad passion ensued. But things got complicated when Beth became pregnant. Dave tried to use his influence to cover up the scandal that was sure to follow, but he ended up destroying Hugh's life and doing irreparable damage to his own family for years to follow.

No doubt, you have figured out that this story is a modernized version of the Biblical account of King David's affair with Bathsheba, a classic example of how affairs happen. (2 Sam. 11:1-27) David was in the wrong place at the wrong time. Bathsheba was not a stranger. Her husband, Uriah, was one of David's "mighty men," a battle-hardened soldier who had fought side by side with David on many occasions. Her father was one of David's trusted advisors. Which raises the question, how does David, described in Scripture as "a man after God's own heart," and with a beautiful wife of his own, get involved in such a sordid mess? How does any Christian leader, for that matter? That's what we'll be considering in the pages that follow.

Where Affairs Begin

Most extramarital affairs take place between people who have known each other previously. A large percentage of them begin in the workplace. This makes sense. Most men spend more waking hours with or around their female coworkers in the course of a week than they do with their wives. Relationships do develop. Things happen. I have counseled too many people (including Christians) whose affairs began on the job. Especially vulnerable are those whose occupations take them on the road frequently, such as airline personnel, sales people, professional athletes, or musicians. Vulnerability plus opportunity is a dangerous mix.

Following work-related infidelity, the most likely situations for potential affairs are with friends, neighbors, family, or church members. Once again, familiarity breeds interest. Unfortunately, my counseling history has included people who have been involved in sexual relationships with their spouse's best friend, their sister-in-law or brother-in-law, someone who lived down the street, or a person with whom they served in a church ministry. You can imagine the horrendous fallout from these affairs.

Then, there are old flames that are reignited when someone runs into a former dating partner by chance, at a reunion, or through social media. These are especially combustible if the former lovers were separated by life circumstances and never had the opportunity to consummate their relationship. It's the old familiar "I wonder what my life would be like if I had married so and so" syndrome.

A more recent phenomenon involves persons who meet one another via the Internet. In some cases, it leads to a physical encounter, but most often, they simply have romantic or sexually explicit conversations online, or engage in cybersex. Skyping or FaceTiming adds a visual dimension. It's easy for a person to excuse this kind of behavior as harmless. After all, there isn't any *actual* physical involvement.

Questions for Personal Reflection or Group Discussion

1. Do you personally know anyone who has had an affair or been the victim of their spouse's infidelity? Where did it begin?

2. What were the repercussions of the affair? Did the marriage survive?

3. Have you ever found yourself attracted to someone other than your wife? How did you handle that attraction?

What is an Affair?

What exactly is an affair? Does it have to be physical? No. Let me give you a definition:

"Marital infidelity is the violation of one's marriage vows by engaging in a romantic relationship with someone other than your spouse, which may or *may not* include sexual contact."

There are basically three kinds of affairs: (1) those which are *strictly sexual*, including one-night stands, the use of prostitutes, or the acting out of a sexual addict; (2) those which are *strictly emotional*, where there is attraction and romantic feelings, without sexual involvement, or the fantasies of pornography (to be dealt with later); (3) those which combine *both* the emotional *and* sexual.

In practical terms, a man can have an affair for the sex alone or *primarily* for the sex. But women typically fall in love first, and *then* get involved sexually (although this is changing in our society). Most men who get involved in affairs are *not* unhappy in their marriages, but *after* the affair starts, they will begin to pull away from their wives as their romantic feelings shift. On the other hand, most women who engage in extramarital relationships *are* unhappy in their marriages, and pull away from their husbands emotionally *before* the affair begins. When sex is introduced into the relationship, it tends to become the primary focus for men, and the depth of emotional intimacy begins to decline at that point. (True of premarital sex as well).

An affair that begins as a friendship, and then leads to sexual involvement, is the most complicated kind, and the hardest of which to let go. The feelings are deeper. The concern for the other person is stronger. When the affair comes to light, and the person decides to end it for the sake of their marriage (and children), it often doesn't end smoothly. And it's difficult for the cheated-on spouse to understand the feelings that may still remain for the "other woman." From her perspective, the cheating partner ought to be more concerned about *her* feelings, not the feelings of the one who ruined their marriage!

With all the problems it creates, what makes infidelity so attractive? The primary attraction is in the nature of the relationship itself. If you compare an affair to an established marriage, it looks something like this: An affair is a new romance; a marriage is old and familiar. An affair is secretive, exciting, and risky (it gets the adrenalin pumping); a marriage is open, routine, and predictable. An affair is socially forbidden; a marriage is socially acceptable (stolen fruit tastes sweeter). An affair is a fantasy where each person is idealized; a marriage is reality, where the weaknesses and foibles of each partner are well known. An affair is free of responsibility; a marriage involves great responsibilities. To sum up (as someone has well said), "The grass is always greener on the other side of the fence because *you* don't have to mow it."

Questions for Personal Reflection or Group Discussion

1. What do you think of the differences between men and women regarding the connection of an affair with love for one's spouse? Does that make sense to you? Why, or why not?

2. Is it surprising to you that affairs can be non-sexual?

3. Does reading the above description of the differences between affairs and marriages help you understand the attraction of an affair? Discuss.

How Affairs Begin

It's good to understand how affairs begin if we are going to avoid them as Christian men. First of all, as indicated earlier, there is *vulnerability*. Many things can make you vulnerable, such as your family history, if one or both of your parents were involved in affairs. Or you may be having problems in your marriage, which is really not the cause, but it can contribute to *either* of you being vulnerable. It could also be unmet personal needs, which leave you open to another person coming along and meeting those needs: things like the need for affirmation or attention, excitement, or romance. Lastly, it might simply be the influence of the world around you, where other people, maybe even friends of yours, are fooling around.

A second factor that contributes to infidelity is *opportunity*. As mentioned earlier, most affairs take place with people we already know. I once asked an airline pilot friend if what they say about pilots and flight attendants is true. He told me that there *was* a lot of hanky-panky going on in his profession. But, he added, it wasn't that people in the airline industry had lower morals than others; it was simply a matter of greater opportunity: working together, eating meals together, staying in the same hotel away from home, etc.

The third factor is a lack of inhibitors that could head off a possible affair. One of those is the commitment level of your marriage. You would assume that Christian men are very committed to their marriages "for better, for worse . . . 'til death us do part," etc. But, as you know, some still get involved in affairs. Were they really committed, day in and day out, or were those just words spoken at a church altar?

The influence of friends and families is also helpful here. Are they people who, by word and example, encourage marital faithfulness? Would they also care enough to confront you if they saw the danger coming? I know a Christian businessman who saw his married partner (also a Christian) getting too friendly with one of the young women on their staff. Rather than considering it none of his business, he confronted his partner with Christian concern and turned his friend away from a possible disaster (see Galatians 6:1-2 for the Biblical principle).

Other inhibitors are a person's morals, values, and spiritual condition. Research has found that people who were sexually active before marriage are more likely to cheat after marriage. I am amazed at how many Christian couples today are following the moral standards of society, rather than Scripture, and choosing to live together before marriage. The Christians involved in affairs that I have counseled have also admitted that their relationship with the Lord was not where it should have been at the time that the affair began—another inhibitor.

The Anatomy of an Affair

The typical scenario goes something like this: As you spend time with a person, you discover common interests and shared experiences. After a while, a friendship begins to develop. You may also find yourself attracted to her, or the attraction may have been there from the start. This makes you want to get to know this woman better (self-deception is common at this point). You may then begin to fantasize about her, or to compare her with your wife. This is very dangerous, because the tendency is to compare her strengths with your wife's areas of weakness.

As the relationship grows, you find ways to spend more time with her (perhaps over lunch), and the conversations begin to get more personal, maybe even sharing about your marriage(s). This is *never* good, no matter who is doing the sharing, you or the other woman. Feelings begin to develop. At this point, you are on a very slippery slope, and you need to get off quickly, or an affair is likely to follow.

Crossing the line takes place when you tell the other person you have feelings for her. If it is mutual, she will confirm her feelings toward you. You have now gone through a flashing red light, and unless the brakes are firmly applied, it will lead to touching and kissing. One expert has observed, "It's a bigger step to the first kiss, than from the first kiss to the bedroom." I agree. Kissing leads to heavy petting and then to intercourse and a full-blown affair.

But, going back to our definition stated above, the affair *really* began when the romantic feelings shifted out of the marriage and toward someone else. It may never get physical (more common with Christians who have strong moral standards), but it can be just as destructive to a marriage. This type of affair is easily rationalized because of the lack of physical involvement, but, in reality, the person has emotionally left the marriage. And not satisfying one's sexual desire can make the attraction even stronger, as you fantasize how wonderful it *would* be, if sexual intimacy finally did take place.

Questions for Personal Reflection or Group Discussion

1. How vulnerable to an affair do you think your marriage is right now?

2. How might your work situation and or schedule provide you with too much opportunity?

3. How strong are the inhibitors in your life?

4. Are there attractive women in your life that you have to spend a lot of time with (say at work), or with whom you may be too friendly (you need to be brutally honest with yourself)?

Warning Signs

As the above process is going on, there are several warning signs, and you'd be wise to pay attention and heed them. One sign is anticipating being with this person and taking extra care in your personal grooming. Another is desiring to be alone with her, say at lunch, rather than having other people around. Thinking about her when you are apart is yet another big warning signal. Sharing more than you should about yourself and your marriage is an even larger red flag, and starting to have romantic feelings toward her should be a signal for you to *run!*

Two other warning signs are also very important: One is hiding the relationship from your wife. When the another woman knows more about your wife than your wife knows about her, this is not good. The other is your wife's jealous feelings. If she doesn't tend to be jealous by nature, and she is picking up on things in your behavior or the behavior of another woman toward you, *listen to her.* Wives know their husbands well, and they understand other women better than men do. They are very intuitive when it comes to picking up on emotional vibes and flirting behaviors.

Avoiding Infidelity

In addition to paying attention to the warning signs, there are several positive steps you can take to prevent slipping into the dark and dangerous waters of an extramarital relationship:

Step One: Deal with your personal issues.

If you come from a family with a history of affairs, or have been sexually abused or abandoned, or are struggling with depression or low self-esteem, it would be helpful for you to work through these issues with a counselor. Also, if you are going through a time when you are angry with your wife; feeling stressed out, lonely, tired; or your ego has taken a hit for any reason, recognize that you are vulnerable, and take steps to be extra careful in this area.

Step Two: Build a strong marriage.

Work on developing more intimacy, resolving any conflicts, and practicing forgiveness with your wife. Learn and use her love language. Spend time and money on your marriage. If a man would invest as much time, money, and attention on his wife as he does on the "other woman," there would a lot fewer affairs. Read the previous chapter on marriage if you want more specific suggestions for improving your marriage. The real question isn't, what are you *getting out of* your marriage? But rather, what are you *putting into* it? The more you invest, the deeper your commitment and satisfaction will be. And this will also help protect your wife from wandering. When women feel truly loved, they rarely look elsewhere. (Caution—don't assume that, if your marriage is good, you can't be tempted in this area.)

Several years ago, there was a prominent Christian leader who was highly respected for his ministry and his marriage. He and his wife held seminars and wrote books about marriage. Their friends and acquaintances thought they had the best relationship of any couple they knew. When this man became involved in an affair, everyone was shocked. After ending the affair, he placed himself under discipline with other Christian leaders. Later, in a radio interview, he was asked, "How did something like this happen to you?" His answer is classic. He replied, "I once was asked in an interview, if Satan could bring me down, how would he do it? I replied, 'I don't know how he *would* do it, but I know how he *couldn't* do it. He couldn't do it through my marriage, because we're too strong there.'" He went on to say, "What I learned from this experience is, *an unguarded strength is a double weakness.*" This is so true. It isn't just our weak areas that need protecting, it's also our strengths. Many a military battle has been lost due to overconfidence, which leads us to . . .

Step Three: Be alert and protect yourself.

Some of the following may seem a bit radical, but you can't be too careful in this area. To begin with, avoid friendships with attractive women. They may even be your wife's friends, but to you they should be just acquaintances. If you feel an attraction, tell your wife (especially if it's someone she knows). It will break the fantasy spell, and she can help you sort out your feelings and also run interference for you.

Don't discuss personal issues with another woman; save it for your wife, a male friend, or a trusted counselor.

Don't allow yourself to fantasize about other women (real or imagined). Especially avoid pornography (to be dealt with in the next section).

Don't flirt. It isn't harmless; it sends the message, "I'm available."

Establish boundaries for yourself, and hold closely to them. Stay away from risky situations like coffee breaks, lunch, long conversations, or traveling alone with a woman other than your wife. Billy Graham was a great role model here. He was so protective of his reputation and his ministry that he wouldn't even get on an elevator alone with a woman.

Avoid secrecy; be open and honest with your wife about your whereabouts, activities, and conversations.

Finally, always stop to consider the long-term consequences. Keep your brain in gear, and be wise concerning possible outcomes.

Step Four: Stay spiritually aware and strong.

There's nothing like living examples to stir the mind and impress the heart. We began this section with the *negative* example of King David.

The best *positive* example we have of dealing with sexual temptation is the story of Joseph and Potiphar's wife, recorded for us in Genesis 39. Here's what happened:

> "Joseph was a strikingly handsome man. As time went on, his master's wife became infatuated with Joseph and one day said, 'Sleep with me.' He wouldn't do it. He said to his master's wife, 'Look, with me here, my master doesn't give a single thought to anything that goes on here—he's put me in charge of everything he owns. He treats me as an equal. The only thing he hasn't turned over to me is you. You're his wife, after all! How could I violate his trust and sin against God.'" (Genesis 39:6-9, MSG)

Here we have an unmarried young man in his early twenties (hormones raging), being seduced by an attractive woman; and he resists her advances! And the way Joseph (unlike David) handles this temptation is a beautiful example for every man who is being sexually tempted.

First, he thinks about how *others* would be affected by his actions, namely, Potiphar, his boss, who trusts him implicitly. And every one of us, before even contemplating an affair, ought to consider how *our* actions would impact those who trust us: our wives, our children, our friends, and those who look up to us as Christian men. But the *primary* consideration for Joseph (and for us) was that an affair was *just plain wrong*. He couldn't do it and sin against God. His relationship with the Lord was more important than the temporary pleasures of a sexual encounter. And so it should always be for us as well.

Questions for Personal Reflection or Group Discussion

1. Have you experienced any of the warning signs mentioned above? How did you deal with them? Have you ever noticed a friend or colleague showing one or more of them?

2. Think about (or discuss) the four steps for avoiding infidelity discussed by the author. Which one(s) do you need to work on?

3. How will you begin and who will you be accountable to?

Going Further: read and reflect on (or discuss) the stories of David (2 Samuel 11:1-14) and Joseph (Genesis 39:6-12). Notice the social position of each man; what each one did or didn't do to protect himself from temptation; how each man responded to temptation; and the end result of their actions. What lessons can you take away from these stories?

The Pornography Plague

He sat in front of me, a shell of a man. A pastor with a beautiful wife and young children, he had been arrested on sex charges, which had led to the loss of his church position and severe damage to his marriage. The church leaders were forced to let him go, but they had gone out of their way to help restore him spiritually and to heal his relationship with his wife. I never encountered a more reluctant counselee. Broken, but not repentant, he didn't know what he wanted to do. Whatever help was offered to him, he failed to follow up on. He was hooked on illicit sex, and he couldn't, or *wouldn't*, let it go. He left his family and moved out of the area. We don't know where he is. A lost soul. And it began with his use of porn.

The best advice I can give you regarding subject of pornography is to "avoid it like the plague," because *it is a plague*. A plague is defined as "a highly infectious, epidemic disease" (American Heritage

Dictionary). Spiritually speaking, pornography fits that definition. It enters the mind and infects the soul. And pornography use has reached epidemic proportions in our society. Few men have not been exposed to it. Many have major struggles in this area, and Christians are not exempt, even leaders in the church. More than anything else I can think of, the enemy of our souls is having a field day undermining the spiritual lives of men through porn.

What is Pornography, and Is It Really That Bad?

Technically speaking, pornography is material that is predominately sexually explicit and intended primarily for purposes of sexual arousal. Experts distinguish between hardcore porn that shows people engaged in sexual activities, and soft porn that simply shows naked bodies. As Christians, holding to a higher standard, I think we also need to include things like subtle sex scenes in R-rated movies, the Victoria's Secret catalog, and the swimsuit edition of Sports Illustrated. In other words, *anything* that fills your mind with images that lead to sexual arousal ought to be considered porn.

Pornography is a multi-billion-dollar business, generating more revenue each year than the NFL, NBA, and Major League Baseball *combined*! It is truly America's pastime. And it is largely an American product, with almost 90 percent of it being produced in our country, primarily in Las Vegas and Hollywood. Unsuspecting young women go to these cities hoping to break into show business, and are preyed upon by unscrupulous porn producers who offer them an alternative route to their dreams. Once involved, their morals begin to break down, many ending up hooked on drugs as a way of dealing with their guilt and shame. Men who view pornography don't stop to consider that the young women they are lusting after are somebody's daughters.

Some marriage counselors, even Christian ones, recommend couples use porn to enhance their lovemaking. Their thinking is that porn use is okay as long as people follow it up by having sex with their spouse. This kind of thinking is majorly flawed for two reasons: (1) Getting sexually aroused by watching someone else, and then turning to your wife to satisfy those artificially created desires, is simply using her body as a sexual outlet, rather than treating her as person. (2) You can become addicted to pornography viewing it with your partner, as easily as watching it alone.

Questions for Personal Reflection or Group Discussion

1. Have you ever considered that material (like the SI swimsuit edition) should be classified as pornographic for Christians?

2. Are you surprised at how big the porn business is and how much of it is produced in our country?

3. The average age of first exposure to porn is around ten years old. When did you first encounter it, and how?

4. Did you ever consider that the young women used to make porn are somebody's daughter and primarily victims? How would you feel if you knew that men were leering at pictures of your daughter?

The Dangers of Porn Use

Pornography is highly addictive. Researchers have compared it to using crack cocaine. Like other addictions, it is chemically induced. The only difference is the chemicals are being produced *inside* the brain, rather than taken in from outside. Those chemicals give one both a sense of euphoria and the feeling that this is something important. They also, as mentioned earlier in this chapter, serve as a bonding agent between a person and the object of their sexual desire. In marital sex, all of this is good; it's part of God's wonderful design. But you can also bond to pornographic images, and that's tragic.

In addition to its chemical workings, it is important to realize two other functions of the brain. First, the brain never forgets. It *never* forgets. Whatever goes in, stays in; it only takes the right trigger to bring memories to the surface. In the words of brain researcher William Struthers, in his book *Wired for Intimacy*, "Food is consumed and digested by the body. Porn is consumed by the senses and digested by the brain. However, there is no process for waste products to be removed."

A second characteristic of the brain is that it is a habit-making machine. If you consciously had to think about every little thing you do in the course of a day, from tying your shoes to driving your car, you'd be exhausted by noon. And so your brain conserves energy by turning repeated actions into habits. This is great, if your habits are good ones, but not so great when the habits are harmful.

This combination of euphoric chemicals, adrenalin-charged desire, and intense physical pleasure, added to the brain's storage capacity and habit-forming tendencies, produces a *tremendously high potential for sexual addiction*. And like all addictions, the hunger is never satisfied. It takes more and more porn, in more explicit and perverted forms, to get the same high. This can lead a man to thoughts and behaviors in which he never dreamed he'd ever engage.

The Internet

One of the most dangerous parts of porn is its easy access via the Internet, and the fantasy world it introduces. Internet use itself is potentially addictive, but cybersex has opened a whole new world to pornography producers and consumers. Porn is now available 24/7 on any PC, laptop, tablet, or smart phone a person may possess, anywhere they have Internet reception. Thus, this insidious plague finds its way into libraries, offices, our children's bedrooms, and even pastors' studies. And it's inexpensive to boot.

Equally dangerous as its easy access is the virtual fantasy world cybersex offers to users. In this make-believe existence, a man can choose any partner who appeals to him—one who is *always* available and ready to do *whatever* his mind can conjure up. This is in direct contrast to the world of *real* human beings, where his wife may not always be available, and who has needs and desires of her own. Many men become so engrossed in this sexual fantasyland that they lose interest in real intercourse with their wives. How tragic! How sad. God created sex to be relational and other-focused, but using pornography encourages men to isolate themselves in their own little self-centered, internal world of lust.

Questions for Personal Reflection or Group Discussion

1. Sexual addiction has been compared to crack cocaine. Does this surprise you?

2. Do you know of anyone who is sexually addicted?

3. Do you still look at porn occasionally? Regularly?

4. Could you see yourself becoming addicted (this takes brutal honesty to admit; like all addictions, there is a lot of denial and rationalization involved)?

5. Consider how easily porn is accessed via the Internet. How might you protect yourself and your children (especially those with cell phones)?

Porn is Anti-Relational and Anti-Women

Apart from its addictive potential, pornography use also destroys relationships. After viewing digitally enhanced female bodies, lacking normal imperfections and blemishes, your wife's body may begin to be less attractive to you. Or, as previously mentioned, you may simply be using her body for release after the images on your computer have stirred your sexual desires, even running those pictures in your mind while having intercourse with her. Another problem is that men using porn often want their wives to duplicate what the women they view on the screen are doing, and their wives are often uncomfortable complying (if they do at all). This is simply manipulation for one's own selfish pleasure.

And perhaps even more serious, men who ingest pornography begin, after a while, to look at their wives (and women generally) as sexual objects, depersonalizing them. This is extremely disrespectful. How would you feel if someone was only interested in your *body*, disregarding you and your needs as a *person*? This kind of thinking, of course, is completely contrary to God's command for us to love and respect our wives, and to show the same consideration for all women.

Pornography also perverts God's purpose for sex as an expression of love, and it gives men a distorted view of women's sexuality. Mark Driscoll in his book *Real Marriage* observes the following:

> "It teaches that women really enjoy whatever any man does to them sexually, (sending the message) that all women want sex from all men, all the time, in all kinds of bizarre ways and are essentially nymphomaniacs."

This, of course, is not true, as any married man can testify. But it's one of the primary reasons for the date rape epidemic on our college campuses today, where porn use is extremely high. Young men watching porn are led to believe that if a woman says "no," she doesn't really mean it. Thus, pornography blunts the conscience and encourages anti-social behavior.

At the extreme end of the spectrum are rapists and serial killers like Ted Bundy who, just before his execution, told of the lifelong addiction to porn that led to his abhorrent criminal behavior. He also said that the other serial killers he had met in prison were all hooked on pornography as well (source: taped interview with Dr. James Dobson).

Pornography also leads to extramarital affairs. More and more I'm finding, as I work with men who have been unfaithful, that it began with the use of porn. It makes sense. After a man has been filling his mind with images of women other than his wife, and bringing himself to a sexual climax lusting after them, the next logical step is doing it with a real live woman. And unless he is content to stay in his fantasy world, this is often where it ends up.

Even if it doesn't lead to a physical affair, wives who learn that their husbands are into pornography often feel and react the same as if it were. This is especially true of Christian women, who understand Jesus' teaching about "adultery in the heart." In some cases, it has also led to divorce. But even short of divorce, it does real damage to the marital relationship. A wife feels degraded and unattractive, like somehow there's something wrong with her, that she isn't attractive enough for her husband. Otherwise, why would he have to be looking at porn?

The Spiritual Impact

As Christians, the most serious damage caused by porn use is spiritual. It is clearly a violation of Jesus' command not to "look lustfully at a woman," which amounts to internal adultery. (Matt. 5:28) Filling our minds with thoughts that exploit and degrade women offends

God's standard of holiness, and loads us down with a burden of guilt, shame, and self-hatred. This, in turn, deadens our spirits to the moving of God's spirit, and we begin to lose our taste for spiritual things. Ultimately, like all habitual sins, it leads to spiritual bondage. (John 8:34, 2 Pet. 2:19)

In light of the above, I can only conclude with this: If you have never used porn of any kind, consider yourself blessed. Don't let your curiosity or any other motive lead you there. If you *are* involved in using pornography, break that habit before it becomes an addiction. If it's already an addiction, you need to get professional help. In the words of the apostle Paul, "Flee from sexual immorality . . . Do you not know that your body is a temple of the Holy Spirit, who is in you, whom you have received from God? You are not your own; you were bought at a price. Therefore, honor God with your body." (1 Cor. 5:18-20)

Questions for Personal Reflection or Group Discussion

1. Have you ever stopped to think of how looking at porn affects the way you view women, including your wife?

2. Have you considered that, instead of enhancing your marital sex life (as some advocate), you may actually be damaging it?

3. Think about (or discuss) how using porn is both emotionally and spiritually cheating on your wife.

Going Further: Read Matthew 5:27-28, Job 31:1-11, and 2 Peter 2:17-19. Reflect on them or discuss them in a group. What are the dangers they point to, and what are the strategies mentioned for dealing with lust?

Handling Sexual Temptation (And Other Kinds)

Temptation is a fact of life. We might as well face it; no matter how old we are, sexual temptation is something we'll always have to wrestle with. As an older man, I can speak from experience. My own struggles, enlightened by Scripture, have taught me a few things about myself, about the nature of temptation, and, especially, about how to deal with it. Although in this section we will have sexual temptation primarily in mind, the same principles apply to temptations in other areas of life as well.

Know Yourself

To begin with, it's important that you know yourself well enough to be able to resist temptation. We tend to be blind to our own weaknesses. As the Psalmist observes, in speaking of the wicked, "For in his own eyes he flatters himself too much to detect or hate his sin." (Ps. 36:2) It's real easy for us to see sin in others, not so easy to detect it in ourselves. (Matthew 7:3-5)

James 1:14 specifically points out how temptation works: "Each one is tempted when, *by his own evil desires*, he is dragged away and enticed." (italics mine) Notice that it begins with our desires, the things we like or want. The source of the temptation may come from the outside, but it begins with sinful urges on the inside. Jesus said that sinful desires come out of the heart. (Mark 7:21) You can't be tempted by something you don't want or like. For example, I love cookies. Put a plate of Oreos in front of me and resistance would be futile. But if those cookies were coconut macaroons, I wouldn't have any trouble at all passing them up, because I dislike coconut. Temptation follows desire, which is why men are sitting ducks when it comes to our sexuality. Sexual desire almost never goes away.

That being said, it's good to ask yourself when this temptation is strongest for you. Is it when you are around certain people, or find yourself in certain situations or places, or perhaps in a particular mood or frame of mind? I once dated a girl in high school who, after becoming a Christian, could not listen to certain kinds of music. It stirred up feelings in her connected to former sinful behaviors. Association plays a strong role in what tempts us as well. It's wise to anticipate tempting situations before they occur and to have a game plan for dealing with them.

For example, I was counseling a man who was struggling to overcome a drinking problem. He was doing well, but was worried about a trip to his company headquarters, where all the regional managers gathered quarterly. These meetings usually ended with everyone going to dinner and consuming a lot of alcohol - especially his boss. We came up with a plan, which was to have him speak up first and ask for a soda when the waiter came around for drink orders. Returning from his trip, he laughingly reported how well the plan had worked. When he ordered his soft drink, several other men around the table followed suit, and his boss ended up drinking much less than usual. The moral of the story is, have a plan. As the old saying goes, "Those who fail to plan, plan to fail."

And at those times when you are feeling vulnerable because of loneliness, boredom, stress, etc., have alternative activities you've worked out in advance to divert your attention. This can be as simple as walking away from your computer, picking up the phone and calling your wife or a friend, going for a walk or to the gym, grabbing an interesting book or game, or, of course, reading your Bible or praying. I have also found that singing praise songs helps (pick your time and place for that one). But again, have a plan and rehearse it in your mind.

In addition to knowing your weaknesses, it is wise not to be overconfident about your strengths. In 1 Corinthians 10, Paul writes about sins committed in the past by the people of Israel, in spite of the clear evidence of God in their midst. He tells us that these were recorded for us as examples. Paul then concludes, "So, if you think you are standing firm, be careful that you don't fall." (v. 12) That's good advice. (Remember our example above). Our human tendency in areas that we're strong, especially where we have overcome a sin or weakness, is to venture too close to danger. Several times a year, people fall over a precipice in the Grand Canyon. In spite of signs warning them not to get too close to the edge, they just feel compelled to look over. It happens to us spiritually as well. We flirt with trouble, and before we know it, we've fallen headlong into sin again.

Know Your Enemy

As Christians, sometimes we forget that we are engaged in a spiritual battle. We have an enemy called Satan, and there are two things about him we should always keep in mind. First, Satan is a liar. Pay attention to what Jesus said: "He was a murderer from the beginning, not holding to the truth, for there is no truth in him. When he lies, he speaks his native language, for he is a liar and the father of lies." (John 8:44) Jesus describes Satan's lying nature five different ways in this one verse! I think we need to pay attention to what he is telling us: *deception is Satan's favorite weapon.* It was deception that he used at the beginning of history to lead Adam and Eve into sin. And deception is what he tried to use with Jesus in the wilderness. But the Son of God saw through him and responded with truth.

Remember the next time you are tempted: *you are being lied to.* I'm sure you're well aware of the things he typically whispers in our ears: "You deserve it," "It's good for you," "No one will find out," "No one will get hurt." All of them lies. Someone has said, "Satan has a limited playbook, but he knows how to run his plays to perfection." He's the Vince Lombardi of evil. He appeals to the desires we already have and, too often, we buy into his lies. This is why the first piece of God's armor Paul urges us to put on is "the belt of truth." (Eph. 6:14)

A second thing to keep in mind is that Satan is out to destroy you. Peter reminds us, "Your enemy the devil prowls around like a roaring lion looking for someone to devour." (1 Pet. 5:8) He will pretend to be your friend (like he did with Eve), but his ultimate goal is to bring you down. Paul tells us that Satan "masquerades as an angel of light," (2 Cor. 11:14) but he's really the prince of darkness. He hates God, and he hates us because we're created in God's image; and especially because, as Christians, we are God's children.

Think about it. On a human level, if you knew someone was lying to you, that they hated you, and were out to destroy you, you would avoid them. That ought to be our response to Satan every time he tempts us, as well. Tell him to get lost, like Jesus did. (Matthew 4:10)

Responding to Temptation

Beyond knowing ourselves (desires, weaknesses, sinful tendencies) and being aware of our spiritual enemy, are there specific things we can do to combat temptation? Thankfully, yes. To begin with, we need to *be completely honest* with ourselves. Satan's deception is one thing; self-deception is something else. There are all kinds of defense mechanisms we tend to use when being tempted by something we desire. For instance, there are *rationalizations*. These are all the reasons we feed our minds while talking ourselves into giving in. Then, after we've yielded to temptation, we use *justification* to excuse ourselves for what we've just done. Or, if we're not able to justify our sin, we *minimize* it by telling ourselves, "It's really not that bad. I don't do it that often; and after all, everybody else does it." And if the sin has become a habit, we can always fall back on *denial*: "It's not really a problem. I can control it." Sound familiar?

The Bible says, "The heart is deceitful above all things and beyond cure. Who can understand it?" (Jer. 17:9) John puts it even more pointedly when he writes, "If we claim to be without sin (denial), we deceive ourselves and the truth is not in us." (1 Jn. 1:8) We need to own up to our skewed thought processes and quickly recognize the rationalizations we use that lead us into sin.

If we should give in, it's essential that we *quickly* own up to it. Thus, John immediately adds in verse 9, "If we confess our sins, he is faithful and just and will forgive us our sins and purify us from all unrighteousness." He goes on to say that he's not encouraging us *to* sin, but wants to let us know that *if* we do, there is an answer for us in Jesus Christ, the one who died for our sins. (1 Jn. 2:1-2) When we justify and minimize our sins, it keeps us from making things right with God, and this just sets us up for Satan's next attack.

At the same time, God does not want us to beat ourselves up with a guilty conscience either. This also plays into Satan's hands. He's "the accuser," (Rev. 12:10) the one who wants to make us feel like we're no good and unforgiveable. He knows that guilty people are easier to tempt. Since we already feel bad about ourselves, we figure that it makes no difference if we sin some more. I believe that God is far more anxious to forgive our sins than we are to confess them. (Ps. 103:8-14)

It's also good to know that our temptations, although strong at times, are not out of the ordinary. Listen to what Paul writes in 1 Corinthians 10:13:

> "No temptation has seized you except what is common to
> man. And God is faithful: he will not let you be tempted

beyond what you can bear. But when you are tempted, he will also provide a way out so that you can stand up under it."

Your temptations are everyday stuff. Every man has to deal with them. You are not being singled out for special attention. But take note of the second part of that verse. In his faithfulness, God will *not allow* us to be tempted beyond our ability to handle it. *And* he always provides an escape route, *if* we will take it. And that's the issue: do we take it early on, while we're still thinking straight? Because if we wait until the pull of temptation builds up strength, our sinful nature won't *want* to take it!

With habitual sins, it's important not to fight the battle alone, having people to whom you are accountable. It might be your pastor, a close friend or two, or a whole group of men who are struggling with the same issues. This is one of the reasons that AA and other addiction programs have been successful. Being with people who understand and will "hold your feet to the fire" is very helpful. Paul encourages us to "carry each other's burdens as followers of Christ," (Gal 6:2) and James urges us, "Confess your sins to one another and pray for one another that you may be healed." (5:16) The church I attend has a group of men that meets weekly, early in the morning, to support and encourage each other in their struggle with sexual temptation. Perhaps this would be helpful for you as well. If your church doesn't have such a group, you may want to talk to your leaders about starting one.

Questions for Personal Reflection or Group Discussion

1. How well do you know yourself? Are you consciously aware of your areas of weakness?

2. What steps do you take to either avoid temptation or, when tempted, to deal with it?

3. Could knowing that Satan is a liar who wants to destroy you help you in resisting temptation? How?

4. Why do you think it's so hard to confess our sins to God when he is so willing to forgive?

5. It's good not to struggle with this issue alone. Is there an accountability group of Christian men in your church, or elsewhere, who could help you stay clean? If not, consider starting one yourself.

Wave the White Flag

In the military, when one side realizes they are going to *lose* a battle, they raise a white flag. That white flag sends a double message: (1) We give up; we are going to stop fighting. (2) We surrender to your will. Ironically, for us, *losing* is the key to *winning* the spiritual battle with sexual temptation, or any other temptation, for that matter.

First, we *give up* doing what we've been doing. In Christian terms, this is called repentance, a word often misunderstood. Repenting does not mean just feeling sorry for what we've done (although true godly sorrow does bring repentance, 2 Cor. 7:10). We can be sorry, but not really want to change. In some cases, we're sorry we got caught! Or we may be sorry someone was hurt. But *sorry isn't enough*. True repentance means to turn around and go in the other direction, to "cease and desist" our sinful behavior. We cannot win the fight against sin, especially sexual sin, because most of that battle is with ourselves. We have to *give up*, instead of *giving in*. And if our sin is habitual, this can be particularly difficult, which leads to the next part.

Second, we **surrender** to God's will. He is not the enemy our sinful thinking makes him out to be. (Rom. 8:7, Jas. 4:4) He wants to set us free from the bondage of our sin. (Rom. 6:6-7; 7:24-25) I have never seen anyone overcome an ingrained habit of sin until they became so sick of it, they were willing to give it completely over to God. And, I should add, you can't simply give him one area of your life and hold on to the rest. It doesn't work that way. So Paul tells us, "Do not offer the parts of your body to sin . . . but rather *offer yourselves* to God . . . and offer the parts of your body to him as instruments of righteousness." (Rom. 6:13) "Therefore, I urge you, brothers, in view of God's mercy, to *offer your bodies* as living sacrifices, holy and pleasing to God . . ." (Rom. 12:1). God wants every part of us.

Surrender is more than a decision, more than a commitment, although we often use those terms when speaking about our relationship with God. Like raising the white flag in a military battle, we *yield* to his control, inviting him to do with us whatever he wishes. The good news is, (despite our fears) he only chooses to do us good. Not always pleasant, but always good, because *he is good*.

With God in control, we now have the full resources of his grace and power available to us for dealing with sin and temptation. (2 Pet. 1:3) Where we aren't strong enough to resist and overcome, he is. But this doesn't happen automatically. We still have to cooperate with his Spirit who lives within us by lining our will up with his will. (Phil. 2:12-13) This is called obedience. We choose to do what we know he wants us to do. But realizing our limitations, we *trust* him to do for us, and through us, what we can't do by ourselves. The Christian life is a life of faith and obedience from beginning to end. As the old hymn says, "Trust and obey, for there's no other way . . ."

Pursue God

There are many books that discuss how to deal with temptation. Most of them focus on avoidance, and much of what they advise is good. For instance, looking away when you notice an attractive woman, *before* you begin mentally undressing her or fanaticizing about sex with her, is a good strategy. In fact, Job says, "I made a covenant with my eyes not to look lustfully at a maid." (Job 31:6) But avoidance isn't enough. In fact, when we concentrate on *not* doing something, our focus is *still* on the thing we don't want to do! And this can work against us in moments of weakness.

Instead, we need to pay attention to Paul's words to Timothy: "*Flee* the evil desires of youth, and *pursue* righteousness, faith, love and peace, along with those who call on the Lord out of a pure heart." (2 Tim. 2:22) And note also what he wrote to Titus: "The grace of God . . . teaches us to say 'No' to ungodliness and worldly passions, and to live self-controlled, upright and godly lives in this present age." (Titus 2:11-12) Fleeing *and* pursuing. Saying "No" to sin *and* "Yes" to God are so important. If our attention is focused on our relationship with Christ, it will go a long way toward lessening the appeal of sin to us.

The purpose of pursuing Christ is to increasingly know Christ. In Philippians 3:10, Paul shares his own goal in life: "*I want to know Christ* and the power of his resurrection and the fellowship of sharing in his sufferings, becoming like him in his death." And his prayer for the Ephesians also ought to be our prayer for ourselves:

> "I pray that out of his glorious riches he (the Father) may strengthen you with power through his Spirit in your inner being, so that Christ may dwell in your hearts through faith. And I pray that you, being rooted and established in love, may have power, together with all the saints, to grasp

how wide and long and high and deep is the love of Christ,
and to know this love that surpasses knowledge—that you
might be filled to the   measure of all the fullness of God."
3:16-19

Paul prays for them to be "*strengthened with power* through God's
Spirit" within (the most important element in resisting temptation).
But then he goes on to say that, "being rooted and established in love,"
they might be able to grasp and *know the fullness of Christ's love.* There
it is: our *motivation* for overcoming sin. If we understand how deeply
we are loved by Christ, and are focused on knowing and loving him
in return, sin loses its appeal, and temptation loses its strength. Why
would we exchange something lasting and deeply fulfilling at the core
of our being for some empty pleasure that won't last beyond the present
moment? We need to pursue God. That's where *real* pleasure is to be
found. (Ps. 16:11)

Questions for Personal Reflection or Group Discussion

1. Are there temptations in your life that you have struggled with
unsuccessfully? Have you given up trying?

2. Are you willing to give up the sin and surrender, or do you
still love it too much? Does true repentance and surrender make
sense to you? Try to picture what your life would be like without
that sin. Recognize that God wants you to enjoy that kind of life.

3. Does pursuing Christ versus merely trying to avoid temptation make sense to you? What would that look like in your
practice of spiritual disciplines (see Chapter One) and your
day-to-day behavior?

Going Further: read and reflect on (or discuss) I Corinthians
10:1-13, James 1:13-15, and 2 Peter 1:3-9. Notice the nature of

temptation and the divine resources available to you in your struggle with temptation and sin.

Additional Resources:

On Marital Sex

Robert & Rosemary Barnes, *Great Sexpectations: Finding lasting Intimacy in Your Marriage.*

Zondervan, 1996.

Edward Eichel & Philip Nobile, *The Perfect Fit.* Donald I Fine, 1992.

Christopher & Rachel McCluskey, *When Two Become One: Enhancing Sexual Intimacy in*

Marriage. Revell, 2004.

Douglas E. Rosenau, *A Celebration of Sex.* Thomas Nelson, 2002.

On Adultery

Dave Carder, *Close Calls: What Adulterers Want You to Know About Protecting Your Marriage*, Northfield Publishing, 2008.

Shirley P. Glass, *Not "Just Friends": Rebuilding Trust and Recovering Your Sanity After Infidelity*, Free Press, 2003.

Stephen M. Judah, *Staying Together: When an Affair Pulls You Apart*, InterVarsity Press, 2006.

On Pornography

Patrick Carnes, et al., *In the Shadows of the Net: Breaking Free of Compulsive Online Sexual Behavior*, Hazeldon Foundation, 2001.

Craig Gross, *Eyes of Integrity: The Porn Pandemic and How It Affects You*, Baker Books, 2010 (includes free accountability software).

John Freeman, *Hide or Seek: When Men Get Real with God About Sex*, New Growth Press, 2014.

Heath Lambert, *Finally Free: Fighting for Purity with the Power of Grace*. Zondervan, 2013.

Thomas Whiteman & Randy Petersen, *Your Marriage and the Internet*, Revell, 2002.

On Temptation

Stephen Arterburn, *Every Man's Battle*: *Winning the War on Sexual Temptation One Victory at a Time*, WaterBrook Press, 2000.

Andrew Comiskey, *Strength in Weakness*: *Healing Sexual and Relational Brokeness*, InterVarsity Press, 2003.

Steve Gallagher, *At the Altar of Sexual Idolatry*, Pure Life Ministries, 1986.

Douglas Weiss, *Clean: A Proven Plan for Men Committed to Sexual Integrity*, Thomas Nelson, 2013.

"We have worked, we have worked hard; but the question comes to us – "What have we worked for? Who has been our master? With what objective have we toiled?"

—*C. H. Spurgeon*

Chapter Six: Integrity at Work - Balance

God is a worker. His eternal activity is well documented. As recorded in Genesis 1, he created our world and the entire universe by speaking it into existence. And God continues to work in the world through his control of nature. (Ps. 104, Job 38:25-39:30) He also worked in history on behalf of his people Israel: delivering them from slavery in Egypt, preserving them for forty years in the wilderness, and giving them one military victory after another against stronger nations determined to destroy them. And he still oversees the nations of the earth. (Ps. 2, 105:1-15; Dan. 2:20-21, 4:17)

Jesus, God's Son, was also a worker. He spent most of his life as a carpenter, and later had a ministry of teaching and healing. (Mark 6:3, Matt. 13:55) He considered that ministry to be the work he was sent by the Father to do, and which the Father himself was doing through him. (John 5:17, 17:4) But even before taking on our humanity, Jesus was working with the Father in creation. As Paul tells us, "All things were created *by* him and for him. He is the head of all things, and in him all things hold together." (Col. 1:16-17) And the work of Father and Son continues, as the spirit acts *in and through us*. (2 Thess. 2:13, 1 Pet.1:2, Phil. 2:12-13, Col. 1:29)

Our Work

If the persons of the Triune Godhead are workers, it's safe to say that the work we do is a reflection of God's image in us. Contrary to what some may think, our work is *not* the result of sin entering our world. It's true that Adam's sin made his work more difficult, and our sin makes work more difficult for us as well (think of how much easier our jobs would be if everyone was unselfish, loving, and cooperative). But the work itself is not our problem.

From the beginning of creation, God gave humans work to do. Genesis tells us, "God blessed them and said to them, 'Be fruitful and increase in number, fill the earth and subdue it.'" (1:28) "The Lord God took the man and put him in the Garden of Eden to work it and take care of it." (2:15) Adam's work was mental as well as physical, for God also gave him the task of studying and naming all the animals. (Gen. 2:19-20) In sum, we were made to be coworkers with God in his creation. And while he brought everything into existence out of nothing, we create and build things with the basic materials he has provided.

Hopefully, you get fulfillment and satisfaction from your work; that sense of a mission accomplished or a job well done. This is as it should be, the way God intended in the first place. And there should also be a feeling of having contributed something of value to your fellow workers, as well as to society at large.

Scripturally, work is highly valued. The first persons who are recorded as having been filled with the spirit were the craftsmen who constructed the Tabernacle. (Ex. 31:1-5) The Book of Proverbs is especially strong on the value of work, and highly critical of those who are lazy, calling them "sluggards." (Pr. 6:6-9, 20:4) In the New Testament, John the Baptist's instructions to those converted under his ministry focused on doing their jobs honestly and helping the poor. (Luke 3:10-14) And when Jesus left his carpentry business to begin his ministry, he told parable after parable in which the main characters were working people: builders, field hands, vineyard workers, etc.

All of this to say, that your work and mine was not designed to be drudgery, nor a punishment. Rather, it is the means by which we provide for the needs of our families, as well as for those who cannot provide for themselves. Paul makes this clear in his writings where he tells people who have been stealing (i.e.takers) should work and "do something useful with their hands," becoming *givers* instead. (Eph. 4:28) Paul also gave the Thessalonian church this rule: "If a man will not work, he shall not eat." And he commanded those who were idle in that church "to settle down and earn the bread they eat." (2 Thess. 3:10-12)

Work Addiction

In contrast to Paul's rule, most of us probably lean in the other direction: we work *too much*. At the extreme, over-workers are called "workaholics." These folks are addicted to the emotional satisfaction they get from their jobs, which may include an adrenalin high, recognition and praise, status and power, or all of the above. They're easy enough to spot because they are usually at work, thinking about work, talking about work, or regularly contacting their workplace. As with any addiction, the workaholic is trying to deal with an emptiness in his or her life, or may be simply driven by the rewards that hard work can bring.

An acquaintance of mine (we'll call him Jim) was like this. As a kid growing up, Jim's parents were dirt poor, and he determined early on that this would never happen to him. So he worked long hours at his law practice and became financially well off. But this wasn't enough. Jim's fear of being poor kept driving him . . . until he met Christ. Through his relationship with the Lord, he found a new security and could finally relax and rest in him. Several years ago, he moved to a country home in a western state and, the last I heard, was working only four days a week and thoroughly enjoying it.

The workaholic is a man who is overly identified with his work. Fixated on his job, he looks at everything and everybody through a vocational lens. Anyone or anything that can help him in his work has his interest and attention. There is no room in his life for hobbies, and weekends and vacations make him "antsy" to get back on the job. He can't separate himself from his vocation. He is a worker. That's his identity.

Another way to spot a workaholic is by watching the approach he takes to other things he does. He works at everything. If playing golf or other some other game, he works hard to beat the completion. If he's on vacation, he has the whole time organized and filled with activities, so he can feel a sense of accomplishment. Even in his spiritual life, he works real hard at being a good Christian, not comfortable to simply relax and enjoy his relationship with the Lord.

In this sense, he is like Martha, rather than her sister Mary, in the incident recorded for us in Luke 10:36-42. Jesus was invited to stay in the sisters' home, where he was engaged in a conversation with Mary. Meanwhile Martha was all stressed out trying to prepare a nice meal for him, without the help of her sister. Finally, exasperated by the situation, Martha pleaded with Jesus, "Lord, don't you care that my sister has left me to do the work by myself? Tell her to help me!" His answer is classic: "Martha, Martha, you are worried and upset about many things, but only one thing is needed. Mary has chosen what is better, and it will not be taken away from her." If you are inclined to over-work, even in your service for God, it's good to keep in mind that the Lord is far more interested in *you* as a person (including spending time *with* you) than in anything you might be doing *for* him.

Questions for Personal Reflection or Group Discussion

1. How does seeing God, as the one who created us to be workers, affect your view of your own occupation?

2. Are you inclined to work too much, and how does this manifest itself?

3. Do you think you lean toward being a workaholic? Does that concern you?

Causes of Work Addiction

Experts studying this issue seem to agree that the roots of work addiction are formed early in life. Workaholics often come from homes where love was mostly conditional. If they lived up to their parents' expectations, they were praised and felt loved. But if they didn't perform, they experienced rejection and disapproval. Some never receive acceptance and approval from their parents, and will spend a lifetime trying to gain it.

I once counseled a man whose father had been a small-time gangster, in and out of jail while my client was growing up. Fred (not his real name) was forced to take various jobs as a kid, just to help his mother put food on the table. On top of this, his father always put Fred down, telling him he would never amount to anything. So Fred set out to prove his "old man" wrong. Obsessed with the desire to "be somebody," he found something he was good at and worked tirelessly to build a successful business. Just when his business was about to take off, his father died. Fred never got to show him that he "*was* something."

His anger and disappointment affected his marriage, which was why Fred and his wife were seeing me. I tried to help him see that his father was the problem, not him, that even if he *had* lived, his father wouldn't have been able to acknowledge Fred's success. His dad's own sense of failure made him put Fred down.

Fred's experience, while a bit extreme, points out one of the main reasons men become addicted to their work—to build up a weak sense of self-esteem. For these men, work is where they get recognition and praise. It's at work where other people answer to them and depend on their skills. It's at work where they prove their self-worth and are rewarded for their efforts. So they put in long hours on the job and feel good about themselves in the process.

Other men have lives that are painful or depressively boring outside of work. For them, work is an escape from a mundane lifestyle away from the office. Perhaps they have an unhappy marriage, or find parenting to be a frustration rather than a joy. So they look to their work to get their juices flowing, to stimulate their minds, and enable them to forget the rest of their life. Plus, long hours on the job give them an excuse to stay away from home.

For still others, their work is a search for identity and meaning. In our culture, we get much of our identity as men from what we do for a living. When meeting another man, the first question we typically ask is, "What do you do?" Then we tend to label him, depending on his answer and level of success. Thus, if a man's job is the only place where he's feeling competent and fulfilled, he can easily become fixated there in order to satisfy his need for meaning in life. Some men are so identified with their job that, without their position, they're totally lost. As a prominent businessman once told me, after selling his business, "You go from a hero to a zero in a New York second." He ended up buying another business.

As Christian men, we need to resist our society's tendency to place value on ourselves (or others) on the basis of what we do for a living. This is a challenge, especially for professionals, who are used to having people refer to them as "reverend," "doctor," "professor," etc. Titles do not make the man, nor do positions such a CEO, president, or VP. Our identity as followers of Christ should come, first and foremost, from our relationship with him; and other relationships as well. Who we are as husbands and fathers, sons and brothers, fellow believers and friends ought to certainly have priority over who we are, or what we do, at work.

The fear of failure also seems to be the force that drives many business and professional men, especially entrepreneurs. But whatever the motivation, there is within most men (even if they are not work addicts) a strong desire to be successful, with all the benefits that come with it, including respect, financial security, and a sense of accomplishment.

Symptoms of Work Addiction

Workaholics spend long hours on the job, bring work home with them, and even go into the office on weekends, if they can. They see themselves as indispensable. Business owners who have no one to be accountable to (except their wives) are particularly susceptible. They love the rush they get from closing a big deal, tackling a major project, or beating out the competition. They become adrenalin junkies, looking for their next high. Constantly needing to prove themselves, they can't relax. Never sure if they've done enough, they continually struggle to show they "still have it."

The work addict constantly compares himself to others. He can't allow others to be more successful, so he keeps pushing himself to get or stay ahead of the competition. Compulsively driven, he's always in a work mode. More than just a hard worker, he gives the impression that he *has* to work or he'll fall apart. Impatient and rushed, he has no tolerance for situations or people that are too slow, requiring him to wait. Continually in a hurry and very time-conscious, he is always checking his watch. He's unable to relax or rest, because for him there is no "off" switch. His restless mind is always working, which may even lead to problems sleeping at night.

Workaholics have trouble saying "no." Not wanting to risk people's disapproval, they won't admit that anything is too much for them to handle. Every new challenge is an opportunity to prove themselves. They can't stand idleness. When forced not to work because of a holiday or mandatory vacation, they experience adrenalin withdrawal, making them feel depressed. Work addicts also become overly serious, because work is serious business. The playfulness and sense of humor they had when they were younger gets lost. They're really not much fun to be around.

Personally, this strikes a little close to home for me. While I don't believe that I am a workaholic, if I *were* to become addicted to anything, this would be my "drug" of choice. Years ago, while traveling, my wife said to me, "I like you better when we're on vacation." Thinking that I'm a pretty nice guy *all* the time, I was surprised by her remark, and asked, "Why?" She replied, "When you're working, you're intense and serious most of the time. On vacations you're more playful and fun. You're the man I fell in love with." That was a wake-up call for me, and I determined not to be so consumed by my work, although it's something I have to fight. Maybe you do too.

Finally, a work addict has distorted priorities. Like all addicts, he slowly loses touch with reality. He lives a life of denial and rationalization, believing that doing well at work is all that really matters. A workaholic may claim to work long hours to provide well for his family or give more money to the church, but in reality, he's addicted to his job. If he were to ask his family whether they would rather have him at home more or enjoy the "extras" he provides, I think he'd find they would choose to have him home.

Unfortunately, workaholism has long-term negative effects. For one thing, living on an adrenalin high all the time puts a lot of stress on the body. The old saying, "Everything that goes up must come down," is true of body chemistry as well. It's also mentally detrimental. Anxiety, forgetfulness, misdirected anger, and loss of perspective are common symptoms. And families are disrupted by the work addict's lifestyle. The neglected wife pours herself into the children or a career of her own. Sons grow up trying to please their dads and are afraid to fail. Daughters may seek affection in the wrong places because Dad isn't available to provide it. Both may end up into drugs.

Last, but not least, the work addict's spiritual well-being is affected. Work has become his idol. As someone has well said, "His ultimate concern is for something other than the One who *is* ultimate." They struggle with doubts about their salvation, because in the workaholic's world, everything is based on performance. The unconditional love and acceptance of God, and the grace offered to him through Jesus Christ are difficult truths for him to embrace—because he didn't earn it.

Do the Scriptures have anything to say about this issue of overwork? Absolutely. The classic passage on this was written by the writer of Ecclesiastes, who tried to find meaning in life through his work on many large projects:

> "So my heart began to despair over all my toilsome labor
> under the sun. For a man may do his work with wisdom,
> knowledge and skill, and then he must leave all he owns to

someone who has not worked for it. This too is meaning-less and a great misfortune. What does a man get for all the toil and anxious striving with which he labors under the sun? All his days his work is pain and grief; even at night his mind does not rest. This too is meaning-less. A man can do nothing better than to eat and drink and find satisfaction in his work. This too, I see, is from the hand of God, for without him, who can eat or find enjoyment? To the man who pleases him, God gives wisdom, knowledge and happiness." (Ecclesiastes 2:20-26)

Notice first, his observation that, for all the work a man may do, eventually he will leave what he owns to someone else. This is particularly relevant for men who build a business from scratch and then leave it to the next generation. Studies show that most family businesses do not make it past the second generation. Because they have not put in the hard labor to get it started, they tend to squander what has been left to them.

Secondly, the writer describes his work as "anxious striving," "pain and grief," and something that kept him awake at night. This is classic workaholism, where a man reaches the point where his work (like any addiction) is no longer enjoyable, but he doesn't know how to get off the treadmill.

His third point is that a man is better off enjoying the simple things of life, including the basics of food and drink that God provides, and "find(ing) satisfaction in his work." God intended work to be satisfying, not "toilsome labor."

Finally, he makes it clear that "wisdom, knowledge and happiness," including the enjoyment derived from work, comes from "the hand of God" and nowhere else. So driving ourselves to be successful or to fill some emptiness in our lives through our work just isn't going to bring us what we're searching for.

Questions for Personal Reflection or Group Discussion

1. Which of the motivations for working listed below come closest to describing you?

(a) Need for self-esteem

(b) An escape from a mundane life outside of work

(c) A search for identity and meaning

(d) A fear of failure.

2. Can you see any of the symptoms for work addiction manifested in your life? Which ones?

Overcoming Work Addiction

1. Get perspective: As with any addiction, the starting place to finding freedom is to face the problem. This involves honest introspection and asking ourselves hard questions. Ecclesiastes 4:8 describes a man who was all alone and had no heir to whom to leave his wealth:

> "There was no end to his toil, yet his eyes were not content with his wealth. 'For whom am I toiling,' he asked, 'and why am I depriving myself of enjoyment?' This too is meaningless[,] a miserable business."

Those are questions that those of us inclined toward work addiction should ask ourselves. Who are we working for? How much work or wealth is enough? When do we stop and examine ourselves and our work pattern? When do we start finding enjoyment in our work, or find another kind of work we *can* enjoy?

Recognizing this problem involves facing the distorted thinking involved with any addiction—the minimizing of our behavior ("I don't really work that much"), or the excuses we feed ourselves and others ("There's no one else who can do it," or "If I don't work long hours, I could lose my job"). Rationalizations will keep us from really dealing with the issue.

Jesus said, "What does is profit a man if he gains the whole world and loses his own soul? And what will he give in exchange for his soul?" (Matt. 16:26) Many men in our society are willing to sell their souls to a company, professional group, or even a church, while pursuing the elusive goal of success (however they define it). I know a pastor who worked long hours to grow one of the largest churches in his denomination, but neglected his family in the process, much to his regret later on. And the work addict's physical or mental well-being is also sacrificed on the altar of self-achievement.

2. Slow down: Dealing with "hurry sickness" is also important. There is a direct correlation between time-urgency, elevated adrenal levels, and stress-related illnesses. When adrenal levels are high in non-emergency situations, it increases cholesterol and fat deposits, thickens the blood, increases gastric juices, and raises blood pressure. Learning to take our foot off the gas pedal is necessary for overcoming a work addiction. This is difficult because hurrying becomes a habit, and habits aren't easily changed. In reality, addictions are simply habits taken to an extreme, where they begin to run our lives. The only way to overcome any habit is by replacing it with a new one. Developing a habit of slowing down is part of the cure.

3. Change your schedule: Track how you spend your time in half-hour increments for a week. Seeing how much time you spend working will probably be an eye-opener. Then, take a hard look at your schedule, and make a commitment to initiate major changes. Asking your wife and/or a friend to hold you accountable also helps. Decide which parts of your job you need to do well, which parts can be less than perfect (or delegated), and which can be eliminated altogether. Also decide how many hours you will work, and when you will relax or play. Then cultivate healthy activities for "off" times. Someone has wisely said, 'If you don't plan your time, others will plan it for you." A good plan allows you to get more balance in your life (we'll look at this later).

4. Pay attention: Watch your choice of words. Talking about how busy you are only adds to the sense of pressure you feel to get everything done. Learning to say "no" is also important in holding off additional work. If "no" is too difficult, try saying, "I'll get back to you." This buys you time to look at your schedule and make a thought-out decision versus an impulsive one. Examine your working space. Clutter and stacks of papers remind you of all you haven't done. This is a particularly difficult habit to break if you depend on visual reminders, like I do.

5. Learn to relax: Take breaks in your work to phone a friend, listen to music, or take a walk outside to enjoy God's creation. Relaxation exercises like slow, deep breathing, or tightening and relaxing muscles can help ease tension and stress. Alternately, grab a few minutes to pray or read a devotional book. This will also enable you to keep perspective. When at home, don't overload yourself with projects. There are always things that need to be done if you are a home owner, but many of them can wait. Taking time to unwind and enjoy your family should be your priority.

6. Increase frustration tolerance: All addicts have a low tolerance for frustration, and workaholics are no different. They seek for immediate gratification and are upset by delays. Deal with it by accepting your impulsiveness as unhealthy, and asking God to help you overcome it (patience *is* a fruit of the spirit).

One way to practice patience that you might want to try is to deliberately choose frustrating situations, like getting in the longest checkout line at the supermarket. If you *choose* the action, you won't feel angry about it. This happened to me while Christmas shopping (I didn't happen to choose the long line; it was unavoidable). At first I was irked, but then I relaxed and struck up a conversation with the people in front of me. The conversation was so pleasant that the time passed quickly and my stress disappeared.

If you are a work addict, or moving in that direction, hopefully these suggestions will be helpful to you. But along with changing your routine, the most important thing you can do is to pray about your problem. God is in the business of change, and he can help you create a healthier pattern and attitude toward your work, if you ask him.

Questions for Personal Reflection or Group Discussion

1. Even if you don't consider yourself addicted to work, are there suggestions listed above that could be beneficial to incorporate in your life?

2. Which ones, and how do you think they would help you?

3. Think about or discuss how you might put them into practice right away.

Rest

For Christians, work is a given. But so also is rest. The same God who spoke the entire universe into existence, also rested when his work was finished. As a spirit being, God didn't rest because he was tired; he ceased his creative activity to step back (as it were) and survey all that he had accomplished. "And it was very good." And so, we are told,

"God blessed the seventh day and made it holy, because on it he rested from all the work of creating that he had done." (Gen. 1:31-2:2)

This seventh day rest was later incorporated into the laws God gave to his people, Israel, as the Fourth Commandment. The reasoning behind the commandment was based on God resting on the seventh day and blessing it. (Exod. 20:8-11) I find it interesting that, even though it *is* one of the Ten Commandments, many Christians violate the Sabbath rest all the time. They wouldn't think of stealing or murdering someone, but somehow working seven days a week is okay. I guess they feel six days isn't enough to get everything done; that the extra day is necessary for their survival.

The Israelites thought that way too, and had to learn the Sabbath principle by experience (incidentally, the word Sabbath means "to stop or cease"). During their wilderness wandering for forty years, God fed them daily with manna from heaven, along with instructions concerning the use of this heavenly food. First, they were to collect only what they needed for that day, and not to hoard it for the next day. God would provide. If they tried to save it, it would turn rotten. Secondly, there would not be any manna on the seventh day—the day of rest—for God would give them enough on the sixth day to carry them over. This would be the only time the manna would stay fresh an extra day.

In spite of these very specific instructions from God, some of them had to learn the hard way. As the saying goes, "Some people believe signs; others just have to touch the electric fence." So some of the Israelites tried to hoard manna during the week, and sure enough, it rotted. And they also went out looking for it on the Sabbath, only to find nothing. (Ex. 16:20-27) God was teaching them an important lesson: *they didn't need to work seven days a week because he would take care of them.* We need to learn this lesson too.

One summer, while working my way through college, I was putting in a seven-day week. I found it really tiring not having a break. One week just ran into another, and I came to realize that I needed a day to rest. That's when I personally learned the value of the Sabbath principle, one I have tried to practice ever since. It isn't always easy to do. In graduate school several years later, I now had a wife and two young children to support, along with my studies to keep up with. But we set aside Sunday as a day of worship, rest, and family time together. No studying, even if I had a test on Monday. I'm so thankful we did that. Looking back, I feel as though that practice helped preserve my health, my sanity, and my family.

I am convinced that God commanded us to rest one day a week because we were created with a need for our bodies and minds to regroup. Athletes in serious training know this, and we should practice it also. God required the Israelites to give their servants and working animals a day off to recoup as well. (Ex. 20:10) And they were also told to stop working the soil one year out of every seven, so it too could rest. (Lev. 25:1-5) Once again, as he did with the manna earlier, God promised them a bumper crop on the sixth year to carry them over during the year the land rested. Even today, as a practical measure, farmers have learned not to exhaust soil by overworking it. It seems that God has built the Sabbath principle into all of his creation.

But the Sabbath day does not only have physical benefits. It also has emotional and spiritual benefits. It's not simply for rest, but also for reflection. As God surveyed his creation after its completion, our Sabbath should be a day of reflection as well. It's a day to step back and get a perspective on our life and work. This is hard to do when we're up to our ears in frantic pursuits. The Sabbath is especially a day to get God's perspective through worship. For the Jews, it was (and is) the seventh day, Saturday. Later on, Christians began honoring Sunday (the day of Christ's resurrection) as a day for rest and worship. The most important part of our Sabbath rest is to stop and think about God—his goodness and provision for us all week—and also to confess our sins, renew our commitment, and gain strength and insight for the coming week.

In the book of Deuteronomy, Moses repeats the Ten Commandments as part of his farewell address. But when he comes to the Sabbath commandment, he relates it, not to God's rest at creation (as in Exodus), but to their slavery in Egypt. (Dt. 5:15) In essence he seems to be saying, "There was a time when as slaves in Egypt, you never got a day off, and never had a chance to worship Jehovah. Now that you have that opportunity, be sure you don't neglect it, and the One who has given you that freedom."

In our culture, there was a time when Sunday was recognized as a day of rest and worship. As a boy, I can remember that stores were always closed on Sunday, except those run by Jewish merchants, who closed on Saturday. After college, I was working in management for a large department store in Detroit when some retailers, including ours, decided to open on Sundays for the first time, *only* during the Christmas season. They were trying to get an edge on their competition. I remember standing in the store one Sunday and thinking to myself, "This is stupid. We have to light and heat this big building and pay the sales staff to be here, but customers aren't going to spend any more money than before. They're just going to spread it out over seven days instead of six."

Now, of course, most stores are open seven days a week *all* year, and merchants are also cutting into holidays (like Thanksgiving), when stores have traditionally been closed. In contrast, one has to respect the Christian leadership at Chick-fil-A for their policy of closing on Sundays. And they're doing it in an industry where weekends are normally the busiest time. God seems to honor them for that. They were recently named America's favorite fast-food chain.

Does God take his Sabbath commandment seriously, even if many of us don't? Absolutely! You can't read through the Old Testament prophets without recognizing that a major reason for God's judgment on Israel was their neglect of the Sabbath. (Neh. 13:15-18, Ezek. 20:19-21) For example, we are told that God sent the Israelites into exile for 70 years because they had not rested the land every seventh year during the 490 years they occupied it. So now the land would lay uncultivated for 70 years to make up for it. (Lev. 26:33-35, 2 Chr. 26:20-21)

Rest versus Legalism

If *not* observing the Sabbath is one extreme, being legalistic about it is the other. The Pharisees of Jesus' day were guilty of this. They developed so many rules and regulations about Sabbath-keeping that it became a burden, instead of the benefit God intended. Time and again, Jesus and his disciples were criticized by this group for their failure to keep all their Sabbath rules. In reply, Jesus declared himself to be "Lord of the Sabbath" and reminded them that the "the Sabbath was made for man, not man for the Sabbath." (Mark 2:27) A balance is needed between violating the commandment and losing its beneficial purpose.

When I was young, my parents didn't allow us to play sports on Sunday, because that was a big part of our everyday lives. We lived across the street from a park, and it was difficult to see our friends out there playing various sports while we rested in the house. During this time, one of my buddies from church invited me to visit his uncle's farm upstate for a weekend. These Christian farmers honored the Sabbath principle by only doing necessary work on Sunday (like milking the cows), and my friend's aunt fixed a picnic lunch on Saturday night for the next day so she wouldn't have to cook on Sunday. Dishes were left in the sink to be washed on Monday.

I found all of this very interesting, since our biggest meal at home was always cooked on Sunday after church, and the clean-up afterwards was a major chore. But the real amazement for me came after our picnic lunch, when the kids went outside and played every sport imaginable on a Sunday afternoon! Years later, better understanding the *principle* behind the Sabbath command, I came to realize that for farm kids, who worked hard six days a week, playing sports was their way of relaxation and rest.

And so, for us as well, how we honor the Sabbath, in addition to worship and reflection, will be determined by what is relaxing and recharging for us and *different* from our everyday work. For the businessman who sits behind a desk all day, working in his garden with God's soil and plants might be just what he needs. On the other hand, if a man's business is landscaping, that's the last thing he should be doing. He could better gain the benefits of the Sabbath by taking a nap, reading a good book, or visiting with family or friends.

Incidentally, while Sunday is a good day to honor the Sabbath because of the opportunity to worship, it might not be the best day for you, especially if your job requires you to work on Sunday. But *do* find a day to keep for rest. You won't regret it.

Questions for Personal Reflection or Group Discussion

1. Have you ever had the Sabbath principle explained to you before? What do you think?

2. Are you in the habit of honoring a Sabbath rest one day a week? What do you do on that day?

3. If you don't have a Sabbath built into your schedule, what steps can you take to make it a priority and make it happen?

Vacations

Vacations should also be part of our thinking about the Sabbath. While Jesus never took a vacation in our sense of the word, he did feel the need to get away at times. (Mark 6:30-31) There's nothing like an extended break from our work to gain perspective and recharge our batteries. Going to a place where you can take in the beauty of God's creation only adds to the benefit. But it's important to not approach vacations like we do our work: keeping a strict schedule in order to pursue a bunch of activities. As mentioned earlier, there are people who do this. If I'm somewhere new on vacation, I also tend to want to take in everything. My wife, on the other hand, likes to kick back and relax. Fortunately, we learned to compromise on this while on our honeymoon, and I'm thankful we did. It helps me slow down and really unwind.

Not checking phone messages or emails as much as possible (ideally not at all) while on vacation is a good way to turn off my brain and separate from my work. During those kick-back-and-relax days (when not sightseeing), I also get to read things not related to my job: a good piece of fiction or a biography, or something that helps me grow spiritually. I usually come back home rested and with a different perspective on my life and work than when I left.

The root word for vacation is "vacate" (or leave). Many men, especially those who own their own businesses, don't seem to be able to separate themselves from their work while on "vacation." Which really, then, isn't a vacation; it's just a temporary relocation of their office. As Christians, we should take a page out of the Israelites experience, and recognize that God can provide us with everything we need when we take time to rest, *if we trust him.* And that's the issue. Can we trust God to take care of our work while we're not there? If you were to have a breakdown or become ill for a while, the company would probably survive. Why wait until then to find out? As much as we hate to admit it, *no one* is indispensable.

Our highly driven society would lead us to believe that we have to out-work our competitors in order to get ahead, or to even to keep up. But that's leaving God out of the equation. At some point, it's important to realize that, if we are in the business God wants us in, he will make sure (like he does with Chick-fil-A) that we stay in business, as long as we are honoring him. This includes keeping the Sabbath.

Work as a Calling

The word "calling" in connection with someone's profession typically makes us think of pastors, missionaries, evangelists, or other church-related vocations. Or if it isn't specifically Christian work, the helping professions come to mind. People like doctors, teachers, or social workers will sometimes speak about feeling "called" to do what they do. Somehow, we don't associate being called to jobs like manufacturing, sales, or engineering. And yet, our word "vocation" comes from a Latin term that means "calling." So technically, whatever your vocation is, that *is* your calling.

For Christians, calling has another, more primary meaning. The Bible tells us that we have been called to be followers of Jesus Christ. Paul uses this term over and over in reference to believers. (Rom. 1:7, 1 Cor. 1:2, Gal. 5:13, Eph. 4:1) Putting our faith in Christ at the beginning of our spiritual journey was a response to God's call. We now live lives of trust and service to a new master and king. And that calling supersedes and includes any other claim on our time, attention, and energy, especially what we do in the workplace. Our main goal in life is best summarized in what Jesus referred to as the greatest commandment: "to love God with all our heart and soul and mind and strength, and to love our neighbor as ourselves." (Matt. 22:37-39) Our challenge is, how do we live out this law of love in our everyday lives, at home, at church, in the community, and where we work?

The way this is done is fleshed out in the chapters that follow, but it's important to recognize here that what you do for a living is not of lesser value or importance than people whose calling is different from yours. The problem is, when we think of callings in Biblical terms, we envision men like Abraham, called out of Ur to go to a foreign land; or Moses, called by God through a burning bush to set his people free; or Paul, who was knocked off his horse on his way to Damascus and called to be an apostle to the Gentiles. Great stories—but they are the *exceptions*, rather than the rule. Most believers, even in Biblical times, were ordinary people doing ordinary jobs, but making an extraordinary difference in the families and communities where they lived and worked.

This was clear, for instance, in the ministry of John the Baptist. When people came to be baptized by him, they asked, "What should we do?" He replied to tax collectors not to collect any more than they were required to, and he told soldiers not to extort money or accuse people falsely, but to be content with their pay. (Luke 3:12-14) Both of these professions were looked down on by the Jews, but John didn't ask them to *change* jobs; he told them to change the way they were *doing* their jobs. They were now to perform their duties in a way that was honoring to God. The same was true in the ministry of Jesus. He called Matthew to leave his tax-collecting profession and become an apostle, but left tax-collecting Zacchaeus where he was, impressed by his promise to be honest. He called Peter, Andrew, and the Zebedee brothers to leave their fishing business, but left a Roman Centurion, whose faith he admired, in his profession.

Think about it. Can your pastor reach the people you work with every day? You may be the only Christian the people around you know. Your workplace is your mission field. Wherever you are, even if only temporarily, is where God has placed you to be salt and light. It's in your present context that you can be an example of what it means to work honestly and hard. It's there where you can show love and concern for the people who work with you. It's at work that God may open up opportunities to share your faith and meet others' needs in the name of Christ. All of us should view our work, whatever our profession, as our spiritual and primary calling.

One of the best examples of this is a man I met a few years ago. The son of missionaries to Japan, Rick felt God was calling him to be a missionary to that country as well. While in his last year of seminary in the USA, he was working part-time in a Japanese restaurant, when the manager was let go and Rick was offered the job. Although he had no business training or experience, he turned an establishment that was losing money into a profitable venture. Someone was so impressed that Rick was approached to go to work for a Japanese auto parts company at a six-figure starting salary! This was certainly not what he felt God had called him to do, so he prayed about it and sought godly counsel from his seminary professors. They suggested that perhaps God was leading him in another direction, and he should try it for a year to confirm one way or the other. If business wasn't God's call, he could always go back to Plan A.

So he went to work for this company and quickly rose through the ranks to become president of their North American division. Rick told me that he knew this was where the Lord wanted him, because his ability to solve business problems was strictly a gift from God, as was his ability to speak Japanese fluently. Although his parents ministered in Japan, he had spent his formative years in an MK school in another country and had never learned Japanese when he was young.

His position took him to Japan for regular meetings with high level executives in the auto industry. They were intrigued by this American who knew their language so well and would ask him about his background. When he told them that his parents were missionaries in Japan, their curiosity was piqued and they wanted to know more. This gave him opportunities to share his faith. Rick began to realize that, if he had been a missionary to Japan (Plan A), he would never have had a chance to share Christ with men at this level of society. As a bonus, his job took him all over Asia, where he could connect with his former classmates from the MK school, who were now serving as missionaries. Rick was able to minister to them, both with encouragement and financial support for their various mission projects.

There's an additional twist to this story. Ted came to work for Rick while *he* was finishing seminary in preparation for pastoral ministry. Having a strong math background, Ted was given a job in quality control, and was so gifted at his job that he soon became a vice president in the company and the head of quality control for the whole international operation. Rick said to me, "My job enables me to share Christ with executives; Ted's job gives him the opportunity to share his faith with engineers." God does indeed work in mysterious ways.

Rick and Ted's stories illustrate two convictions I have come to embrace over the years: First, don't try to put God in a box to fit the way we think he should work in and through people's lives. His call comes in many ways. Second, God's call on our lives also takes many different forms, including working in the so-called "secular world" and having an impact for Christ with people who might never enter a church.

Questions for Personal Reflection or Group Discussion

1. What do you do on your vacations? Do you truly vacate or just move your office?

2. What can you do to make them more restful and reenergizing?

3. Have you ever considered your work as a "calling"? Does viewing it this way give you a different perspective?

4. What opportunities can you envision for serving God in your workplace?

Balance

One of the most difficult things for men to do is maintain a balance between work and the other areas of our lives. There are several reasons for this. For one thing, we feel a strong sense of responsibility to take care of our families' physical and financial needs, and work is necessary for us to do this. Secondly (as indicated earlier), our profession contributes largely to our sense of identity as men. And for many business and professional men, our work is the place we get a lot of satisfaction and fulfillment. Also, if you have your own business, there is the added pressure of needing to satisfy customers or clients, as well as providing income for the people who work for you. Put it all together, and it's easy for our jobs to dominate our lives and schedules, leaving other areas to get "the short end of the stick." But., even if we would like to get more balance, where do we begin?

It always comes down to a question of priorities; one we have to wrestle with in every area of life. To do this, it's helpful to ask a few key questions: What's more important to me, my relationships or my work? If I were to die tomorrow, who would miss me the most? Lying on my deathbed, would I want to be surrounded by my family or my coworkers? How many family activities have I missed because of my job? How often do I neglect my spiritual life during times when the pressures at work are greater than usual? Am I making time for exercise and leisure activities?

It's hard to get a realistic look at our lives when we're in the middle of the fray. So, it's good to step back from time to time in order to gain a more objective viewpoint. When I left the church I was pastoring to teach at a seminary, I was able to get a hindsight perspective on my pastoral work that I couldn't have while engaged in it. I came to realize that, if I were to do it all over again, there were a number of things I would do differently. But under the day-to-day responsibilities of the position, I just kept plugging along, without taking adequate time to evaluate, let alone change, what I was doing.

During that first year of teaching, I read an interview with former Dallas Cowboys coach, Tom Landry, who was asked if he missed coaching. His answer was surprising and insightful. Landry replied that he loved being a coach, but he didn't realize how much pressure coaching involved until he got out from under it. He said, "Now that I know what normal feels like, I wouldn't go back to that for anything."

Men, in particular, are not very good at getting in touch with our bodies. Under an adrenalin rush, we can drive ourselves to the point of physical and mental exhaustion. Stress becomes an accepted feeling for us. We even claim to work better under pressure. But the truth is, as discussed earlier, we need to rest, both physically and mentally. We need time with family and friends. We need quiet times of fellowship with the Lord. We need enjoyable times of recreation. We need balance.

A realistic look at your schedule by tracking the hours you spend on the various areas of your life (as suggested earlier) will enable you to actually see the imbalance. The results may surprise you. The question is, how do we cut down at work (I doubt if anyone is overbalanced at home)? To begin with, a famous quote by President Dwight D. Eisenhower will help us gain perspective: "The things that are urgent are rarely important, and the things that are important are rarely urgent." This is so true.

There are things that are both important and urgent, things that absolutely have to be done and can't be put off. Sometimes we have to put in more time at work to keep a contractual promise or to help a patient, client, or parishioner in crisis. At home, if your wife or child needs emergency medical care, it simply can't wait. These things are obvious, but they're usually not the problem. The real problem is treating things as urgent that really aren't, and neglecting things that are very important over the long run.

As a counselor, I sometimes get phone calls from people who feel they absolutely have to see me right away. After asking a few questions concerning the nature of their problem, I usually find that they have neglected dealing with this issue for years. Now, that it has finally come to a head, they're feeling an urgency to fix it. But unless this person is suicidal or in harm's way, I am quite comfortable meeting them the next day or another day that works for me, rather than getting caught up in *their sense of urgency*. Ironically, there have been a number of times that I have adjusted my schedule to fit such a person in, only to have them fail to show up, or even call.

The problem for most of us is that the so-called "urgent" often crowds out what is truly important. Spending quality time with our wife and children is really important, but it often gets pushed aside because it lacks a sense of urgency. The same is true of the time we spend developing our relationship with the Lord, or taking care of our physical and mental health with exercise and leisure activities.

One of the reasons balance is so difficult to maintain is that our families are often more forgiving than the people at work. Failing to meet the expectations of customers, clients, or upper management (depending on who we answer to) could hurt our chances to grow our businesses, or advance in our careers. On the other hand, our wives and children might complain about our work hours, or family events missed, but after a while they will probably suffer in silence, no longer expressing their hurt and disappointment. They'll just assume Dad isn't going to show up, and won't plan on it. The sad result is what I hear from clients over and over: "I never really knew my dad. He was working all the time." Or, "Our marriage broke up because he was never home."

Besides deciding what's important to you, the key to having balance is using your personal calendar. Start by planning ahead and scheduling time for the important things in your life. Then, as much as possible, work your job schedule around those priorities. This will take some creativity on your part, but it can be done. Pray for God to help you with this process. It's easier to do this if you're working for yourself. But if you are in middle management, answerable to others, you'll have a bigger challenge, especially if you're working for a boss who's a workaholic and expects his staff to be also.

In that case, you may have to manage your time on the job better, so that the quality and quantity of your work doesn't suffer, even though you are working fewer hours. Frankly, there are probably time-consumers (non-essential things) that can be delegated or eliminated, if you take a hard look at them. Getting more family time and rest will also enable you to be more efficient when you're on the job. And your subconscious mind will be processing work problems while you are not at the office.

At some point, you may have to explain to your boss why you are changing your pattern, but be sure your work speaks for itself. And you may trigger in him the need to take a hard look at his own work pattern. If he is unsympathetic to your changes, then requesting a transfer, looking for another job, or starting your own business may be your only options. But if you're serious about resetting your priorities, I think God will honor and take care of you, whatever you decide.

The apostle Paul wrote to workers in the Colossian church was, "Whatever you do, work at it with all your heart, as working for the Lord, not for men . . . It is the Lord Christ you are serving." (3:23-24) When at work, give it your best. But notice the words, "whatever you do," which includes your responsibilities to your wife, children, and the fellowship of believers, all which are addressed earlier in his letter. Work is necessary and important. But it's not as important as other areas in your life. Fight for balance. It's a fight that has great rewards if you win, and one you can't afford to lose.

Questions for Personal Reflection or Group Discussion

How much balance do you have between work-related and other activities?

2. Try charting your work schedule for a week to find out.

3. What do you need to change in order to gain more balance? Write out your priorities and come up with a specific plan to address them.

Going Further: Read Ecclesiastes 2:17-26, Deuteronomy 5:12-15, and Matthew 6:25-34. What principles do you find in these passages that you can apply to your life and work? What changes might you have to make?

Bottom Line (What Did Jesus Do?)

Jesus lived with balance. There was a rhythm to his life between work and rest. You can't read the gospels without noticing how often he would get off by himself after a period of intense ministry. And he was never in a hurry. He even deliberately delayed responding to a desperate message from his friends to come and heal their sick brother. He was so tuned into his Father's will that he waited until Lazarus died before going and performing his greatest miracle, glorifying God through it. (John 11) That's the key: becoming centered on doing what God wants us to do, being sensitive to his spirit at work in our lives. Then we can find that inner peace and direction that only he can give.

Additional Resources

Lynne M. Baab, *Sabbath Keeping: Finding Freedom in the Rhythms of Rest*. InterVarsity Press, 2005.

James E. Dittes, *Men at Work: Life Beyond the Office*. Westminster John Knox Press, 1996.

Alan Fadling, *An Unhurried Life: Following Jesus' Rhythms of Work and Rest*. InterVarsity Press, 2013.

Martin C. Helldorfer, *Work Trap: Rediscovering Leisure, Redefining Work*. Twenty-Third Publications, 1995.

Barbara Killinger, *Workaholics: The Responsible Addicts*. A Firefly Book, 1991.

Doug Sherman & William Hendricks, *How to Balance Competing Time Demands*. NavPress, 1992.

"When man loses the sacred significance of work and of himself as a worker, he soon loses the sacred meaning of time and of life."

—*Carl F. H. Henry*

Chapter Seven: Integrity at Work - Motives

We work for many reasons, but mostly because we *have* to. It's how we support ourselves and our families. If you own your business, you also provide jobs and needed income for your employees. But if we weren't paid for what we do, we probably wouldn't be doing it. Even those in the helping professions can't afford to do their work for nothing. We may also get a sense of accomplishment and satisfaction from our work. But creating income is still the main reason we roll out of bed and hit the ground running every workday.

Money is Not the Bottom Line

Even though income may be the *prime* motivator for most people's work, money is *not* the bottom line for Christians - at least it shouldn't be. Is it necessary? Absolutely. Is it comforting to have financial resources over and above what we need to live on? Yes, that can be a real benefit to us, and others. But, as followers of Christ, we ought to have a different view of money than the world around us. Some Christians see wealth as something suspect, if not evil, because of the many warnings in Scripture about its dangers. Others are oblivious to Biblical teaching on this important topic, and handle their funds like any of their nonbelieving neighbors. Both of these perspectives need correcting.

The Scriptures have a lot to say on the subject of wealth. There *are* warnings of its dangers, to be sure, but there are also instructions concerning its benefits and potential use for good. The Biblical perspective on money seems to revolve around three issues: (1) how we *attain* our wealth, (2) what our *attitude* is toward money, and (3) how we *use* our financial resources. We'll look at each of these issues in turn.

Attaining Our Wealth

It's a given that any wealth we have as Christians must be acquired honestly. Ultimately, all riches belong to God. He owns everything. (Ps. 50:10-12) And he is the one who provides us with everything we need. (1 Tim. 6:17, 2 Cor. 9:10-11, Phil. 4:19) Our part is to make sure we are working diligently for our financial resources, (Prov. 10:4, 1 Th. 4:11, 2 Th. 3:6-12) but at the same time not overdoing it. (Prov. 23:4)

Getting our money *dishonestly* is roundly condemned in Scripture. For example, Solomon says in Proverbs 13:11, "Dishonest money dwindles away, but he who gathers money little by little makes it grow." Jeremiah adds this thought, "Like a partridge that hatches eggs it did not lay, is the man who gains riches by unjust means. When his life is half gone, they will desert him; and in the end he will prove to be a fool." (17:10) Bribery, extortion, and cheating are simply out of bounds for the people of God. (Ex. 23:8, Matt. 21:12-13, Luke 3:12-14)

So then, for followers of Christ, having money is a good thing, as long as we gain it legitimately. This would ordinarily be through our work, but could also come by way of an inheritance or investments. In addition to how we attain it, the way we view money is also important, which is considered next.

Our Attitude Toward Wealth

Interestingly enough, the Scriptures have more to say concerning our attitude toward and use of money than about how we acquire it. First, there's the issue of how much it's desired. Needing it is one thing, but *wanting* it too badly is something else. In 1st Timothy Chapter 6, we have two classic Biblical passages on the Christian perspective and use of wealth, which are extremely helpful. In the first passage Paul writes the following:

> "But godliness with contentment is great gain. For we brought nothing into the world, and we can take nothing out of it. But if we have food and clothing, we will be content with that. People who want to get rich fall into temptation and a trap and into many foolish and harmful desires that plunge men into ruin and destruction. For the love of money is a root of all kinds of evil. Some people, eager for money, have wandered from the faith and pierced themselves with many griefs." (vs. 6–10)

Notice how Paul began with the attitude of contentment. He says that being content has great advantages, as long as we have a godly perspective on material things. Contentment was something Paul learned personally through the everyday struggles in his life. In his letter to the Philippians, he writes, "I know what it is to be in need, and I know what it is to have plenty. I have learned the *secret* of being content in any and every situation, whether well-fed or hungry, whether living in plenty or in want. I can do everything through Him who gives me strength." (4:12-13) Paul's secret? He learned to rely on the strength of God, regardless of his circumstances.

This quality of contentment contrasts directly with how our society views things. We live in an economic world where *discontent* is the name of the game. Advertising is designed to create a sense of dissatisfaction with what we have. The people behind those ads try to convince us that we *need* to have the latest clothes, appliances, cars, and cell phones. Judging from the lines of people who camp all night outside of retail stores, in order to be one of the first ones to buy the latest gadget being promoted, those ads are pretty effective. But this incessant drive for the latest and the best leaves one anxious and empty, for in reality we can never get enough. (Eccles. 6:7) Materialism never satisfies a person's deepest needs.

Secondly, Paul reminds us that we will leave this world the same way we came in: with *nothing*. Wealth and material goods are temporary. I was reminded of this years ago when I went to an estate sale. The belongings of the deceased (a farmer) were spread all over the lawn for people to examine, before they were sold to the highest bidder. Among the items was a roll-top desk that still had the former owner's personal papers and reading glasses on it. I heard that there were family members present who wanted to bid on that desk. I hoped that they got it for sentimental reasons. But whoever purchased any of the items being auctioned off that day would still have to leave them, eventually, to someone else.

In our materialistic world, it's too easy to get caught up in trying to keep pace with our friends and family members regarding the amount of "stuff" we own. And when attics, garages, and basements are full, we rent storage lockers to handle the overflow! But how much of it do we actually *use*, let alone need? And the more we own, the more we have to worry about. Will it be stolen? We'd better lock it up. Will it be damaged? We'd better insure it. And, of course, we also have to maintain it. The bottom line is: there's real freedom in simplicity, genuine relief in contentment. Having less also gives us more time to use on the really important things of life—like our relationships.

Paul tells us next (v. 8) that having the basics in life ought to be enough to make us content. Notice he says, "We *will be* content with that," rather than we *should* be content with the minimum. Numerous studies have been done on what makes people happy. One area explored is wealth, because so many people believe that having more money would bring them happiness (consider the number of people who gamble money they can't spare while playing in state-run lotteries). Interestingly enough, what researchers have discovered is that, if people are below the poverty line and their income is raised to where they can care for their basic needs, their happiness increases significantly. But beyond those basic needs, no matter how much a person has, their increase in happiness is very little.

Not surprisingly, Paul was right. If our basic needs are met, it doesn't get any better than that. Think of when you were just starting out in your work and/or married life. You probably didn't have much to spare. You struggled and saved for the things you wanted, especially for your first house. Are you happier now that you have accumulated a lot more stuff, than you were during that time? Probably not. Life was simpler then, and that had real advantages.

One of the "traps" (v. 9) of wanting to get rich is that money can be addictive. The writer of Ecclesiastes points out that "whoever loves money never has money enough, whoever loves wealth is never satisfied with his income." (5:10) In modern vernacular, the famous quote by industrialist John D. Rockefeller sums up this attitude. When asked how much money is enough, he replied, "Just a little bit more." This attitude of greed is something Jesus warned us about in Luke 12:15, when he said, "Be on your guard against all kinds of greed; a man's life does not consist in the abundance of his possessions." When the pursuit of wealth becomes the driving force in a person's life, it eventually replaces God as one's master. Which is why Jesus also warned, "You cannot serve both God and Money." (Matt. 6:24)

In verse 9 of 1 Timothy 6, Paul issues his own warning. He talks about "people who want to get rich" and the pitfalls that result from that desire. It isn't *being* rich that's a problem; it's the *desire* for wealth that creates difficulties. He describes this desire as "a temptation and a snare." Our desires set us up for temptation (James 1:14-15 makes this very clear). We can't be tempted by something we have no desire for. And wanting to be rich entices people in a variety of ways. Gambling is one way. Investing in get-rich-quick schemes is another. Borrowing money they can't pay back to indulge in things they can't afford also pushes people into debt, with all of its problems. For many, growing credit card balances create a major "snare."

Paul then states that there are "foolish and harmful desires that plunge men into ruin and destruction. For the love of money is a root of all kinds of evil." (vs. 9b–10a) This is the *dark side* of pursuing wealth for its own sake. Think of the many evil things that are done for money: bribery, stealing, cheating on taxes, producing and selling pornography, prostitution, abortion clinics, sex trafficking, selling illegal drugs, pollution of our environment by uncaring manufacturers; payment of excessive bonuses to CEOs who deliver profits by firing employees and overworking those who remain; the unreasonable demands of union bosses that force businesses to close, costing laborers their jobs; and even murder. Someone has well said, if you want to get to the root of any evil, "just follow the money."

Continuing, Paul says, "Some people, eager for money, have wandered from the faith and pierced themselves with many griefs." This may be the greatest evil of them all—the loss of one's spiritual bearings. I have known a number of believers who got caught up in the pursuit of wealth in various ways, only to end up spiritually bankrupt. Having money, along with the prestige, power, and privileges that go with it, can easily go to a person's head. They begin to think they don't need God, that they can handle life on their own terms. After a while, money becomes the most important thing in life, usurping God's place. As stated above, "You cannot serve both God and money." Jesus goes on to conclude, "What is highly valued among men is detestable in God's sight." (Luke 16:13, 15) Proverbs 30:7-9 sums it up well:

> "Two things I ask of you, O Lord; do not refuse me before I die: Keep falsehood and lies far from me; give me neither poverty nor riches, but give me only my daily bread. Otherwise, I may have too much and disown you and say, 'Who is the Lord?' Or I may become poor and steal, and so dishonor the name of my God."

Questions for Personal Reflection or Group Discussion

1. How important to you are the things that you own? Being honest, how would it affect you if you were to lose it all tomorrow?

2. On a scale of one to ten (ten being the most), how content are you with your present standard of living? If you would like to have more wealth, what drives you?

3. Do you ever feel like your wealth and possessions own you, rather than you owning them? If you were to downsize tomorrow, where would you begin?

Handling Our Wealth

After encouraging Timothy to "fight the good fight of faith," (v.12) Paul returns to deal with the issue of wealth again in 1 Timothy 6:17-19.

Here he addresses believers who are already wealthy and writes about how they should deal with it.

> "Command those who are rich in this present world not to be arrogant nor to put their hope in wealth, which is so uncertain, but to put their hope in God, who richly provides us with everything for our enjoyment. Command them to do good, to be rich in good deeds, and to be generous and willing to share. In this way they will lay up treasure for themselves as a firm foundation for the coming age, so that they may take hold of the life that is truly life."

He begins by helping them (and us) get a proper perspective on wealth. He points out that there are two things to avoid in viewing the money we have: arrogance and misplaced hope. Arrogance is a temptation to which the rich person can easily fall victim. Other people treat you differently when you are wealthy, and this special treatment can make you think that you are, in fact, special. We've all met people who were full of themselves because they had money, expecting to be catered to, and looking down their noses in distain at us common folks. Paul reminds the wealthy that it is God "who richly provides us with everything for our enjoyment." (v. 17b) Everything we have is ultimately a gift from him, so there is no room for pride on our part, only humble gratitude for his generosity.

For those who might reply "Yes, but I've worked hard for the financial success I enjoy," it's good to consider God's words through Moses to the people of Israel: "You may say to yourself, 'My power and the strength of my hands have produced this wealth for me.' But remember the Lord your God, for it is he who gives you the ability to produce wealth." (Deut. 8:17-18) Every talent and opportunity we have in life, including life itself, come from the hand of God, and it's good to keep that humbling thought in the forefront of our minds.

Money should also not be our source of security, says Paul, because it "is so uncertain." (v.17) How very true. Is there any such thing as a truly "safe investment"? Story after story could be told of people who invested in "a sure thing" and lost their shirts in the process. Instead of putting our hope in wealth, we are told to put it in God. Not only is he the one who provides us with everything we have, but he also is in total control of this world and its resources. He is more than able to take care of his own. In the Sermon on the Mount, Jesus reminds us that we don't have to worry about how we're going to obtain the basics in life. Our heavenly Father, who feeds the birds and clothes the flowers, "knows that we need them." (Matt. 6:25-34)

It's interesting to me that all American currency has the words "In God we trust" on every bill and coin. This started in 1861, when Secretary of the Treasury Salmon P. Chase, at the urging of a minister in Pennsylvania, made the following recommendation: "No nation can be strong except in the strength of God, or safe except in His defense. The trust of our people in God should be declared on our national coins." Congress passed it into law that same year. It's ironic that, in today's society, our trust seems to be more in the almighty dollar than in almighty God, whose name is inscribed on it. Jesus said (while holding a coin with a Roman inscription on it), "Give to Caesar what is Caesar's, and to God what is God's." (Matt. 22:21) If Jesus held an American coin today, would he also ask us, "Whose inscription is this?" and would he tell us to give God what is his, namely, all of it? Wouldn't he remind us that, in the end, we are only stewards of God's temporary gifts to us?

Having dealt with the issues of pride and security, Paul now instructs Timothy regarding how those who are blessed with wealth should handle that blessing. He writes, "Command them to do good, to be rich in good deeds, and to be generous and willing to share." (v. 18)

Someone has said that money is a terrible master but a good servant. So much potential good can be done with funds put in the right hands and the right places. There are many worthy enterprises (especially Christian ones) that could do so much more to help people, if they had adequate financial resources.

Several years ago, an article in Christianity Today discussed this very issue. The author pointed out that, if you took the number of professing Christians in this country and multiplied it by the average American's salary, and then figured a 10 percent tithe on that total, the amount available for God's work would be astounding. I don't recall the actual amount (which was in the billions), but it would be enough to fund churches, Christian schools, missions, and other Christian ministries many times over!

Obviously, many Christians have never experienced the joy of tithing. They feel they can't afford to give even 10 percent, forgetting where it *all* comes from in the first place. Giving to God is humbly acknowledging what he has given to us; and expressing gratitude, while supporting his kingdom work here on earth. It's recognizing that the wealth we have, like everything else, belongs to him, and it's simply on loan to us to be used for good. This is Stewardship 101.

On the other hand, many Christians feel that, as long as they are giving a tithe (10 percent) of their income to God's work, they are free to spend the rest as they please. But the question is, are we "rich in good deeds"? Are we "generous and willing to share"? (v.18) Being generous requires *more* from those of us who have been on the receiving end of God's generosity. In fact, there are some whom God blesses with wealth because they have the gift of generosity. I recently ran into a former seminary student of mine who ended up in business after several years of full-time ministry. God blessed his business to the point where he and his wife were able to double, then triple, and quadruple their tithe, while supporting a variety of ministries. He told me, "God has given us the gift of giving, so he keeps providing us with the resources to do it." And, I might add, he's having the time of his life in the process.

Not only is giving the appropriate thing to do, but Paul tells us it's wise investing on our part: "In this way, they will lay up treasure for themselves as a firm foundation for the coming age, so that they may take hold of the life that is truly life." (v. 19) Think about it. The way we use our financial resources on earth has an impact on eternity. Paul calls it "the life that is truly life." Another translation for "truly" is "really." When we look at people who have all the "trappings" (interesting word in light of v. 9) of wealth, we sometimes say, "Man, that's really living." But Paul is reminding us that *real living* is found in the life to come, *if* we have laid "a firm foundation" by the good and generous things we have done with what God has "richly provided" for us here.

Questions for Personal Reflection or Group Discussion

1. Which presents the greatest temptation for you, having pride about your financial status or depending on money for security?

2. How generous are you with your income? Do you give 10 percent or more to your church or other ministries?

3. How much have you used it to "do good deeds" and been "willing to share"?

4. Has it ever occurred to you that your use of money in this life is making an investment in the next? How would consciously keeping that thought in mind affect the way you use money?

Ambition

Ambition is another reason people work and is also highly valued in our American culture: doing great things and gaining recognition.

Most of the great accomplishments in the world are the result of ambitious people. Who wouldn't want employees who are highly motivated? And don't we all want our sons and daughters to have enough drive to accomplish something significant in the world? And yet, ambition is a double-edged sword. It can be good or bad, depending on a number of things: What are we ambitious for? What motivates our driving desire? What are we willing to do to achieve our goals, and what is the cost of pursuing them? As Christians, our single overriding goal should be the same as that of the apostle Paul:

> "So we make it our goal to *please him* [the Lord], whether we are at home in the body or away from it. For we must all appear before the judgment seat of Christ, that each one may receive what is due him for things done while in the body, whether good or bad." (2 Cor. 5:9-10)

For Paul, who had a highly successful career in his religious profession, living for this present life was impossible. Having met the risen Christ, he was now driven by a new purpose, and new goals to pursue. None of us have been called to be apostles, but being called to follow Jesus should involve the same mindset that Paul had. While we all have different gifts and callings, our underlying ambition ought to be the same: to please God.

Is it possible to be successful in a so-called secular environment, while at the same time pleasing the Lord in all we do? I believe it can be done, as long as worldly success is not our primary goal, *and* if it fits the plans that God has for our lives. When we, as Christians, declare that "Jesus is Lord" (Rom. 10:9), it means that he has the final say over whatever we do with our lives, including our careers.

Ambition involves having goals and a deep desire to reach those goals. So it all boils down to motive: Why do we want to have that new home, or build a bigger business, church, or professional practice? Why do we strive to attain a higher position in the corporate, educational, or ecclesiastical world? Is it to satisfy our own ego needs, or to build the kingdom of God? The highway of life is littered with the shattered careers of people who were ambitious for the wrong reasons, or who tried to attain their goals the wrong way. As Christians, we know that "the heart is deceitful." (Jer. 17:9) There's no end to our ability to rationalize our actions.

If our goal is simply to achieve vocational success and all the benefits that come with it, we will be tempted to compromise our morals and values in the process. Instead, as is clear from Scripture, our ambition should be to do the best job we can, i.e., to strive for excellence. Paul writes to workers in Colossians 3:23-24:

> "Whatever you do, work at it with all your heart, as working for the Lord, not for men, since you know that you will receive an inheritance from the Lord as a reward. It is the Lord Christ you are serving."

I recently heard a great example of this attitude. A man was on an airline flight where one of the passengers was drunk and unruly. The cabin attendant was able to handle the situation with such patience and grace that this man was greatly impressed. On his way off the plane, he stopped and asked the young woman for her name, explaining that he wanted to send the airline a letter of commendation on her behalf. To which she replied, "Oh, I don't work for the airline; I work for Jesus Christ." She had it right.

Someone has observed that success is mostly a byproduct. If our goal is simply to be successful, we probably won't hit it. But if, on the other hand, our goal is to do our best to accomplish something worthwhile with our God-given abilities, we probably *will be* successful in the process. That was the apostle Paul. His ambition was "to preach the gospel where Christ was not known," (Rom. 15:20) and in the process, he planted churches all over the Mediterranean world, and jump-started the universal spread of Christianity. That's ambition at its best. But then there's the other kind . . .

Selfish Ambition

In the New Testament, the word for selfish ambition is used almost twice as much as the one for legitimate ambition. Selfish ambition is self-explanatory. It's striving for goals that are all about *us—our* desires, *our* dreams, *our* reputation, *our* position, etc.—without regard for others. Paul lists selfish ambition among the "acts of the sinful nature" in Galatians 5:20, along with things like sexual immorality, idolatry, hatred, and drunkenness. Obviously, this is a serious sin to avoid.

James insightfully puts selfish ambition together with bitter envy in his letter, (3:14, 16) for envy often drives ambitions that are self-centered. In fact, Solomon, who achieved more in his lifetime than most men ever will, observed that "all labor and all achievement spring from man's envy of his neighbor." (Eccles. 4:4) We may feel that he overstated his case a bit, but wanting what someone else has (or more) *is* a key component in self-centered ambition. It's Paul again, who gives us the best perspective on this problem in his letter to the Philippians:

> "Do nothing out of selfish ambition or vain conceit, but in humility consider others better than yourselves. Each of you should look not only to your own interests, but also to the interests of others." (2:3-4)

Notice how Paul puts selfish ambition and vain conceit together. Both of those qualities are self-seeking and self-promoting. Those who are full of themselves (conceited) often have a sense of entitlement, justifying the ambitions they pursue at other people's expense. Paul then gives us the antidote: to humbly consider others better than ourselves—the direct opposite of selfish behavior.

Paul is not saying that others *are* better than us, or that we should go about feeling inferior to everyone with whom we deal. To *consider* means to regard something as true; it's a perspective, an attitude. He goes on to spell out what that means: looking out for other people's interests as well as our own. (v. 4) In other words, it's okay to have ambition and goals for ourselves, as long as we're not stepping on other people in the process. Instead, we need to consider their interests, desires, and goals, too. For Christians, it's not just about us. It's also about others.

In verse 6 of the same chapter, Paul goes on to write about following Jesus' attitude: our Lord did not "*consider* (same Greek word) equality with God something to be grasped, but made himself nothing," taking on human nature and living an obedient life that led to the cross. Clearly, Christ was not thinking selfishly. He had *our* interests in mind when he died for *our* sins. James throws further light on this word when he opens his letter by saying, "*Consider* it pure joy, my brothers, when you face trials of many kinds" Why? "Because you know that the testing of your faith develops perseverance." (Jas. 1:2-3) Once again, to "consider" is a matter of perspective, enabling us joyfully look beyond our present difficulty to the end result.

Should we be ambitious? Yes, but also humble and considerate of others in the process. In my own experience, some of the most successful people I have met, in a variety of fields, have also been humble, because they were godly. Even in the business world, there are enduring organizations that people love to work for, built by leaders who avoided the spotlight and quietly strove for excellence. Jim Collins wrote about them in his best-selling book, *Good to Great*.

The Cost of Ambition

Even if our ambitions are for the right things, motivated by the right attitude, and pursued in the right way, there is still one other issue to consider: what price are we willing to pay? Jesus asked, "What does it profit a man if he gains the whole world and loses his own soul?" (Mark 8:36) This is a good question for us to ponder. Too many men have sacrificed marriages, families, friends, and health while pursuing ambitious career goals.

The rationalizations are numerous. Most commonly heard are, "I'm doing this for my family" (who would rather have them home more), or "I'm working hard now so I can retire early or more comfortably" (a retirement they may never live to see if they keep pushing themselves). One that is sometimes used by Christian men is, "I want to have a more prominent position so that I can have more influence for Christ" (in reality, climbing the corporate ladder leaves little time for developing relationships of real influence).

Let's be brutally honest. Our ambitions are really not as selfless as we would like to believe (again, "the heart *is* deceitful"). While we might take care not to step on anyone's toes while pursuing our goals, we may well be neglecting other things in the process. This is where the challenge of balancing priorities comes into play. For example, many men find it hard to turn down a promotion. The extra income or opportunity for advancement (or both) is just too enticing. But if time for our wives and children, church and community, and even personal care of our physical, emotional, and spiritual needs gets short-changed, is it really worth it? Most positions with a larger paycheck also mean greater responsibility. This typically means longer hours, additional stress, and perhaps more travel. Is this a price you are willing to pay?

Every once in a while, I meet a man who turns down a job advancement because it would either require more hours than he wanted to spend, or a move to another state. He didn't want to short-change his family, or pull up his wife and children's roots, or leave their extended family. In some cases, it was the fellowship of believers in his church or a ministry he was involved in that he didn't want to sacrifice. I've always admired the commitment that enables a man to make that kind of choice. I'm sure it isn't an easy one, with friends, coworkers, or even his boss telling him he's crazy to turn down such an opportunity. But his priorities were straight, and there were no regrets. I've yet to meet a man who, in the twilight of his life, wished he'd spent more time at the office and less at home or church. It's always the other way around.

As I write this, I am thinking about my friend, Bob, a former NHL hockey player and coach. While working with the youth in his church, the leaders asked if he would consider a position as the youth pastor. After praying about it with his wife, he decided to accept the challenge. When he went to resign his coaching job, he was asked, "How much are they paying you? We'll pay you more." He wanted to laugh out loud. If they only knew he was taking a huge pay *cut* to take on this new position, they would think he was out of his mind! Today, Bob is the senior pastor of that church and having an effective ministry, both as a pastor and Christian counselor. And no regrets!

Questions for Personal Reflection or Group Discussion

Being brutally honest, consider the following questions:

1. How ambitious are you when it comes to your work, athletic competition, or other ventures?

2. Do you ever find yourself running over others to accomplish your goals?

3. Think about (discuss) the value of also considering others' wants and needs.

4. What benefits have you gained, and what price have you paid for your ambitions?

Competition

We can't think about ambition without also considering the idea of competition. We live in a highly competitive society. In fact, it has been estimated that the United States is probably the most competitive country in the world. Many assume that this is a natural part of the human psyche, but that just isn't true. Being competitive is something we *learn* from the time we are very young. Fathers especially push their children to be more aggressive (starting in pee wee sports) for fear that their young ones won't excel in athletics, or life.

And it isn't just in sports that kids have to compete. There are spelling bees and art contests and striving for the best grades. Later there is competition to belong to the "in group," or gain the affections of a certain attractive girl or boy. We compete to make the school team, land the lead role in the school play, or be accepted into the National Honor Society, and get into the best colleges. We teach our children how to compete because "it's a dog-eat-dog world" out there, and we don't want them left behind.

Our society itself is competition-obsessed. There's little doubt that sport is the *real* religion of America. More people attend sporting events than attend church. And sports are all about competing, whether it's baseball, football, golf, or NASCAR races. But it's not enough to simply cheer for our favorite team or player; we need fantasy leagues where we can compete against each other, feeding off of their performances. Even recreational activities like skate-boarding, mountain biking, or fly fishing have become contests to see who's the best. TV programing is filled with reality shows where people contend with one another to see who can sing the best, survive harsh elements, win the bachelorette, or even lose the most weight. And kids' games, video or otherwise, are always designed to have a winner and a loser.

Of course, the world of work is also a highly competitive one. Employees compete for positions or promotions, businesses try to outdo one another for contracts and customers, and even the helping professions are not exempt. Ever notice the number of advertisements for doctors and hospitals competing for patients, lawyers vying for clients, or schools trying to attract students to their campus? This was unheard of a few years ago. Unfortunately, even churches often fall into the mindset of competing for members. And sadly, judging from what they advertise, it appears they are appealing primarily to a shrinking Christian population, even though there are still plenty of unconverted sinners to go around!

Interestingly, our society rarely questions the value of competition. We assume that it's a good thing. Three things in particular are heard in its defense. **First**, it is said that competing is the best way to have a good time. While it's true that competition can enhance an experience by getting the adrenalin flowing, in the end, the only people having a real good time are the winners, not the losers. In any competition there are only two options: win or lose. And there are usually more losers than winners.

Of course, those who don't come out on top learn to be good sports about losing. This is part of sports etiquette. One doesn't want to make the winner feel bad about winning. But the losers *do* feel bad, especially if they *really* wanted to win, or were *expected* to win.

Just witness the tears of the losing team at the end of a tournament. Talented young athletes, who won far more games than they lost, and who may have played the final game very well, end up feeling bad about themselves because they didn't win it all.

Second, we are told that competition builds character, that a person develops discipline, perseverance, and courage in the crucible of competitive endeavors. Again, much of that is true. But the other reality is that losing can tear down one's self-esteem, making us feel like lesser persons. Only one person or team gets to win the championship, or have the lead role in the play, or give the valedictory speech at commencement. Everyone else loses.

Alfie Kohn, who has written a classic (and very helpful) book entitled *No Contest*, observes, "We compete to overcome doubts about our capabilities, to compensate for low self-esteem." This is particularly damaging for children, who see losing as failure. I've seen my grandchildren beating themselves up after losing a game, even if they personally performed very well. Their contribution just wasn't good enough for their team to win. And, make no mistake, competition is all about winning. In the business world, as well as sports, to be successful, one has to win the sale, have the best bid, get the big contract.

The sad part is that this need to win more often brings out the worst, rather than the best, of a person's character. When it's all about performance, and winning is the name of the game, some people will stoop pretty low in order to come out on top. In sports, consider the use of performance-enhancing drugs that has become such a problem and has tainted our record books, or the wholesale cheating that takes place in our classrooms so that students can get a better grade and outdo the competition to get into the better colleges or to land a better job. Or consider our political system, where the best candidate for the job doesn't necessarily win. Instead, it's the one most able to charm the public, or who has enough financial backing to destroy the other candidate with last-minute lies.

In the world of commerce, where most of you make your livelihood, how many scandals have we witnessed in recent years? Aside from the major ones that hit the news, there are those that go on every day. People lie on their resumes in order to gain an edge for a position. Others lowball a contract bid in order to beat out their competition. Then they cut corners on the actual job, or add expenses to the agreed-upon price in the name of unexpected overrides, or they deliver an inferior product that looks the same on the surface but doesn't perform as well. Of course, there is also the use of bribes, a tactic as old as history, (Isa. 5:23, Ezek. 22:12, Mic. 7:3) not to mention the neglect of safety standards that would add to the cost of doing business, or the common ploy of paying workers under the table in order to avoid taxes.

Consider also the large retail chain that opens a store in direct competition with an established local merchant. The large retailer then lowers his prices to a point where the little guy can't compete and is forced to go out of business, leaving the market to the large chain, which can then raise its prices because there's no competition. "That's just business," you might say. But is it ethical? Is it fair? And aren't we as Christians called to a higher standard than what is commonly practiced in the world? The list goes on and on, all in the name of winning, beating out the competition. Competition and character don't necessarily go together.

A **third** argument in favor of competition is that it improves performance. To a large extent, that is true, but to some degree, it's not. Since competition is about beating the other person, if that can be done with little effort, little effort will be expended. It is also about *not losing*. When we are trying not to lose, there is a certain amount of anxiety involved. And while a little anxiety is helpful, a lot of it works against a person performing well. How often have you seen a sports team or individual athlete leading in a game, only to tighten up and blow it at the end because they were anxiously trying *not* to lose! As Kohn points out, "Trying to avoid failure is not the same as succeeding."

In the business world, trying to keep up with or beat the competition results in things like DC10 airplanes shoddily assembled, pharmaceuticals rushed to market without adequate testing, the environment polluted rather than taking measures to prevent it, stories released by the press without checking the facts, or contracts automatically going to the lowest bidder, who (as mentioned) too often cuts corners on the products made or the buildings constructed.

Competition versus Cooperation

From a Christian perspective, the biggest problem with competition is that it creates an adversarial relationship with the person or persons we are trying to defeat. I was watching an ESPN special the other day about the rivalry between basketball players Magic Johnson and Larry Bird, one that began when their teams met in the NCAA title game. It carried over into their pro careers to the point where they actually *hated* each other. When their teams met, it became a bitter personal battle between these two Hall of Fame players. That's the dark side of competition.

Whether playing on a church league team, or watching Christian schools in athletic competition, I have observed how easy it is for Christians to be reduced to less-than-Christian behavior in the heat of competition. Church softball leagues are formed in the name of Christian fellowship, but in reality, little fellowship with the other team actually takes place. We want to beat them! If we're seeking real fellowship, why not get together with another church and divide the players up so that each team is a mixture of the two churches, and then play a friendly game? To make it more interesting, have both teams go out for pizza together after the game.

This idea hit me after my own personal experience. Our church was in a softball league scheduled to play another team that came up a player short. So, as pastor, I volunteered to play on the other side. It was fun. I got to meet and talk with the guys from the other church, and there was a lot of good-natured trash talk aimed at me from my own parishioners. I never enjoyed a game more. In a world of endless competition, there ought to be places where we can set competing aside, especially in the context of Christian fellowship.

Biblically, competition is something that is rarely mentioned and not encouraged. In the New Testament, only Paul uses the term, and then, only twice. In 1 Cor. 9:25, he uses an example of the training required for an athlete to compete and how he trains himself spiritually to attain "a crown that will last forever." And in 2 Timothy 2:5, he discusses the need for Timothy to endure hardship like a soldier in combat, an athlete in competition for a crown, or a hardworking farmer. Notice the emphasis is not on competing *against* someone, but competing *with* other Christians *for* something available to everyone.

The New Testament is filled with athletic metaphors like run, (Heb. 12:1) race, (Gal. 5:7) fight, (1 Tim. 6:12) strive, (1 Tim. 4:10) struggle, (Eph. 6:12) and wrestle. (Col. 4:12) But in each of these instances, it has to do with the spiritual battle we are all engaged in against the enemy of our souls, and against our own sinful nature, *not* against other people.

In contrast, the emphasis of Scripture is on *cooperation*, not competition. Not only does cooperation create and build relationships, but it improves performance. Kohn points to numerous studies showing that students learn more in an atmosphere of mutual cooperation than one where they are competing with each other. Work settings are also enhanced where teamwork and cooperation are encouraged, versus pitting employees or departments against one another. Employee or salesperson of the year awards may light a competitive fire under a few people, but it only discourages most because they know they can't compete. Plus, the lack of recognition for the good job *they* did (under perhaps more difficult conditions) makes them want to exert less effort next time.

In the broader business sector, some of the best work has been done by companies working together on a project, rather than competing with each other for the whole piece (think of the space program). This also includes working with other businesses for the good of the community. For example, Beckett Industries in Ohio wanted to address the problem of people who are chronically hard to employ (from generations of living on welfare, and lacking even a basic understanding of how to hold a job). Together with other companies in their area, they formed Advent Industries, which not only trained potential employees in particular job requirements, but also taught them basic life skills, and lifted their standard of living. That's cooperation.

Also problematic, a competitive atmosphere sets up situations for pride on the part of winners and envy on the part of losers. Both attitudes are condemned in Scripture. I often tell the men I work with, "Don't bother praying for your favorite sports team to win. Winning makes you proud, and losing makes you humble. You *know* which side of the equation God is on." (James 4:6 and 1 Peter 5:5)

When it comes to our work (as mentioned earlier), the emphasis of Scripture is on *excellence*: doing the best you can with the abilities you have been given. Can any of us expect more than that from our children, our employees, or ourselves? Proverbs 14:23 says, "All hard work brings a profit," and Ecclesiastes 4:9 cites the advantage of cooperative ventures in declaring, "Two are better than one, because they have a good return for their work." In Ephesians 6:7, Paul urges slaves (the primary labor force in the Roman empire) to "serve whole-heartedly, as if you were serving the Lord, not men." Even in the discussion of spiritual gifts, the emphasis is upon giving one's best effort (Rom. 12:8, 1 Pet. 4:10-11); and time and time again, the hard work of Christians is commended. (Rom. 16:12, 2 Cor. 6:5, 1 Thess. 5:12, Rev. 2:2)

The reality is that if we strive for excellence—focused on our own performance rather than on beating someone else—we will probably do quite well in whatever venture we find ourselves (also mentioned earlier). Competition is about comparisons. The winners compare themselves with the losers and feel superior; the losers make the same comparison and feel inferior. Scripture discourages us from making comparisons. Galatians 6:4 says, "Each one should test his own actions. Then he can take pride in himself, without comparing him to somebody else." Paul reminds us in 1 Corinthians 12 that we shouldn't compare our giftedness with someone else's. God has given each of us the abilities He wants us to have, and each plays an important part in the body of Christ.

Questions for Personal Reflection or Group Discussion

1. Have you ever seriously considered the down side of competition as outlined above? As you look back on your life, what has it felt like personally to be on the winning side and the losing side of competition?

2. From a spiritual perspective, think about (or discuss) the potential dangers of competition and the advantages of cooperation.

3. Can you visualize areas where a cooperative structure might be beneficial?

Overcoming Our Successes

In our competitive, win-at-any-cost Western culture, success is the name of the game. This is a major motivator for men, because we all want to be successful, and desire that for our children as well. But what do we really mean by success? And specifically, what does it look like for you personally?

I think there are *three levels* to success. First, there is the basic level of simply reaching a goal, achieving what you set out to do. It can be anything from repairing a lawn mower, to breaking 80 in your golf game, to winning that contract you have been working on for weeks. These are the small successes that bring a certain amount of satisfaction to everyday life. They're a good thing.

Secondly, there is the cultural perception of success that applies to our jobs and how well we perform them. Thus, if you climb high on the corporate ladder, build a very profitable business or professional practice, write a best-selling book, pastor a large church, or are elected to a significant political position, you are considered successful by society. This kind of success is usually rewarded with wealth, recognition, power, or any combination of the three.

For a Christian, this kind of success comes with potential pitfalls and dangers. The first one is pride. The Bible says, "Woe to you when all men speak well of you." (Luke 6:26) When the accolades come, along with the special treatment accorded to the successful, it takes a very well-grounded person to resist getting a swollen ego.

Then there are higher expectations on the part of others. For example, if you have been successful in not only meeting but exceeding your sales quota, you are briefly applauded, and then the bar is raised higher for next year. Or if your performance has earned you a promotion and raise, you will be expected to work even harder and longer in your new position. At times those expectations are self-inflicted, with our own internal pressures pushing us to live up to our new status or position, or what *we* think others are expecting of us.

Another problem with success is complacency, the tendency to rest on our laurels; or worse, to think that the only one way to accomplish something is the way we've done it in the past. There are countless stories of people and businesses that refused to adjust to new circumstances because the old way had been so successful for them. And in today's rapidly changing world, they are soon operating behind the curve instead of ahead of it.

In addition, there's the reality that success is temporary at best. Every athlete knows they are only as good as their next home run or touchdown pass. And every big business deal needs to be followed by new ones. As former Miami Dolphins coach Don Shula once said, "Success [is] not forever and failure is not fatal." Thus, there is that ongoing pressure to keep performing.

Many men who have been successful in their careers have paid a heavy price for it by neglecting other areas of their life. The business landscape is littered with dysfunctional families, broken marriages, ill health, addictive behaviors, shortened lifespans, and spiritual neglect or ruin. A number of years ago, I was talking to an acquaintance who ran an organization that supplied counselors for corporate employee assistance programs. As a psychologist and CEO, he made himself *personally* available to work with corporate executives and their families, who wouldn't feel comfortable using one of his employees. He shared with me that the typical corporate head worked about eighty hours a week. I asked him, "Where do they find time for their families?" He replied, "They don't. That's the problem." As an example of how bad it could be, he me told of a CEO who instructed his secretary to call his daughter and wish her happy birthday on his behalf. Wow! An extreme example, to be sure, but it shows how far the hunger for success can push a person.

There is a third kind of success that goes beyond one's occupation and whatever level we might attain there. This one should be of primary interest to every Christian man: being successful *as a person*, while living a life that makes a real difference in your circle of influence. You can call this legacy or by some other name, but the question is: at the end of your life, what do you want to be remembered for? Do you want to be one of those men whose adult children often tell me in counseling sessions, "I never really knew my dad; he was always working"?

I have often thought that when I come to the end of my life, it really won't matter how many degrees I earned, or what positions I held, or what honors may have been bestowed upon me. All of that, while impressive in an obituary, won't compare to what my family and friends have to say about me. But even that pales in importance to the only commendation that will echo through eternity: God's words, "Well done, good and faithful servant."

Real success then, from a Christian perspective, is living a life that brings glory to God. It means a lifetime of service to our Lord and to others in his name. In the workplace, it means helping others to be successful. At home, it requires loving our wives as Christ loved the church, and nurturing our children in the ways of the Lord while modeling for them what Christian manhood looks like. At church, it's using the gifts and resources God has given us to serve others and advance his kingdom. And in the community, it involves finding ways to love our neighbors, share our faith, and strive to leave this world a better place.

Benefitting from Our Failures

If success, as defined by our culture, is fraught with potential land-mines, failure has some surprising benefits. Failure is really the other side of success. I once asked a group of businessmen (most of them entrepreneurs) what motivated them in their work: the desire for success, or the fear of failure? To a man, they said, it was the fear of failure. While we certainly try to avoid failing at our endeavors, when it happens (and we all do fail at times), it is not the end of the world. In fact, some of the most successful men in history saw more failures in their lives than successes. People like Winston Churchill or Abraham Lincoln, who experienced many political losses in the course of their careers before rising to the top and leading their nations during critical periods of history. Or consider Thomas Edison, who failed hundreds of times to invent an electric light bulb before he finally succeeded, changing the modern world forever.

In reality, where success can lead to negative spiritual traits such as pride, envy, and complacency, failure has the potential of developing genuine character. To begin with, it humbles us. We realize that we are not as good or talented or competent as we thought we were. From a spiritual standpoint, we could not be in better company. Think of the outstanding leaders in the Bible who had to be humbled before they could be used by God: Joseph, Moses, David, and Peter, to name a few. At the top of the list would be our Lord himself, who didn't need to *be* humbled, but who "humbled *himself* and became obedient to death, even death on a cross." (Phil. 2:8) Humility is a quality highly valued by God. (Mic. 6:8, Matt. 23:12, 1 Pet. 5:5-6)

Failure, whether on the job, in our families, or in our personal lives, also drives us to be dependent on God for his strength and guidance; exactly the place God wants us to be. The experience of most Christians I know, myself included, is that we really don't come to a point of surrendering to God and his will until we have tried to do it our way and failed, perhaps over and over again. The apostle Peter was pretty brash and full of self-confidence, until he failed miserably. Then, after Jesus picked him up and dusted him off, Peter waited for divine power, and became the dynamic leader of the early church we see in the book of Acts. (John 21:15-19, Acts 2:1-4, 14-41)

In addition, failure provides a great learning experience, if we use it to that end. There are people who never seem to learn from their mistakes, but the wise man stops and reflects on what happened, so he doesn't repeat the same error again. This is true not only with mistakes we may make in planning and execution on the job, but also, more importantly, in making judgment calls concerning the *people* with whom we work and live. Especially crucial are mistakes in moral judgment, where a failure to understand a situation, learn from it, and correct it can be disastrous.

Failure, like any other kind of trial, also has the potential for spiritual growth and maturity. It would be nice if we could become more Christ-like without going through the "school of hard knocks," but it doesn't seem to work that way. For example, James 1:2-4 tells us that trials should be faced positively because they test our faith and produce perseverance and maturity. Paul says essentially the same thing in Romans 5:3-4, where he declares that suffering produces perseverance and perseverance produces character. Peter adds that the grief we suffer in trials is used by God to test the genuineness of our faith, like gold refined by fire. (1 Peter 1:6-7) It's safe to say that the difficulties we face in life are God's way of bringing out the best in us. Think of your own spiritual journey. Isn't it true that you grew a lot more during times when your back was against the wall, and you were forced to depend on God and his resources? Failure can be spiritually beneficial (see Chapter Eleven on Integrity Under Fire).

As Christians, we *are* going to have times when we fail, just like everyone else; especially when we are taking risks (often necessary in business and in life). The important thing is that we handle our failure with grace. This involves, for one thing, owning up to it, not making excuses, or trying to fix the blame on someone or something else. It also involves not taking ourselves too seriously, which means, whether we succeed or fail, we don't blow it out of proportion. As John Maxwell says, "Failure isn't fatal, and success doesn't completely define you." It also means that we don't allow failure to defeat us. In the words of Ben Stein, "The human spirit is never finished when it is defeated. It is finished when it surrenders." Failure should drive us to learn from our mistakes and figure out why it happened.

In the area of relational or moral failure, we need to remember that God is a God of grace, and he is not at all surprised when we blow it. He anticipates that, as fallen human beings, we are going to mess up royally at times. In fact, the word for sin in the Bible (*hamartano* in Greek) means "to miss the mark" or "fall short of a goal." In other words, it is spiritual failure. But the good news (gospel) is that there is pardon or forgiveness for our sins. God doesn't want us to wallow in guilt. That's Satan's ploy. Rather, God convicts us of sin (points it out by his spirit) so that we can deal with it and get on with our lives, learning and growing in the process. We can fail at some task, or even experience failure in our business careers, but the one area in which we cannot afford failure is to fail at life.

Questions for Personal Reflection or Group Discussion

1. What do you think about the potential problems with success? Have you encountered any of them, and how did you handle it?

2. Consider the idea of succeeding as a person. What does that look like for you?

3. How have you handled failure in the past? Can you see the potential benefits of *not* landing on your feet?

Going Further: Read Philippians 2:2-8 and 1 Timothy 6:6-10, 17-19. What principles can you pull out of those passages that would help you in your approach to business and wealth? Think or talk about their practical application.

Bottom Line (What is Your Primary Motive?)

When it comes to your work, then, it's good to ask yourself, "What is my primary motive?" Is it to make money, even *a lot* of money? Is it to make a name for yourself with your friends or business associates? Is it to feed your ego-driven ambitions to be "successful" in the world's eyes? Or is it simply to find satisfaction in using your gifts and abilities? Ultimately, as stated above, a Christian's motive has to be to bring glory to God, in our work as well as in every other area of life. When this is what drives us, we won't have to worry about the rest. God will make sure that our basic material needs are met, that we find satisfaction in our work, and that we make a difference in the lives of others in ways that really matter.

Additional Resources

Joshua Becker, *The More of Less: Finding the Life You Want Under Everything You Own*. WaterBrook Press, 2016.

Alfie Kohn, *No Contest: The Case Against Competition*. Houghton Mifflin, 1986.

John C. Maxwell, S R. Graves & T. G. Addington, *Life@Work: Marketplace Success for People of Faith*. Thomas Nelson, 2005.

John C. Maxwell, *Failing Forward: Turning Mistakes into Stepping Stones for Success.* Thomas Nelson, 2000.

Greg McKeown, *Essentialism: The Disciplined Pursuit of Less.* Currency, 2014.

Paul David Tripp, *Sex & Money: Pleasures That Leave You Empty and Grace That Satisfies.* Crossway, 2013.

"People need to be valued. They need love, dignity, and respect shown to them. Because these needs are basic to everyone, actions aimed at meeting these needs are always right."

- Wayne T. Anderson

Chapter Eight: Integrity at Work - People

Work always involves people. They may be partners, supervisors, employees, vendors, or customer/clients, but (unless you are a veterinarian) they are all people; people with various personalities, ambitions, expectations, and problems. And while, as a business or professional man, you may also have to deal with buildings and equipment, for the most part, the biggest challenges you will face each day will involve people. That's what this chapter is about.

Power and Position

Power is not a word we often use when talking about relationships, but in reality, power is involved in *every* relationship. One definition of power is "the ability to influence other people." And, certainly, each of us influences, and is influenced by, others every day. As a family counselor, I frequently observe the power dynamics in families. And I have come to understand that the healthiest marriages are those in which each partner feels that the relationship has a *balance* of power. When one is overpowered by the other, it creates either a power struggle or an unhappy subservience. Neither is good. And then there are those dysfunctional families where the parents have abdicated power, and the children seem to be in control—a real disaster!

In the workplace, it's clear that bosses typically have more power than those who work under them, but employees also influence supervisors, who depend on them for their production. And customers and stockholders hold power over businesses, including the executive management.

Power, like many things in life, has the potential for either good or bad. Leaders who use their influence to bring about positive results for those under them, as well as for society as a whole, are to be commended. But the adage of Lord Acton, "Power corrupts, and absolute power corrupts absolutely," is too often true. Examples of political leaders, business owners, athletic coaches, teachers, and even clergymen who have abused their power are too numerous to need mentioning. The focus in this chapter is on the influence you have over those who work for you, and how to use that power positively and effectively as a follower of Christ.

Leadership and Power

Those who study how organizations work often discuss the differences between *positional* and *personal* power. If you hold a particular title, office, or position within a company or group, this gives you power over the people under you, but that doesn't make you a leader. As someone has wisely observed, you're not a leader unless someone is following you. Those in positions of authority may be able to force compliance to a certain degree, but their *real influence* will be minimal. And employees have ways of undercutting supervisors they don't like or respect.

Truly influential leaders are those who have personal power. Sometimes, it is someone with no *official* position of authority. Take, for example, the impact that a factory worker may have on his fellow employees. Because of the respect he has earned from his peers, he could have more *real* influence than the foreman, who has positional power, but may lack that respect. And if there's a union involved, that worker will probably be elected as their representative.

Personal power is attained partly by having the skills and competence to handle a position. But, mostly, it is gained by how you treat other people, especially those you are trying to lead. For Christians in leadership, this is good news, for the Bible is largely a book that teaches us about relationships—first with God, and then with other people—both those we like, and those who don't like us. And the Scriptures give us two primary models for leadership that we neglect to our own peril: shepherd leadership and servant leadership.

Questions for Personal Reflection or Group Discussion

1. Do those in leadership positions in your workplace (including you) lead mostly with positional or personal power?

2. If it's positional, how does that seem to be working?

3. If it's personal, what did they (or you) do to gain that respect?

Shepherd Leadership

Because Israel was largely an agricultural society during Biblical times, and sheep herding was one of its primary industries, the responsibilities of a shepherd were well known. Interestingly, the Bible portrays God as the shepherd of his people, not only in Psalm 23 where David begins with "The Lord is my shepherd . . ." but in other places as well. Jacob, at the end of his life, while blessing his son, Joseph, refers to

"God, who has been my shepherd all my life." (Gen. 48:15) And God is referred to, and refers to himself, as Israel's shepherd in Psalm 28:9, Isaiah 40:11, Jeremiah 31:10, as well as Ezekiel 34:12-16. He also refers to the leaders of Israel as shepherds, especially David, (2 Samuel 5:2, Psalm 78:71) and was angry at those who failed to shepherd rightly. (Ezekiel 34:2-10) On the same theme, God spoke of a promised future shepherd for his people, (Ezekiel 34:23, Micah 5:4, Matthew 2:6) clearly a reference to Jesus Christ.

In the New Testament, Jesus had compassion on the crowds of people who came to listen to his teaching "because they were like sheep without a shepherd." (Mark 6:34) In John 10, he refers to himself as the good shepherd who knows and is known by his sheep. He knows their names, and they know his voice. As the good shepherd, he also lays down his life for the sheep, because he cares for them. (John 10:1-1-15) Hebrews 13:20 also refers to Jesus as "that great Shepherd of the sheep," and Peter calls him "the Shepherd and Overseer of your souls" and "the Chief Shepherd." (1 Peter 2:25, 5:4) This is the same Peter who Jesus commanded three times to take care of his sheep as proof of his love. (John 21:15-17) This shepherd model is then passed on to other leaders in the church by Peter, (1 Peter 5:1-3) and also by Paul. (Acts 20:28-29)

So, what does **shepherd leadership** look like? And how does that apply to us who work in a highly technological society, far removed from Biblical times and sheep herding? **First** of all, as Jesus taught, a shepherd leader *takes responsibility* and *really cares* for those who are under his supervision. This is largely a matter of attitude. Jesus contrasts this role with the hired hand who cares nothing for the sheep and runs away at the first sign of danger. (John 10:12-13) The shepherd leader is committed to those under him and to their well-being. Among other things, this would include providing favorable working conditions, fair wages, and caring concern when they are hurting. I was teaching at a seminary when my first wife was dying of cancer. I'll never forget the kindness shown to me by both the dean and president of the school, who told me, "You do what you need to do for your wife; we'll cover your classes for you." That kind of caring increased both my respect for, and loyalty to them.

Second, the shepherd leader *knows his sheep by name*. (John 10:3-4) People appreciate it when others know their name, especially people over them in authority. I have a friend who I lunch with regularly. Jim always makes a point of learning the name of the people waiting on us (if they fail to tell us upfront). Then he uses their name whenever he needs to speak to them. It is evident that they respond differently when they are treated like real persons, rather than simply food dispensers.

Third, the shepherd leader is *willing to sacrifice* for his followers. It's doubtful that any of us will be called upon to lay down our lives, like Jesus did, but the attitude of putting others' needs ahead of our own is a shepherding one, especially when protecting the flock from threats. (John 10:11-13, Acts 20:28-31) What that threat might look like in the context of the workplace will depend on your situation. You might have to put in extra time to help an employee finish a project on time, or go to bat for your people with those above you for better wages or working conditions. Or a more extreme example was one I read about several years ago, where the owner of a manufacturing plant kept his people on the payroll through a serious recession, paying them out of his own personal savings, when there was no work for them to do.

Fourth, Jesus speaks of his flock following him because they know his voice and will not follow the voice of a stranger. (John 10:4-5) Shepherd leaders *talk to their people*. They communicate what they're thinking, rather than having their employees try to guess what they want, or what their values or goals are. People follow a leader because they have come to trust his leadership. This is the difference between a shepherd and a cattle herder. Sheep followed the Biblical shepherd because they felt safe. Cattle are driven from behind, and are intimidated. People would rather work for a shepherd than a trail boss. And unfortunately, the trail boss mentality is still alive and well in too many companies today.

Fifth, shepherd leaders are *not greedy*. Peter says that shepherd leadership in the church excludes greediness. (1 Peter 5:2) This also applies in the workplace. While higher wages are not the primary thing that keeps employees happy, they do resent it when the business owner or supervisor is living "high on the hog" while those who do most of the actual work are not sharing in the company's success. This is also true when it comes to getting recognition for their work. If the boss is taking all the credit for what is essentially a team effort, those under him will feel unappreciated—and rightly so.

Finally, shepherd leaders *lead by example*. (1 Peter 5:2-3) They set the work atmosphere and moral tone for everyone else. Your value system, your ethics, and your treatment of others will trickle on down to those under your supervision. What is significant in the context of Peter's admonition here is that he contrasts leading by example with "not lording it over others," which in turn follows his command to be "eager to serve." This leads very naturally into our second Biblical model, which is **servant leadership**, one that Peter and the other disciples had to learn the hard way.

Questions for Personal Reflection or Group Discussion

1. Had you ever considered the shepherd leadership model as something you could use in the workplace? What are your impressions?

2. Of the six traits listed, which ones do you feel are most important, and why?

3. What difference would they make if exercised in your organization?

Servant Leadership

A lot has been written about servant leadership as a model for business in recent years. Robert Greenleaf, in his book *Servant Leader*, seems to get the credit for coming up with this concept. But as Christians know, it really originated with Jesus. Mark 10:35-45 records an incident involving Jesus' hand-picked disciples. Brothers James and John approached him with the request to have positions of authority in Jesus' kingdom when he comes into power. The other ten disciples are understandably indignant with the brothers over this, so Jesus gets them together and teaches them a very important kingdom truth:

> "You know that those who are regarded as rulers of the Gentiles lord it over them, and their high officials exercise authority over them. *Not so with you.* Instead, whoever wants to become great among you must be your *servant*, and whoever wants to be first must be slave of all. For even the Son of Man did not come to be served, but to serve, and to give his life as a ransom for many." *vs. 42–45* (italics mine)

It's from this passage that we derive the **first** principle of servant leadership: *the way up is down.* We gain both stature and real personal power when we learn how to serve, rather than being served, or "lording it over" others (Jesus' words). It would be great if Jesus' disciples got this lesson the first time, but, like us, they were slow learners. Thus, when they gathered in the upper room for the last supper, they all sat around with dirty feet waiting for the customary foot-washing. There were no servants present, and none of them were willing to lower themselves to do that menial and unpleasant task. So, Jesus did it. John records the scene in his gospel:

> "Jesus knew that the Father had put all things under his power, and that he had come from God and was returning to God; so he got up from the meal, took off his outer clothing, and wrapped a towel around his waist. After that he poured water into a basin and begin to wash his disciples' feet, drying them with the towel that was wrapped around him." (John 13:3-5)

Notice that doing this house-slave duty was triggered by *strength*, not weakness, on Jesus' part. He knew who he was, where he came from, and where he was going. He was conscious of the authority that was his—more authority than any of us will ever wield. And it was from that position of strength that he served - much to the embarrassment of his disciples. From his example, we learn our **second** principle of servant leadership: *it takes real strength to be a servant leader.* If you are worried about hurting your reputation, you'll never pull it off. If you are so insecure that you need to maintain the appearance of being in charge, it just won't work for you.

When Jesus finished his foot-washing object lesson, he applied what they just experienced to their own lives and attitudes:

> "Do you understand what I have done for you? You call me 'Teacher' and 'Lord,' and rightly so, for that is what I am. Now that I, your Lord and Teacher, have washed your feet, you also should wash one another's feet. I have set you an example that you should do as I have done for you ... Now

that you know these things, you will be blessed if you do them." (John 13:12-15, 17)

That last verse contains the **third** principle of servant leadership: *serving others brings a personal blessing.* Even secular researchers have come to the conclusion that the happiest, most fulfilled people in the world are those who serve others. In contrast, think of the people you know who live with a sense of entitlement, expecting others to serve them, and how miserable most of them are.

Above and beyond the foot-washing incident, an even greater example was provided by Jesus the very next day, when he rendered the lowliest, yet greatest service of all, by dying in our place. (Mark 10:45 above) Paul paints the full picture for us beautifully in Philippians 2:5-8, where he describes the extent of Christ's self-sacrifice:

> "Your attitude should be the same as that of Christ Jesus: Who being in very nature God, did not consider equality with God something to be grasped, but made himself nothing, taking the very nature of a *servant*, being made in human likeness. And being found in appearance as a man, he humbled himself and became obedient unto death[—] even death on a cross!"

It's difficult for us, as human beings, to grasp the breathtaking humility that Jesus exhibited in doing what he did. The Lord of creation (Col. 1:16-17) becomes a mere creature. The Author of life (John 1:4) submits to death. The blameless Son of God (Heb. 4:15) endures one of the most painful and humiliating means of execution ever created by the darkened heart of humanity. Accompanied by mocking and jeering, crucifixion was designed to make a brutal, public example of its victims. Jesus willingly submitted himself to that abuse for us.

This, then, is the **fourth** principle of servant leadership: *being a servant leader requires humility.* If you are full of selfish ambition and conceit, (Phil. 2:3) fearful of having your pride dented, you'll never be a servant leader. Only by humbling yourself *at* the cross of the one who humbled himself *on* the cross will you gain the necessary attitude to truly serve. Not without reason, Jesus calls us, as his followers, to a life of self-denial by telling us to "take up (our) cross daily." (Luke 9:23) And Paul reminds us in several places that we no longer live for ourselves. We live for Christ, (2 Cor. 5:15) and in order to serve others. (Gal. 5:13) That leaves our egos out of the equation.

Is humility an effective trait in the workplace? According to Jim Collins, author of *Good to Great,* it is. Collins and his research team examined thousands of companies to discover why some were more successful than others. They found a small handful of organizations that had gone beyond good to attain true greatness. The key to their success was a leader who exhibited two important traits: *humility* and intensity. As intense persons, they were determined to do whatever it took to succeed. But as humble persons, they avoided the spotlight, preferring to work quietly behind the scenes. One mark of this humility is what Collins refers to as the window and the mirror. When things were going well in their companies, they looked out the window to find and recognize the people who were most responsible for that success. But if things were going badly, instead of looking for someone to blame, they looked in the mirror. Their example and accomplishments speak for themselves.

People-Focused Leadership

Clearly, both Biblical models of leadership focus *not* on the leader but on those he leads. Finding out what your people need to be fulfilled and effective in their work will help them grow as persons and your organization to be productive. This involves creating, first of all, a *physically* healthy work environment, where their safety and well-being are primary concerns. It also requires establishing an *emotionally* healthy environment, where people are treated with respect and importance. When there's a job to get done, it's too easy to zero in on the task at hand and neglect the people who are performing that task. In reality, who your people *are* is more important in the long run than what they *do*.

Most organizational models are shaped like a pyramid, with the larger number of workers at the bottom answering to and trying to please their immediate supervisors, who answer to middle managers, and they in turn to upper management, etc. The owner or CEO sits at the top of the heap with everyone trying to keep him happy. If you've read anything on servant leadership, you understand that it turns the pyramid upside down. The one at the top sees himself as servant to those under him, doing whatever he can to help them become the best they can be and do the best work they can do.

Following his example, those in lower management have the same objective: to help those they oversee to be productive, not by demanding, but by assisting through training, encouragement, and (if necessary) working alongside of them, to get the job done. This then flows out into the marketplace, as street-level employees, picking up this servant attitude, do what they can to serve customers and vendors, which ultimately can only help the organization as a whole.

Part of the servant leader model involves a shift in the power structure. Rather than those at the top trying to hold on to their power and maintain control, they share the power with the rest of the team. In fact, they see their task (to use a current buzzword) as "empowering" others in their work. Among other things, this means pushing the decision-making process as far down the line as possible. The reasoning is that those doing a particular job are in a better position to decide how the job can best be done, than those who are above them. This, then, encourages workers to be creative, and to look for ways to improve production and the work environment.

Of course, it requires leaders to *know* the people they are trying to serve. To truly empower people, one has to know their strengths and abilities, as well as their personalities. One employee may be anxious to do a good job, but needs to acquire more skills to pull it off. Another may have the skills, but lack the confidence, and would be helped by getting encouragement from you as their supervisor, along with the freedom to fail until they get it right. Still another may be very competent and highly motivated, so the best thing you could do is leave them alone to do their job (people hate to be micromanaged) and simply acknowledge their performance from time to time.

It also means knowing enough about a worker's interests and family life that you can ask how their daughter in college is doing, or how the weekend fishing trip went. That kind of personal interest shows you care about them as real people, not just as cogs in the corporate machinery. Knowing your people also enables you to pick up on any changes in mood or personality that are out of character for that individual. This can be important if such changes indicate they are having problems with their work or worried about a situation at home. We all tend to live mostly on the level of our emotions, and those feelings can impact both our job performance and relations with coworkers.

Questions for Personal Reflection or Group Discussion

1. Are you familiar with the servant leadership model? Have you seen it practiced in your own workplace or others with which you are acquainted?

2. Could you see it working in your organization? What would have to change?

3. What do you think would be the most difficult challenge in implementing it?

People-Smart Leadership

If relationships are the most important element of our Christian experience, as well as the key component in the workplace, then we really need to know as much about human behavior as possible. This has been called *social intelligence*. In recent years, researchers have come to realize that not all intelligence can be measured by IQ tests. Some people score very high on those tests because they have the ability to master abstract ideas. But others are intelligent in different ways. I know people who are very bright, but it shows up by being highly skilled with their hands, or by making music or creating art, or in many other ways. One way that has been identified and studied is a person's ability to interact well with others, i.e., social intelligence.

One of the best books I have found on this subject is Karl Albrecht's book entitled, *Social Intelligence: The New Science of Success*. He defines social intelligence as "the ability to get along well with others, and to get them to cooperate with you." He cites four essential qualities: (1) knowing yourself, (2) being sensitive to others, (3) connecting with others, and (4) caring about others. A quick glance at these traits and it's clear that the last three—sensitivity, connecting, and caring—are clearly in line with the teaching of Scripture. And knowing yourself is important, because if you are not aware of your own behavior, you will not understand others' actions or how yours may be impacting them. Notice the focus is on other people, fleshing out the concepts of leadership discussed above. In his book, Albrecht discusses five necessary skills of social intelligence in the form of an acrostic, the first letter of each spelling out "S-P-A-C-E."

1. Situational awareness: The ability to read social situations and interpret people's behavior in those settings, picking up on feelings and intentions, appreciating their points of view, and seeing how they react to stress, conflict, or uncertainty. It involves being aware of where we are, who we are with, and how we ought to behave in that context. For example, how we behave on the basketball court or when attending a ball game is different than how we act at church or at a classical concert. And honestly, how we act when we're with guys is different than when our wives are present. Not necessarily bad, just different.

Awareness of those around us also means noticing how others deal with physical space. We all have different comfort levels when it comes to personal space, and we make others *un*comfortable if we invade theirs. Also involved is seeing how others act in social situations. Are they outgoing and talkative, or more reserved and quiet? My wife is fine when talking with a person one-on-one, especially someone she knows. But if you put her in a group of people she's just met, she will tend to be very quiet and just listen while others talk. Noticing how other people speak is part of being aware of our surroundings as well. Do they tend to process and reply quickly, or are they more likely to ponder what's being said and then respond? Do they express themselves clearly, or is their speech pattern somewhat vague, needing you to ask questions for understanding?

All of this, of course, requires listening and observing, which takes time and attention. In the busyness of our workday, we may feel like we have better things to do, but over the long haul, we really don't. A great example of awareness is recorded in John 4:1-30, where Jesus encounters a Samaritan woman getting water at her local well. Noticing that she was unaccompanied and coming at an unusual time, he senses that she is a social outcast and broaches a conversation by asking her for a drink (something a Jew would never ask a Samaritan). He knows his request will invoke a questioning response in her, which then opens up a discussion that leads to her conversion, and that of many other people in her town. As leaders, we need to pay attention to our people, so we can pick up on those things requiring our attention.

2. Presence: This is how you affect people or groups by your physical appearance, your mood, demeanor, body language, and the way you occupy a room. Some people impact a room by their size or charisma just by showing up. Most of us don't have that quality. But it is important that we, as leaders, first of all *just be there*. Our people need to know that we are available and approachable; not just physically, but emotionally also. Ever talked to someone who you sensed wasn't really listening or didn't really care? Not a pleasant experience, is it?

More than just being there, we need to be there with a purpose. It may be simply to observe, or to get to know our workers and allow them to ask questions, or perhaps to figure out how to improve their work situation. People need direction, and when we as leaders show up, it should be with a sense of direction for the organization, as well as for those who make the organization work.

Respect is also a part of presence—not demanding respect from others, but showing *them* respect. This involves valuing their skills, recognizing their contribution to the company, and being sensitive to their time (in some places, when the boss shows up, everything comes to a screeching halt). But most of all, it involves respecting them as persons: their ideas, opinions, and especially their feelings.

3. Authenticity: This is how honest and sincere you are with yourself and others in any given situation. It's living your values and beliefs. It's dealing with people straight, being real, connecting with others. It means not having hidden agendas, but focusing on other people and their situations, rather than your own. To quote Paul, "Each of you should not look only to your own interests, but also to the interests of others." (Phi. 2:4)

Being authentic involves showing genuine interest in others, especially those you work with and who work for you. It's easy to be interested in our families and friends, more difficult under the pressures of our jobs to do the same for the people at work. It involves tuning into their needs, discovering what they want, and talking about what really matters to them. For a real education in what *not* to do, watch reruns of the TV sitcom *The Office*, where the manager is so clueless about people he does absolutely everything wrong - because it's all about him! When you are authentic, you build trust, which is the basis for every relationship (more about trust in the next chapter).

Look at how Paul describes his work among the people in Thessalonica: "The appeal we make does not spring from error or impure motives, nor are we trying to trick you . . . You know we never used flattery, nor did we put on a mask to cover up greed—God is our witness." (1 Thess. 2:3&5) That's authenticity.

4. Clarity: Your ability to express thoughts, opinions, ideas, and intentions clearly, saying what you mean, and meaning what you say. Your rate of speech, tone, volume, and inflection go a long way toward inspiring confidence and respect. Even more essential is your ability to *listen* effectively.

It's important to be aware of how you use language. Some people are very negative in their use of words. Criticism and sarcasm leap quickly to their tongues. Their opinions and viewpoints are aggressive and dogmatic. They act like there's only one way to look at things— *their* way. They make overly generalized statements, which means they are only partially true. And they give advice that is not asked for, *nor* particularly wanted. These people are easily tuned out by those forced to listen to them. Paul writes, "Do not let any unwholesome talk come out of your mouths, but only what is *helpful for building others up* according to their needs, that it *may benefit* those who listen." (Eph. 4:29, italics mine)

On the positive side, if you give opinions or viewpoints in an undogmatic, gentle, this-is-simply-what-I-think way, you invite others to share *their* perspective, and they are much more likely to hear you. Qualifying what you have to say and offering other possibilities to your own ideas also tends to evoke positive responses from others. A good rule to follow is, saying less is best, and (at times) saying nothing is better. And it is absolutely necessary to think before we speak. In the words of James, 'Let everyone be quick to listen, slow to speak, slow to become angry." (James 1:19) How many times have you wished you hadn't said what you said, or had said it differently? Being a verbal person myself, some of my most embarrassing moments have been because I said something before I really thought about how it might come across to others.

But the real the key to clarity in self-expression is *listening.* One of the biggest problems I observe between the married couples I counsel is the inability to really listen to each other. Failure to listen leads to misunderstanding, especially if one doesn't pick up on the emotions and motives behind the words. It's always healthy to ask questions to make sure you fully grasp what's being said to you, and then to listen closely to the answers. Listening is hard work. We tend to zone out if the other person talks too long; or their words get interrupted in our minds by what we think or want to say next. In the process, we may miss something really important.

Finally, it is always appropriate to speak with an attitude of humility. Before I taught my first graduate course, I asked a seasoned professor for advice. The one piece of advice he gave me was, "Don't be afraid to say you don't know." That's also good advice for managers, ministers, counselors, and other professions. You won't lose the respect of those you're working with by admitting ignorance, but you certainly will if you fake it and they find out. Along with "I don't know," you can add "I was wrong" (even harder to say), and "I changed my mind" (be sure to give the reasons why).

5. Empathy: Being aware and considerate of other's feelings. It means accepting them as they are and for who they are. Identifying and sharing their feelings is part of it, but so also is feeling connected with the other person, having an ability to understand their thoughts and desires. To really do this, you need to be aware of your own feelings. If you don't know how *you* feel in a given situation, there's no way you can understand what someone else might be feeling.

Early in my counseling career, I was working with a young mother whose husband was having an affair. Assuming she was angry (as I would be), I was trying—quite unsuccessfully—to help her get in touch with those feelings. I eventually tried putting myself in her place, and then it hit me. It wasn't mostly anger she was dealing with; her marriage was hanging by a thread, and she was scared! Once I tuned into her fear, she was able to open up emotionally, because she felt that I finally understood.

Part of empathy is being attentive to other people's feelings. As a rule, men are not as good at this as women are, probably because we were taught to *hide* our feelings in order to survive on the playground. And so, we need to learn to be attentive to our own feelings. Then we can more easily pick up on what others are experiencing. But much of this involves not being so single-mindedly focused (another male trait) on the business at hand that we miss the emotional component.

Another aspect of empathy is affirmation. To recognize a person's feelings is one thing, to acknowledge and affirm them is better. A good practice would be to walk around and greet your people at the beginning of each day, with a focus on sensing where they're at emotionally. Simple phrases like, "You look a little tired this morning," or "You seem a little down today," or "You haven't been your usual self the last couple of days; is everything all right?" communicate that you care. It can also help them open up about what may be on their mind. This takes time, and while you may not be a counselor, a little attention to the emotional needs of the people you work with can do wonders for the atmosphere in the office.

Counselors teach their clients the "First Four Minutes Rule" in regard to their marriages (discussed in chapter four). I think this rule can be effective at work as well. If you walk in with a positive, uplifting, and caring attitude, it helps get the day off on the right foot, versus barking orders and jumping immediately into the task at hand.

Questions for Personal Reflection or Group Discussion

1. On a scale of 1 to 100, what grade would you give yourself in social intelligence? How would you score yourself on the individual "SPACE" skills discussed earlier?

2.. On which skill would you score yourself highest, and lowest?

3. Reflect on (or discuss) ways that you could improve your lowest score, and come up with a plan of action. Find someone to hold you accountable (not your wife).

Appreciation

There's another component to empathy that is really important on the job (as well as in other places), and that is appreciation. People need to feel appreciated. And this is especially true in the workplace where they are putting out an effort that they hope will be noticed. Steven Covey has said, "Next to physical survival, the greatest need of a human being is psychological survival—to be understood, to be affirmed, to be validated, to be appreciated."

One of the best sources to read in connection with showing appreciation is a book by Gary Chapman and Paul White entitled *The Five Languages of Appreciation in the Workplace*. Chapman is best known for his popular book, *The Five Love Languages*, and in this book on appreciation, he and White apply the same concepts to manager–employee relations, working off the principle, "Each of us wants to know that what we do matters."

They begin by discussing why employees leave their companies. Research has shown that while 89 percent of managers believe their employees leave for more money, only 12 percent of them actually do. Instead, 70 percent of US workers say they receive no praise or recognition. They are more likely to burn out and leave when not feeling appreciated or supported by their supervisors. My son-in-law recently left his company for that reason.

A Deseret News Service article reporting research on millennials (roughly twenty-two- to thirty-five-year-olds) in the workplace reinforces this thinking. Researchers found that 72 percent of current millennial students desired a job that allowed them to serve a greater purpose, and 71 percent even want their coworkers to be their second family. They want their job to be more than just a source of income. One discovery on this subject by the Pew Research Center was that a high-paying job was the *least* important characteristic desired for their work life, with only 19 percent of millennials valuing it. They "want jobs they enjoy, that offer security, and give them time off for childcare and family needs." Millennials make up 53 percent of the US labor force.

In their book, Chapman and White go on to spell out the five languages of appreciation:

1. Words of affirmation, which is praising people for their accomplishments and affirming their character, focusing on the most effective way to do this, depending on the individual's personality.

2. Quality time, which is simply giving an employee your undivided attention by means of shared experiences (like going to a ballgame together), a meaningful conversation, an open dialogue with a small group of workers, or working side by side on the same project.

3. Acts of service, which involve helping others with their work (fitting the servant leader model). It also means doing it well. If you jump in to help a worker who may be running behind, or is in over their head, they suggest four guidelines: Ask before you help (they may not want it). Do it cheerfully (no one wants reluctant help). Do it their way (don't take over). And complete what you start.

4. Tangible gifts, which are not raises or bonuses. A gift may not be a person's language of appreciation, so you want to give them primarily to those who *would* feel appreciated by the gesture. And make sure it is a gift the person values. Tickets to a ballgame might be appreciated by Joe, but not by Bill, who would rather have a gift certificate to a hunting and fishing store. Or it may not be a thing, but an *experience* (for example, dinner for two with their significant other). It might even be time off.

5. Physical touch, which has to be handled very carefully in today's society. An appropriate pat on the back, a brief handshake, a high-five, or a fist bump may be in order. An extended handshake with words of appreciation or a friendly hug in a time of crisis might be appropriate. It's best to observe the people you work for to see how they respond to touch. And, by all means, know the rules of sexual harassment (a lot of which is perception). The rule of thumb is, when in doubt, don't.

Chapman and White go on to say that "people need to feel appreciated in order to enjoy their job, do their best work, and continue working over the long haul." They stress the need to be observant of other's behavior, to notice what they ask others for, and to listen to their complaints (which reveal their emotional hurts). It's also good to be aware of your blind spot—your primary appreciation language may not be theirs. The authors also stress the difference between recognition, which focuses on performance, and appreciation, which focuses on the value of the person. For them, the key question is *not* whether you appreciate them, but do they *feel* appreciated? That's a question we can all ponder with regard to our wives, children, and friends as well.

Questions for Personal Reflection or Group Discussion

1. Think or talk about a time when you felt really appreciated on the job. How was it expressed, and what emotions did it invoke?

2. In which of the ways described above do you express appreciation to the people you work with?

3. In which areas could you use improvement?

Going Further: Read Ephesians 6:5-9 and Colossians 3:22-4:1. Keeping in mind that slaves were the primary workforce in New Testament times, what do these passages have to teach us about manager–employee relationships?

Bottom Line

When it comes to relationships on the job, the rule, which should be the controlling principle in all our relationships, is, "Love your neighbor as yourself." (Luke 10:27) Jesus said this was the second part of what he called the greatest commandment (the first part being to love God with all our heart, soul, strength, and mind). Ever stop to really consider what this familiar concept means? When we think of "neighbor," we tend to picture the guy who lives next door. But the word that Jesus used in the language of his day literally means "the one near to you."

Who is nearer to you for eight to ten hours, five days a week (or more) than the people with whom you work? So they become your neighbors and, therefore, should be the recipients of your love. Notice we are to love them "as ourselves." This means treating them like *we* would like to be treated, which reminds me of Paul's words to the slave owners in Colossae: "Masters, provide your slaves with what is right and fair, because you know that you also have a Master in heaven." (Col. 4:1) In other words, masters (bosses) were to treat their slaves (the working force of that day) the same way they would like God (the ultimate CEO) to treat them, dealing with them in a way that is right and fair.

And if you think about it, this also means that your wife and children, "the ones near to you" when you are home, are also neighbors to be loved as you love yourself, which is echoed by Paul as he tells husbands in Ephesians 5:33 that each "must love his wife as he loves himself." *All* relationships fall under the command and need for love. Living with integrity means loving people as Jesus loved and *still* loves them.

Additional Resources

Karl Albrecht, *Social Intelligence: The New Science of Success.* Jossey-Bass, 2006.

Henry & Richard Blackaby, *Spiritual Leadership: Moving People on to God's Agenda.* B&HPublishing, 2001.

Dale Carnegie & Assoc., *How to Win Friends and Influence People in the Digital Age.* Simon & Schuster, 2011.

Gary Chapman & Paul White, *The 5 Languages of Appreciation in the Workplace: Empowering Organizations by Encouraging People.* Northfield Publishing, 2011.

Kenneth R. Jennings & John Stahl-Wert, *The Serving Leader: Five Powerful Actions to Transform Your Team,* Business, and Community. Berrett-Koehler, 2016.

"Character is like a tree, and reputation is like a shadow. The shadow is what we think of it; the tree is the real thing."

—*Abraham Lincoln*

Chapter Nine: Integrity at Work - Character

Living with Christian integrity at work calls for Christ-like character. Who we *are* affects, and is more important than, the things we *do*. You can't fake character. Sooner or later, the *real you* will show itself, especially under pressure. People who met Jesus were attracted to his teaching and miracles, but what he taught and did was the overflow of *who* he was. Jesus taught truth because he was *a man of truth*, living in a world of deception (like ours). He healed, fed, and delivered people from demonic oppression because he was *a man full of compassion* for the broken world around him (like ours). His character was exemplary, and showed itself particularly in situations where most men would fold - like being worked over by Satan himself for forty days in the wilderness, or experiencing the terrible humiliation, anguish, and pain of a Roman crucifixion, while also carrying the burden of all our sins.

While none of us will experience what Jesus endured, *our* challenge is to bring Christ-like character to every situation in which we find ourselves. This includes the place we spend the lion's share of our time: at work. Sadly, Christians do not have the best reputation in our society, and one area it has been damaged is in the workplace. I have personally observed too many Christian men in business and the professions whose actions fail to reflect their faith. On Sunday they're praising the Lord at church, but come Monday morning, and it's business as usual, seemingly unaffected by what they claim to believe. This needs to change, if we are going to be true followers of Jesus. And it's not enough simply to use business as a platform for witness by having Christian literature in the waiting room, spiritual posters on the wall, or tracts stuffed in invoices sent to customers. Christian witness requires *real substance.*

My own experience doing business with other Christians has been a mixed bag. Many have provided services with high value and integrity. Others, unfortunately, have produced less-than-good quality in their work, along with an attitude that seems to imply that (since I am a fellow believer) I should tolerate or forgive their slipshod performance. Others I've spoken to have, unfortunately, had similar experiences.

The premise of this chapter (and indeed the whole book) is that our *actions* are every bit as important as our *words* when it comes to our Christian witness at work, in our families, or wherever we may find ourselves. This is the emphasis of Scripture. For example, Jesus said, "Let your light shine before men, that they may *see your good deeds* and praise your Father in heaven." (Matt. 5:16) And Paul says, "Make it your ambition to lead a quiet life, to mind your own business and to work with your hands ... so that *your daily life may win the respect* of outsiders." (1 Thess. 4:11-12) Peter adds, "Live such good lives among the pagans that, though they accuse you of doing wrong, *they may see your good deeds* and glorify God on the day he visits us." (1 Pet. 2:12)

As a leader, you are being watched. It's good to always keep this in mind. Studying the boss is a normal pastime for working people. They want to know what you expect of them, what pleases you, and what you won't tolerate. They do this primarily by noting your behavior and how you react in different situations. And if you are a Christian, you are being scrutinized even more closely, not only by your subordinates, but by everyone else who works with you. Just like with your children at home, a major part of leadership is setting a good example.

Operating Values and Principles

When it comes to functioning as Christians in our vocational world, we have to begin with our values: what's most important to us, and how is that reflected in our dealings with others? As followers of Jesus, our first priority is pleasing him in everything we do. This means *people take priority over profits*. Love is Christ's primary commandment and a responsibility for us all. If you are a business owner, this should be reflected in your company's *stated values*. A few examples might be helpful:

R. W. Beckett Corporation, one of the largest manufacturers of domestic and commercial heating systems in the world, has as its core values *integrity, excellence, and respect for the individual*.

ServiceMaster, one of the world's leading service companies, operates on the following set of what it considers "immutables":

1. Truth cannot be compromised.

2. Everyone has a job to do, and no one should benefit at the expense of another.

3. We should treat everyone with dignity and worth.

4. Our combined efforts are for the benefit of our owners, members, and customers, and not for some select group.

5. We must always be willing to serve.

Fast food restaurant chain, Chick-fil-A, has as its corporate purpose, "To glorify God by being a faithful steward of all that is entrusted to us, and to have a positive influence on all who come into contact with Chick-fil-A." They "firmly believe in treating every person who comes through" their "doors with honor, dignity and respect."

And finally, Interstate Batteries System of America has as their stated business philosophy, "To treat others as we want to be treated, to treat all our business associates with respect, with fairness, with integrity, caring and listening to them, professionally serving them, always being a model of working hard and striving toward excellence."

All of these companies were founded by Christians seeking to operate according to Biblical principles, as reflected in their statements. The challenge for them, and for all of us, is *living up to* their stated convictions. I've had personal contact with three of these companies, and have been impressed by what I have experienced and observed. The questions, then, we all need to ask are: What are *our* personal values when it comes to business? Do they line up with the organization of which we are a part? If we own our business or practice, are these values clearly stated and understood by our employees and those we serve? And more importantly, are they *adhered to*, or are they just nice platitudes on our organization's website? One definition of integrity is having *actions that are consistent with our words.*

Questions for Personal Reflection or Group Discussion

1. What kind of example do you think you present at work? Are there areas in which you would like to improve?

2. What are your personal values when it comes to your business or profession? Are they reflected in the stated values of your business or professional practice?

3. Do you and others consistently live up to those values?

Integrity in Marketing

One area where integrity is important is how we present ourselves as individuals and organizations. This begins with one's resume or vitae during the application process. A common practice in our society today is for people to exaggerate, or downright lie, about their education, experience, and skills when applying for a position. This seems to follow the equally common practice of cheating for higher grades in college. Of course, we all put our best foot forward when trying to sell ourselves, but is what we're selling really the truth?

Most of you reading this book are probably beyond looking for a job, but the principle of honestly presenting ourselves applies in sales and marketing as well. Whether selling a product, a service, or a job proposal, is this done in a manner that is consistent with the truth, including how fast and at what cost you can deliver the goods? A few years ago, my wife and I needed some major work done in our basement. One of the contractors we interviewed for the job made an impressive presentation, complete with full color pictures of all that his company could do. When checking him out with the Better Business Bureau, however, his reputation was anything but good. Great sales pitch, but no substance.

Of course, this same principle carries over into whatever form of marketing your business may do. You want to attract customers by emphasizing your capabilities and strengths. But, again, are you presenting yourself accurately and honestly? Telling them whatever it takes to close the deal is not nearly good enough for a Christian businessperson or professional. If you advertise excellence, speed, friendly service, or whatever, you need to be able to back that up and not oversell yourself. A few years ago, there was a Christian counselor practicing in our area who identified himself in his brochures as Sam Jones, PhD (the name is fictitious). There was just one problem: his doctorate was real, but it was in English literature! A little misleading, to say the least.

Another area where we need to be careful is using our Christian faith to attract potential business. I sometimes hear radio ads or see trucks with the word "Christian" as part of their company name. This bothers me. Should we be employing the name of Christ for personal profit? Doesn't this fall under the commandment about misusing the Lord's name? (Ex. 20:7) If you are in a non-profit, Christian ministry, that's a different story; you want people to know where they can find Christian literature, or Christian counseling, etc. But Christian plumbing or electrical contracting? Really?

Besides the misuse of the Lord's name, there are two other reasons to not use our Christian faith to attract business. First, why would we as believers *want* to restrict our business to other Christians, who might be attracted by our name, but turn others away, who may have negative feelings about our faith? Wouldn't it be better to service non-believers, giving them the opportunity to deal with a Christian who is honest and anxious to provide excellent work performance? And, perhaps, in the process, change their perception of Christianity? We might even have an opportunity to talk about our faith. For example, I have a friend who is a house painter. Painters typically play their favorite music while they work, and he plays Christian music. His music, plus the quality of his work and the way he treats his customers, has opened up numerous occasions for him to share his faith and minister to them in various ways.

Another reason not to use faith words in our name or advertising is that our workmanship and treatment of customers and clients should speak for itself. As Paul writes in Colossians 3:23, "Whatever you do, work at it with all your heart, as working for the Lord, not for men." Treat people as Christ would, do your job with excellence, and you won't have to worry about getting your share of business. The best advertising is still word of mouth, and you will *still* get customers/clients from those who know you in the Christian community, for they will recommend you to one another. I have never advertised myself as a Christian counselor (or at all, for that matter). But I receive a lot of referrals from pastors, Christian friends, and former clients who know me. If asked whether I am a Christian counselor, I reply that I am a Christian who does counseling, and if they want further explanation about my approach, I am glad to share that. But by not advertising my faith, I also get the opportunity to counsel people who aren't Christians, to show them the love and compassion of Christ in the process, and, at times, to share my faith with them.

I once counseled a Christian woman with various struggles in her life, and eventually it came to light that there were marriage issues as well. She agreed to bring her husband, who was not a believer, to our next session. I always ended my meetings with her in prayer. However, I was hesitant to do so with him present, because I didn't want to scare him off before we were able to connect. But she said to me at the end of our joint session, "Aren't we going to pray?" I asked him if he was comfortable with that, and he said it was OK. So I prayed for them that day, and every session thereafter. Several months later, they came in for a meeting, and he told me he had received Christ in church the Sunday before and that my prayers for them had planted the seed that started him on his spiritual journey. It made my day. The point is, we just never know what opportunities God will give us, and how he may use us, just by being who we are as believers, simply doing our jobs.

Here's a humorous and misleading note about advertising our faith. A friend of mine is a building contractor who has a bumper sticker on the back of his truck, which is familiar to most Christians. It reads, "My boss is a Jewish carpenter." We get it. A lot of outsiders don't. One day he received a call from a Jewish woman who got the phone number off of his truck. She wanted to hire a carpenter who was Jewish, like her. Be careful what you advertise, even inadvertently.

Striving for Excellence

As quoted earlier, Jesus talks about others seeing our good works and praising our Father in heaven. (Matt. 5: 16) In the context of our daily business lives, "good works" should be interpreted as *good work*. I think, more than anything else, how we conduct ourselves in *every* situation is the *major part* of our witness to the world. For a Christian in business or one of the professions, this includes the quality of the work we do. Too many believers have ruined their testimony with outsiders, and hurt the reputation of Christians in general, by not only failing to live up to what they claim to believe, but also failing to live up to the work they promised. Our goal should be to strive for excellence in all we do.

Excellence does not mean perfection—that's God's territory. It does, however, mean giving our best effort and using our skills to the best of our ability. Slipshod work should be out of the question for a follower of Jesus. Remember, according to Colossians 3:23 (see above), we are doing it for him, not for ourselves, or even for our customer/ clients. In the long run, excellence also helps the bottom line, but that shouldn't be our primary motive.

As I write, my wife and I are having some remodeling done in our home. We know several contractors in our circle of friends who do this kind of work, but we sought bids from only two of them—both of whom had reputations for doing excellent work, even though they were probably the more expensive ones of the group. Thus far, we have not been disappointed with our choice. The work Tom's company does is excellent, and his workers and sub-contractors are pleasant to have around. While Tom is a Christian, most of his guys are not. But they are trustworthy to the point that we are comfortable leaving the house with them working in it, and their reputation for excellence is well deserved (a reflection of Tom's values).

Questions for Personal Reflection or Group Discussion

1. How do you market yourself and/or your business? Accurately and honestly?

2. If you had to depend on referrals alone, how do you think you would do?

3. On a scale of 1 to 10, how would you rate the quality of the work or service that you provide? What areas do you think could be improved?

Building Trust

Every relationship is built on trust. This includes, first of all, our relationship with the Lord. We usually use the words "faith" or "belief" when discussing spiritual things, but Biblical faith is a combination of *belief* (the intellectual side) plus *trust* (an act of the will), a whole-hearted commitment to what we believe. I often use parachutes as an example. Do I believe a person can strap on a parachute, jump out of a plane, and float safely to the ground? Absolutely! I have seen films and talked to people who have done it. Will I do it myself? No way! Why? Because I don't *trust* parachutes. Why would a person jump out of a perfectly good airplane and trust a silk sheet and some ropes to get them to the ground, unless the airplane wasn't going to make it? My belief in parachutes is only intellectual; it lacks confidence or trust. Our faith in God must include *both* in order to be the genuine article.

Our relationships with other people are also built on trust. You wouldn't have married your wife, nor would your marriage have lasted, if you didn't trust one another. As a counselor, I have found that, when infidelity has occurred in a marriage, the hardest hurdle for them to get over is rebuilding trust again. Trust is essential with your children as well. They need to know they can count on you being there for them, taking care of them, and protecting them. And you need to know that you can also trust them (especially in their teens) when you're not around to supervise. And the people you consider to be your friends are also people with whom you share a mutual bond of trust.

The same is true in the world of business and the professions. Businessmen are not likely to conduct their affairs with people they don't trust, unless their deals are backed up with very binding legal contracts. And the very existence of those contracts shows the basic lack of trust that exists in our business world today.

If you are in one of the professions, trust is even more crucial. Would anyone in their right mind use the services of a doctor, a lawyer, or a counselor that they didn't trust? Would they remain in a church if they didn't trust the pastor? Would they learn anything in a classroom where they had no faith in what they were being taught, or in the person teaching it? It all begins with trust, and there are numerous ways in which trust is built and maintained.

Consistency

To be trusted, one needs to be consistent. People need to know that the person they dealt with yesterday is the same person today. They need to have the confidence that you operate with the same set of values and ethics, the same attitudes and motives, and the same way of treating people every day. Whether you are selling a product or providing a service, those you work for (or with) need to be able to count on the same level of quality in every transaction.

Inconsistency puts people on edge, whether they are your customers or fellow workers, especially those employed by you. My wife once worked for a manager who had a drug problem as well as a dysfunctional home life. When the boss came in the door each day, my wife never knew if it was going to be Dr. Jekyll or Mrs. Hyde. The stress this created in the office was very difficult to handle. An extreme example to be sure, but the principle is still true: consistency in leaders develops trust and creates a more positive work atmosphere (assuming the boss's behavior isn't consistently bad).

Truth-Telling

Probably, more than anything else, trust is built on truth. People don't trust others who aren't truthful, and nothing undermines trust more quickly than deceit. The problem of trust destroyed through marital infidelity was mentioned earlier. One of the reasons it's so hard to rebuild trust in those situations is because of the deception and outright lying that normally accompanies extramarital affairs.

Aside from how it affects our business or personal relationships, deception is an affront to God. The Ninth Commandment is, "You shall not bear false witness against your neighbor." God hates deception because he is a God of truth, and deception is of the Devil. It is the language of hell. In John 8:44, Jesus says the following about Satan: "He was a [murderer] from the beginning, not holding to the truth, for there is no truth in him. When he lies, he speaks his native language, for he is a liar and the father of lies."

Think about that the next time you are tempted to bend the truth. You would be using the Devil's native tongue. Sobering thought, isn't it?

God does not lie. (Titus 1:2) Indeed, he *cannot* lie. (Heb. 6:18) It is contrary to his character. And he expects us, as his children, to be truthful as well. (Eph. 4:15, 22-25; Col. 3:9-10) Jesus, His Son, declared, "I *am* the truth." (John 14:6) More than simply understanding the truth, or teaching the truth, Jesus actually *embodied* the truth. He was the one completely authentic person who ever lived. There was nothing phony or deceptive about him. Unfortunately, *we can* be deceptive; it's part of our fallen nature. Jeremiah 17:9 says, "The heart is deceitful above all things and beyond cure." We can even deceive ourselves. (1 Cor. 3:18; Gal. 6:3; Jas. 1:22,26; 1 Jn. 1:8) Truthfulness does *not* come naturally to us. It has to be cultivated.

There are many kinds of deceptions. The most blatant is the outright lie. Hopefully, as Christians, we have grown beyond that, although, when under pressure, the temptation will always be there. One of the worse forms, not uncommon in business and politics, is slander, which is telling lies about another person. This, of course, is strongly condemned in Scripture, (Eph. 4:29-31, 2 Tim 3:1-5) because it can destroy that person's reputation.

But it's the subtle forms of deceit that we are more tempted to engage in, like misleading someone by telling only part of the truth—the part that puts us in a good light—or failing to correct misinformation when it works to our advantage. Thus, even silence can be a lie. In the early church, Ananias and Sapphira were deceptive by giving the impression they were donating *all* the money they received from the sale of a piece of property when they only gave a part. Peter tells them that, in so doing, they lied to the holy spirit. The penalty was that God struck them dead, an indication of how seriously he saw the destructive nature of deception in the infant days of the church.

Exaggeration or misrepresenting a product or service is yet another form of deception. And pretending to be someone or something we are not is also deceptive, because it is misleading. The Bible calls this "hypocrisy" and is clearly what Jesus reacted to most strongly, (Matt. 23:13-33) especially in the Pharisees.

Lewis Smedes, in his book *Mere Morality*, points out that the key to determining whether or not something is deceptive is a matter of *intention*. One can tell an untruth out of ignorance, believing it to be true. That's not a lie. But if the intention is to deceive or mislead the other person, then it is sin, even if factually true. And it also reveals who we really are: ultimately, it's a matter of the heart. (Matt. 15:18-19)

Promise-Keeping

Related to truth-telling is keeping our promises. The failure to live up to our word can be deceptive, if it is done deliberately. In other words, if we promise something that we know in advance we're not going to follow through on, that is an outright lie. But most of the time, when we give our word, we *intend* to do what we promised, but extenuating circumstances or time pressures may get in the way of our carrying it out. Yet, regardless of the reasons for breaking a promise, it still undercuts the ability of people to trust us, whether business colleagues, our wives, or our children. The bottom line is, if we promise to have a report ready, be at a meeting, deliver a product, or pay a bill by a certain time, we need to make sure it is done. Nothing short of an emergency should prevent it.

This means being careful about what we commit ourselves to. Overcommitment is a constant challenge for busy people. We either underestimate the time and energy required for a certain job, or we overestimate our ability to take on some projects. In business, it's hard to say "no" to a large order, a major buyer, or a potential customer. But we don't do them (or ourselves) any favors by not delivering what we promised, even if our intentions were good. This sort of temptation is particularly strong for those in sales. Salespeople want to close the deal because their livelihoods depend on it, but sometimes they make promises on which their company can't deliver, much to the frustration of those responsible for making good on those promises.

Once again, the Scriptures are clear on this subject. First, they show the propensity of sinful man to not keep promises. Numbers 23:19 contrasts God's actions with man's: "God is not a man, that he should lie, nor the son of man, that he should change his mind. Does he speak and then not act? Does he promise and not fulfill?" Unlike humans, God always keeps his promises. This was one of God's issues with Israel as reflected in Hosea 10:2f: "Their heart is deceitful, and now they must bear their guilt . . . They make many promises, take false oaths and make agreements; therefore, lawsuits spring up like poisonous weeds in a plowed field."

This sounds a lot like our culture today, doesn't it? Add to this Paul's remarks in 2 Corinthians 1:17 where he discusses his honest plans to visit their church, but needs to change those plans for their own good. He writes, "When I planned this, did I do it lightly? Or do I make my plans in *a worldly manner* so that in the same breath I say, 'Yes, yes' and 'No, no'?" (italics mine) Worldly people talk out of both sides of their mouths. As Christians, we shouldn't.

On the flip side, there is the positive instruction in Scripture concerning the need to keep our word. In Psalm 15, David asks the question, "Lord, who may dwell in your sanctuary?" and answers his question with, "He whose walk is blameless and who does what is righteous, who *speaks truth* from his heart . . . who keeps his oath even when it hurts." Sometimes it *is* painful to live up to our promises. We may miss opportunities that come up in the meantime. But in the long run, it's always better because it is the right thing to do. And we will have God's blessing.

Then, of course, there are the words of Jesus in his Sermon on the Mount: "You have heard that it was said to the people long ago, 'Do not break your oath, but keep the oaths you have made to the Lord.' But I tell you, 'Do not swear at all . . . Simply let your 'Yes' be 'Yes' and your 'No,' 'No'; anything beyond this comes from the evil one.'" (Matt. 5:33f) These words are echoed by James 5:12: "Above all, my brothers, do not swear[—]not by heaven or by earth or by anything else. Let your 'Yes' be yes, and your 'No' no, or you will be condemned." In other words, we should say what we mean, and mean what we say. God requires nothing less.

Questions for Personal Reflection or Group Discussion

1. Have you ever had someone violate your trust, in business or on a personal level? How did it feel, and how did it affect your relationship?

2. Think about or share (in a group) your experiences with people who are inconsistent in their behavior.

3. How have you reacted in situations when you have been lied to, or had promises broken? In what areas would you be tempted to compromise the truth, if you weren't a Christian?

Honesty

Another quality that builds trust is honesty. Honesty is a two-pronged virtue. It involves being honest in our handling of things, and honest in what we say. At heart, it means dealing with *reality* minus self-deception. For example, the Bible commands us not to steal. This command reflects the reality that things are the property of certain people. To take something belonging to someone else is to ignore that reality, as well as depriving the owner of what is rightfully his or hers.

Another example is cheating. If you cheat on your tax report, you are taking away the government's right to that income, and cheating on an exam gives you an *unreal* grade and an unfair advantage over students who answered questions honestly. When I was a kid, my parents drummed into us the necessity of being honest, even if a store clerk inadvertently gave us a few pennies extra in change. That early training, reinforced by my Christian faith, has made it easy for me to act accordingly in any situation. I am always intrigued by people's reactions when I correct a monetary mistake on their part. They often seem genuinely surprised by my honesty, which shows just how rare it is in our culture.

I recently had a business transaction that involved a $2000 mistake in our favor. When I called the person I was dealing with to point out the error, she was very grateful for my honesty. I realized that a mistake of that amount would have created a major problem for her with her manager. But it also occurred to me later that this was part of our witness as an organization, especially since we were dealing with this company for the very first time (since we call ourselves Integrity Ministries, we'd *better* show some integrity!). It wasn't just my reputation on the line, but also the reputation of our ministry, and more importantly, the reputation of the Lord we represent.

Handling money is another area of business where as believers we need to be meticulously accurate and aboveboard. Withholding money from those who have provided services for us should be out of the question, whether they be employees or vendors. This also includes taking company materials or equipment for private use. It is too easy to rationalize in this area. If you don't have receipts and need to estimate, it is best to remain on the safe side and put down figures in the organization's favor. Those are the kind of things "when no one is looking" that should set us apart as men with Christian integrity.

When it comes to our words, dishonesty is a close kin to deceit or lying. A prime example would be when something goes wrong that is our fault and we fail to take responsibility for it, "The check is in the mail," when we haven't been to the post office yet, or "You should get that shipment tomorrow," when there's no way that will happen, are subtle ways of covering our backsides. A more honest approach, of course, would be to simply apologize for the delay and give a realistic time for them to receive it.

Another example would be to accept credit for something good we didn't do. One thing that destroys morale in an organization is when supervisors benefit from the success of their departments or businesses, while their employees (who do the lion's share of the work) go unrecognized or unrewarded. The other side of this equation is when we, as leaders, allow blame to fall on someone else for our mistake. People in management positions can usually protect themselves by finding someone under them to be the fall guy. But that's just not honest.

As Christians, who come into a relationship with Christ acknowledging that we are sinners needing forgiveness, we ought to be the first to own up to times when we mess up in dealing with customers, vendors, or colleagues. Making excuses for our behavior isn't acceptable. Taking responsibility for our actions is the way of integrity. It is the necessary way of following our Lord.

Fairness

Justice or fairness in dealing with people is a major theme in Scripture. A key passage in this regard is Micah 6:8, which reads, "And what does the Lord require of you? To act justly and to love mercy and to walk humbly with your God." There is built into our psyche, as humans, a tremendous sense of fair play, which kicks in especially when we feel like people are not treating us right. Our wives feel this way when we give considerably more time and attention to our work than to them. Our children watch very closely to make sure that they receive the same treatment as their siblings. And employees are very sensitive to management practices that are unevenly distributed.

This applies in many areas of business. When raises, bonuses, or promotions are given, is it done on the basis of performance or preference? Favoritism is deadly to the atmosphere and production of any organization. When it comes to giving recognition for a job well done, are only the high achievers being cited, or does everyone doing a good job get commended as well? As indicated in an earlier chapter, it is recognition and praise, more than financial remuneration, that makes people happy at work.

It goes without saying that to show favoritism on the basis of race, gender, ethnicity, etc. is out of the question. Aside from our Christian ethics, there are laws about these things. But one area in which we do need to be extra careful as believers is dealing with other Christians in our employ. We naturally are going to feel more comfortable with others who share our faith, but at work, we need to be sure to treat them no better or worse than those who don't. And it's good to keep in mind that they are watching us also, not only regarding fairness, but to see how well our Christianity functions on the job. You may not be able to disciple them directly at work, but your Christian example will teach them volumes.

Fairness also applies to time off in special circumstances. As mentioned earlier, when my first wife was seriously ill and dying of cancer, my superiors told me to take whatever time I needed to care for her, and they would make sure my teaching responsibilities were covered. I was forever grateful to them for showing me such care, and I knew I wasn't receiving special treatment, for they would have done the same for anyone in my situation.

Which leads to another point—treating people fairly does not necessarily mean treating them all the same. In their book *Situational Leadership*, Ken Blanchard and Paul Hersey explain that treating all persons equally is not really equal. They show that different situations require different approaches when working with employees on the job. For example, new employees may have a lot of enthusiasm but lack in the necessary knowledge and skills to do their work effectively. They will require a lot of focused training and supervision while getting their feet under them. At the other extreme are those who are the highly skilled, highly motivated, who know what's expected of them, and don't need, or want, to be micromanaged. They function best if they are just left alone. In between these two extremes are workers who, for various reasons, may need encouragement or other types of input from their managers. Simply put, the wise leader will give each employee what he or she needs in any given situation.

Questions for Personal Reflection or Group Discussion

1. How honest are you in handling money and company materials (including taxes and expense reports)?

2. How forthright are you in dealing with other people?

3. Can you think of any situations where you may not have been fair in dealing with others through partiality or neglect? Do you respond differently to employees or colleagues who are different, or whom you just don't like?

Going Further: Read Proverbs 6:16-19 and Ephesians 4:22-25, and think about (or discuss) the contrast between these two passages. Also read Colossians 4:1, and notice the emphasis on what is "right and fair" in dealing with those under our leadership. What does that look like in your business?

Bottom Line (The Golden Rule)

There's one principle that seems to cover all we have addressed above. It's found in Matthew 7:12, which says, "So in everything, do to others what you would have others do to you." This teaching of Jesus is popularly known as "The Golden Rule" and is breathtakingly broad in its application. So broad, in fact, that John Maxwell feels it is the only guideline we really need to govern ethical decision-making (*Ethics 101: What Every Leader Needs to Know*, p. 15). Another way of stating it is simply, "Treat others like you would want to be treated." This goes hand in hand with Jesus' command to love our neighbor as we love ourselves.

Many other religions have similar commands; however, they are often stated in negative terms, i.e., "Don't treat others like you wouldn't want to be treated." But stating this in a positive way, as Jesus does, is more powerful and far-reaching. Most laws and rules, including the Ten Commandments, are worded negatively, telling us what we shouldn't do. They were created because people were doing things that were harmful or dangerous to themselves or others. But the Golden Rule or the law of love goes beyond not doing people harm, to actively doing them *good*. For example, I can be commanded to not steal from my neighbor, but *giving* to that neighbor in various ways is beyond what can be demanded or enforced.

As a Christian leader in your workplace, then, the challenge is to deal with your employees, peers, superiors, vendors, and customers the way you would want to be dealt with if the situation were reversed. It's a simple principle. But implementing it will take all the grace God can give you by his Spirit. And he will give you that grace, if you are determined to follow him.

Additional Resources

Wes Cantrell & James R. Lucas. *High-Performance Ethics: 10 Timeless Principles for Next-Generation Leadership.* Tyndale House, 2007.

Raymond L. Hilgert, et. al. *Christian Ethics in the Workplace.* Concordia Publishing House, 2001.

David Horsager. *The Trust Edge: How Top Leaders Gain Faster Results, Deeper Relationships, and a Stronger Bottom Line.* Summerside Press, 2010.

John C. Maxwell. *Ethics 101: What Every Leader Needs to Know.* Center Street, 2003.

Clinton W. McLemore. *Street-Smart Ethics: Succeeding in Business without Selling Your Soul.* Westminster John Knox Press, 2003.

Doug Sherman & William Hendricks. *Keeping Your Ethical Edge Sharp.* NavPress, 1990.

"Everything can be taken from a man but one thing: the last of his freedoms - to choose one's attitude in any given set of circumstances, to choose one's own way."

—*Viktor S. Frankl*

Chapter Ten: Integrity in Our Inner Life

It has been said that it's not what happens to us that matters, as much as our attitude towards it. I believe this is true. Attitudes are crucial to satisfaction, success, fulfillment, and, ultimately, happiness in life. To quote former TV commentator Hugh Downs, "A happy person is not a person in a certain set of circumstances, but rather a person with a certain set of attitudes."

Attitude is one of those words that's more easily understood than defined. Drawing on a number of sources, I would suggest the following meaning: "Attitude is the way we see and evaluate circumstances, people, things, and events. It involves our emotions: positive, negative, or indifferent. These perceptions and feelings are based on previous experiences and their resulting beliefs. Our attitudes greatly influence our behavior."

Let me give you a couple of examples. My attitude toward ice cream is extremely positive. I never met a dish or cone I didn't like. This is based on my experiences going back into childhood, where I tasted the delights of many different flavors in many different settings. For a brief time, it was even the staff of life, the only thing I could eat for several days after having my tonsils removed. How does this influence my behavior? After dinner every night I'm looking in the refrigerator for an ice cream dessert. Even if we have pie or cake or cookies available, everything tastes better with ice cream. And when on vacation, it's not unusual for my wife and me to enjoy ice cream as our entire lunch.

On the other (and a more serious) side, I once had a negative attitude toward Puerto Ricans. I developed this attitude years ago, reading about Puerto Rican youth gangs in New York City. The problem was, I never *knew* any Puerto Rican people personally! In the years since, I have had the opportunity and privilege to develop several friendships with Puerto Ricans, to visit the island and stay with a Puerto Rican family while I was there. In addition, my daughter's closest friend has a Puerto Rican heritage. The result of all this exposure is that my previous attitude has made a complete 180° turn, so that I now feel very warm and positive toward them.

This means attitudes *can* change. You can probably relate your own stories of changes in attitude and behavior based on personal experience and altered beliefs. And this is good news. We don't have to be stuck in old negative attitudes that impact our lives, our relationships, and our well-being, particularly those that are less than Christian.

A Christian's Attitudes

Are there attitudes that are *specifically* Christian, reflecting the character of Christ in us as his followers? There's no question about it. And while many of them are not *uniquely* Christian, they are nonetheless perspectives we need to cultivate if we are going to be like Jesus.

Most of them are in contrast to what we regularly see in the world around us. Some examples include love and compassion versus hatred and indifference, faith and hope versus skepticism and despair, or contentment and generosity versus greed and stinginess. Even with such a brief list, it's clear that a person's perspective mostly reflects either a good attitude or a bad one. Good attitudes come from a heart that has been changed by God, one that reflects his own. These need to be integrated into our everyday lives, by the power of his spirit.

Trust

The most basic Christian attitude is trust (or faith) in God. Having the perspective of being created, loved, and cared for by a heavenly Father, Christians hold a different view of life. It enables us to see what's happening in the world and in our own lives as part of a bigger plan. And it gives us hope where we might otherwise despair, for hope is simply trusting God with our future, whatever it may bring. As believers, we understand that our relationship with God is a personal one, not based on God-pleasing performance, but on God-given grace. (Eph. 2:8-9) And this is the result of what Christ did for us through his life, death, and resurrection. He extends his grace to us; we receive it by trusting in him.

I prefer the word *trust* rather than faith, because faith is typically thought of simply as belief. A person can say that he *believes* in Christ, but what does that mean? That he existed? That he is the Son of God? That he's the savior of the world? All of these are necessary, but not enough. Belief is the intellectual side of Biblical faith, but there's more. To have real faith in someone means to *trust* that person, which involves our *will* and *actions*, not just our intellect.

So, when it comes to our relationship with Christ, believing in his work to redeem us is essential, but exerting our will and trusting that what he did was enough is also necessary. And this attitude of faith and dependence does not stop with our conversion. It is the basis for our everyday relationship with him. We live by faith, depending on him to do for us, in us, and through us by his spirit, what we can't do ourselves. We can trust him. He is trustworthy.

Love

A second attitude basic to Christian experience is love. Our perspective of love begins with the fact that God loves us. This is the essential message of the Bible. It's because he loves us that he sent his Son to die for us, so we might have a relationship with him. His love for us leads to our ability to trust in him. We can't trust someone unless we're sure they have our best interests at heart. And when we receive Christ by faith, he gives us his spirit to live within us. This *both* assures us of God's love, *and* gives us a capacity to love others we didn't possess previously.

More than anything else, we Christians are to be marked by our capacity and willingness to love. Jesus said that everyone would know that we are his disciples *if* we have love for one another. (John 13:35) It is the number one fruit of the spirit, and the baseline against which the use of all our God-given gifts are measured. (Gal. 5:22, 1 Cor. 13)

In marriage, this love is expressed by being considerate and responsive to the needs of our wives in a self-sacrificing way. (1 Pet. 3:7, Eph. 5:25) As fathers, it's displayed through our patience and sensitivity. (Eph. 6:4, Col. 3:21) In the workplace, it shows up by how we treat others, whether those who report to us, (Col. 4:1) or those with whom we do business. (Phil. 2:4) Love even extends to those who treat us badly. (Matt. 5:44)

In a variety of situations, our love for others will be expressed in different ways. It may involve showing compassion, kindness, gentleness, or patience. It could also be exercised by putting up with those who irritate us, or forgiving those who offend us. (Col. 3:12-14) Jesus modeled this love for us at every possible level, and it's his example we are called to follow. But thank God, we aren't left to our own devices. Again, with his indwelling spirit, we have all the resources we need to be truly loving men. (Gal. 5:24, Rom.5:5, 2 Cor. 5:14-15, 2 Peter 1:3-7)

Questions for Personal Reflection or Group Discussion

1. As you consider your own attitudes, are there those you would like to change? Which ones, and why?

2. Are there areas of your life where having a trusting attitude is difficult? Toward God? Toward others? What is it in your past experience that seems to get in the way?

3. Who are the most difficult kind of people in your life for you to love? Have you figured out why? Have you ever prayed about them? How about praying *for* them?

Humility

In our society, self-promotion is the name of the game. This is reflected in the attitude "If I don't promote myself, no one else is going to do it." Whether it's politicians orchestrating public appearances in order to look good, athletes calling attention to themselves after a score, or self-made celebrities doing outlandish things in order to gain the public spotlight, it's all about "Look at me, applaud me." In this environment, a humble attitude is rare, and rarely praised. This isn't new. In the Greek–Roman culture of New Testament times, humility was not considered a virtue, but a weakness. Thus, when Jesus and the apostles taught it as a basic Christian attitude, it was truly counter-cultural . . . and still is.

We can't escape the clear teaching of Scripture on this point. Beginning with the Sermon on the Mount where Jesus declared, "Blessed are the meek," he urged his disciples over and over again to be humble by serving each other. (Mark 9:33-37, 10:25-44) But they really didn't get the picture until he modelled it for them, much to their embarrassment. (John 13:1-17) They were taught to be humble, because he was humble, (Matt. 11:29) which he demonstrated by his death on a Roman cross. (Phil. 2:5-11)

Little wonder that Paul uses this as an example, after urging his Philippian readers to "do nothing out of selfish ambition or vain conceit but in humility consider others better than your selves." (Phil. 2:3) If the Son of God, with all the authority and power of the universe at his disposal, could humbly submit to such humiliation for us, who are we to be anything but humble ourselves?

Self-centered as we're naturally prone to be, this is one of the most difficult attitudes for us to develop. It's important to understand it correctly. Humility does *not* mean thinking negatively about oneself; it's not putting yourself down, or pretending that whatever you accomplish is really nothing. That's false humility. *True humility* is seeing yourself as God sees you. It's appreciating your talents and accomplishments, while also keeping in mind that everything you have—your looks, intelligence, talents, opportunities, health, and life itself—is a gift from God's gracious hand. In the words of Paul, "Who makes you different from anyone else? What do you have that you did not receive?" (1 Cor. 4:7) We are all totally indebted to God for absolutely everything. As Jesus said, "Apart from me you can do nothing." (John 15:5)

In practical terms, this means we can recognize our God-given abilities and be grateful when he uses them to accomplish something good. But it also means we are not in a position to look down on anyone else, whom God has gifted in different ways. Paul says, "Do not think of yourself more highly than you ought, but rather think of yourself with sober judgement, in accordance with the measure of faith God has given you." (Rom. 12:3)

On the other hand, we don't need to be intimidated or feel inadequate by comparing ourselves with others who we may feel are better than us. Paul tells Timothy, "Don't let anyone look down on you because you are young, but set an example for the believers in speech, in life, in love, in faith and in purity." (1 Tim. 4:12) What a great verse! I think we can expand its application even to those who are not so young. Don't let anyone look down on you for *any* reason. God is more interested in the quality of our lives in relationship to him, and any one of us can be an example to others in speech, life, love, etc. We are all God's servants, and he is the one to whom all of us ultimately answer.

One last thought—comparing ourselves with others distorts our thinking. If we feel like we are superior, it breeds *pride*. If we feel inferior, it breeds *envy*. Both are offensive to God. The truly humble man, who is trying to see himself "with sober judgment," will heed the warning Paul gave to the Galatian Christians: "If anyone thinks he is something when he is nothing, he deceives himself. Each one should test his own actions. Then he can take pride in himself, *without comparing himself to somebody else*, for each one should carry his own load." (Gal. 6:3-5, italics mine)

Gratitude

When growing up, our parents taught us to say, "Thank you," whenever a person did something nice for us. We teach our children to do the same. It's the polite and mannerly thing to do. But gratitude is more than simply saying the right words. It's an attitude of heart that expresses the humility discussed above. Ungrateful people have a sense of entitlement. They feel that whatever they have, or whatever is done for them, is fully deserved. The humble person, on the other hand, recognizes that everything is a given by God, and therefore something for which to be thankful.

Pride is what keeps us from being thankful and expressing it to God and to others. It's humbling to be the recipient of another's kindness or generosity. We don't like to feel obligated or dependent. We prefer to do things for ourselves. Most of us would rather be on the giving end, not because "it is more blessed to give than to receive," (Acts 20:35) but because it's more comfortable. It also makes others indebted to us, rather than the other way around. Here's a reality check: we are *all* indebted to God, and to others, on many different levels, much more than we'd like to admit.

Ironically, those who have been blessed with the most are often the least grateful for what they have. Once again, the comparison game rears its head when they see someone who has a little bit more. I have observed that people with very little are often the most grateful for what they have. I think of an elderly English lady named Blanch, whom I knew a number of years ago. Always cheerful and positive, one would think that she was really well off. In fact, she was a widow living on a very meager income, but she always had a heart full of gratitude to God for what she did possess.

A grateful attitude not only recognizes and acknowledges the goodness of God in caring for us, but is also an expression of faith in him. A key passage in this regard is found in Philippians 4:6, where Paul writes, "Do not be anxious about anything, but in everything, by prayer and petition, *with thanksgiving*, present your requests to God." (italics mine) At first glance, the words "with thanksgiving" seem to interrupt the flow of thought, but they are important. For they express the confidence not only that our prayers will be heard, but that they will be answered with a sense of God's peace. (v. 7)

If a friend of yours offered to give you something in the future and you were sure that they not only *could*, but *would* do it, your response would be, "Thank you," even though you hadn't received it yet. Your expression of gratitude would reflect your faith or trust in your friend keeping his word. So it is with God. Our faith in him not only expresses gratitude for past blessings, but a trustful anticipation of future ones.

Questions for Personal Reflection or Group Discussion

1. How has the above discussion altered your way of looking at humility?

2. On a scale of 1 to 10, how would you rate your own humility? What would help you gain a greater sense of humility?

3. How often do you thank God for the many gifts he gives you each day? How might you incorporate that into your prayer life?

4. When was the last time you thanked your wife, your pastor, or the people at work, for how they bless your life on a regular basis? Think of ways you might do this via a conversation or a note (texts are too easy and not very warm).

Contentment

Closely related to gratitude is the attitude of contentment. Given our society's standard of living, you'd think Americans would be the most contented people on earth. But we're not. In fact, we may be among the most *dis*contented. Marketing gurus, who flood our media with various ads, make sure of that. We're *not supposed to be* content with the cars we own, the clothes we wear, the phones we use, or anything else we have. To keep the wheels of our economy rolling, we must (according to them) have the newest and best—our happiness depends on it! Question is, why are so many people who have all the latest stuff unhappy?

As Christians we should understand that, like all other attitudes, contentment is an issue of the heart. In comes from understanding that "a man's life does not consist in the abundance of his possessions," but in being "rich toward God." (Jesus' words in Luke 12:15, 21) The writer of Hebrews echoes Jesus' teaching when he says, "Keep your lives free from the love of money and be content with what you have, because God has said, 'Never will I leave you; never will I forsake you.'" (Heb. 13:5)

In an earlier chapter, we quoted 1 Timothy 6:6-8: "Godliness with contentment is great gain. For we brought nothing into the world, and we can take nothing out of it. But if we have food and clothing, we will be content with that." The reality is that those who have a great deal of this world's goods are not any happier than those whose basic needs are being met, and in many cases (as indicated), a whole lot *unhappier*. Discontented people are also unpleasant to be around. They put a damper on social situations. Did you notice that all three passages quoted above are focused on an orientation toward God? He is the key to contentment. If we have him, we have enough, and *more* than enough.

But contentment extends beyond material things. Are we content with the way God made us, with the talents and abilities he has given to us? Have we found contentment with our positions or status in our families, churches, vocations, or our lives in general? Or are we always wishing things were different, that *we* were different? Does contentment, then, exclude having ambition? Not at all. But it does mean having a realistic picture of our circumstances and limitations.

For example, in my youth, I had a little bit of athletic ability. But had I set my sights to become a professional athlete (as so many kids dream), it would have led to years of frustration and failure. I wasn't that good. I also have some artistic talent, but I came to recognize early on that pursuing art as a career would only have added to the number of starving artists already in the world. Knowing ourselves, including our limitations and weaknesses, as well as our talents and strengths, is necessary to finding real contentment.

As a young man, I also admired people who had attained greatness, especially at an early age. My favorite baseball player was Hall of Famer, Al Kaline, who went right from high school to the majors, and won the American League batting title at age nineteen. That admiration created in my heart the desire to be somebody important, whatever my field, to have my name be known by others. I wanted to be successful in a publicly recognized way. And since I had felt called to the ministry, all of this was for the glory of God, of course!

Then one day God confronted me with the painful picture of what my real motive was. It was selfish ambition, sugarcoated with spirituality. It was all about me. And, in God's eyes, it stunk. But gracious Father that he is, he didn't leave me broken and bruised. Instead, he gently showed me that he hadn't gifted me with the abilities I would need to accomplish the goals I had set for myself. Rather, he had gifted me for a more personal, out-of-the-spotlight kind of vocational ministry. And I'm so glad he taught me that lesson, for in the years since, I have found deep satisfaction in being who I am in Christ, rather than striving to be someone I was not. Contentment is a beautiful thing.

Generosity

Out of gratitude and contentment should flow a generous spirit, for we serve a generous God. "Freely you have received, freely give," Jesus said. (Matt.10:8) When we receive something, we do it with an open hand. And when we give something, our hand is also open to let it go, in contrast to the tightfisted-ness condemned in Deuteronomy 15:7-11. In that passage, lending freely and giving generously are also stressed, with the reminder that those who are poor and needy will always exist (see also Romans 12:8).

The key to having an open hand is to have an open heart. Paul reminds the Christians in Corinth that God wants our giving to be done cheerfully, *not* reluctantly or out of a sense of obligation. (2 Cor. 9:7) He uses the poor Christians in Macedonia as an example for them to follow: "Out of the most severe trial, their overflowing joy and their extreme poverty welled up in rich generosity. For I testify that they gave as much as they were able, and even beyond their ability." (2 Cor. 8:1-3) Again, generosity isn't related to how much we have to give, but having a heart that is willing and truly *wanting* to give.

Those who lack a generous spirit are either greedy, ungrateful, or afraid. Greedy people selfishly always want more and more for themselves, without considering others or their needs. The ungrateful person fails to recognize that he or she is always on the receiving end of God's generosity. And fearful persons worry there might not be enough left for them. Paul addresses this fear in 2 Corinthians 9:8-11, where he reminds the believers in Corinth that God will make sure that they have all *they* need, if they are willing to share with those who are *in* need.

Because, as Christians, we recognize God as the source of all that we have, generosity really comes down to a matter of faith. We know that we are in God's loving hands and that he will care for us, his children. Thus, Jesus declared that those who worry about not having the basics of life are really lacking in faith. (Matt. 6:25-34) And those who are hoarding this world's goods have placed their hearts and their trust in the wrong place. (Matt. 6:19-24) As indicated above, generosity is also related to contentment, for if we're worried that we won't have enough, there's no way we'll part with some of what we do have.

It's good to remember that our heavenly Father is pleased with our generosity, just as we earthly fathers are when we see our children share with others what we have given to them. The Book of Proverbs reminds us that "a generous man will prosper," (11:25) and "will himself be blessed." (22:9) More importantly, when we are generous, God receives thanksgiving and praise. (2 Cor. 9:11-13) And isn't bringing glory to God what the Christian life is all about?

As I write this, I am reminded of an incident I experienced as a pastor. A woman in the church had lost her husband and was in financial need. A friend wanted to help, but didn't want to embarrass her and create awkwardness in their friendship. I suggested she send a cashier's check with a typed, unsigned note, mailed from a neighboring town, instead of her own, which she did. The lady on the receiving end (whom I was counseling at the time), joyfully shared with me later how God had met her need through an anonymous gift. I thought to myself at the time, "Isn't this the way it's supposed to work? The receiver has her need met, the giver has the blessing of helping a friend, and God gets the glory!"

But generosity involves more than just material things. It also involves how much of our time, energy, and abilities we are making available to those who could use them. This starts with our families, then extends to our churches, our friends, our neighbors, and to those we hear about who are needy. I have a friend who is very handy and has about any tool a homeowner could want. His neighbors know this, so if they need to borrow a tool, John is the guy to see. But there's a bonus. John will not only loan them a tool, he'll help them with the job—the most generous person I know with his time and skills.

Questions for Personal Reflection or Group Discussion

1. Have you found real contentment in your life and vocation? In what areas are you discontent?

2. Are you using your God-given gifts and talents? If not, why not? How might you change that?

3. Financially speaking, how much do you really need?

4. What do you have to offer that others need (financial or otherwise), and how do you think God would want you to give it?

Going Further: Meditate on or discuss the following passages: on trust, (Prov. 3:5-7) on love, (Col. 3:12-14) on Humility, (Phil. 2:3-8) on gratitude, (Col. 3:15-17) on contentment, (1 Tim. 6:6-8) and on generosity. (2 Cor. 9:6-11)

A Christian's Emotions

Emotions are simply something we all have. They are built into us by our creator, as part of our essential humanness and a reflection of his image. They are responses to whatever we are experiencing in life. If things are going well, we feel happy. If we experience loss, we feel sad. If we do something wrong, we feel guilty. And so on. So, what does it mean to *feel* in a Christian way? Aren't everyone's emotions the same, regardless of their beliefs? Yes, and no.

It's true that we all have the same set of emotions, but how we react in any given situation is also influenced by what we believe. For instance, everyone goes through difficult times in life, but as Christians, we are encouraged to have joy when this happens. Why? Because we *believe* that God is working through those painful circumstances to make us into better persons. (Romans 5:3-5, James 1:2-5, and Peter 1:6-7) In addition, our sensitivity and how we react to the emotions of others is also a reflection of our Christian faith. Do we understand how others feel, and more importantly, do we care?

This is an important part of life, because how we feel often affects how well we conduct our activities and handle relationships each day. Negative emotions influence our ability to think clearly and relate positively to the people around us, whether at work or at home. And the key to dealing with the emotional side of life is to first handle our *own* emotions: admitting *what* we're feeling, figuring out *why* we're feeling that way, and then deciding *what to do* about it. This is a special challenge for men, because we are not as tuned into our emotional side as our female counterparts. We tend to spend most of our days working with the rational side of our brains while ignoring our feelings.

In this section, we won't try to cover every emotion, an impractical and impossible task in so short amount of space. We will discuss some of the key emotions most men struggle with, and how we can best deal with them as followers of Christ.

Anger

If there is one emotion common to all men, and frequently misused, it is anger. How many times have we lost our cool and, in the process, done or said things that hurt or offended family members or coworkers? Or how many of us struggle with high blood pressure or gastro-intestinal problems because we have learned to sit on our anger and let it eat at our insides? Neither of these approaches is healthy, or particularly Christian.

At the outset, it's important to recognize that anger is a God-given emotion and, therefore, not wrong per se. You can't read the Bible without seeing that God himself gets angry. And when Jesus walked this earth, he also got angry at times. For instance, when he was turning over tables in the temple courts, or lambasting the Pharisees for their hypocrisy or their hardness of heart, I don't think he did it with a smile on his face. He was ticked. So, anger itself is not the problem. It's *why* we get angry and *what we do* with it that counts. When God the Father gets angry or Jesus his Son got angry, it was always in response to something that was wrong or unjust. This is righteous indignation, and we *ought* to get angry in those situations, too. If we *aren't* angered by injustice or abuse, there's something morally missing in us.

In fact, when we get angry, the thoughts that generally run through our minds are, "That's not right!" or "That's not fair!" It's this sense of injustice that is part of God's image in us. But, in reality, most of our anger is self-focused, a feeling that *we* are being treated unjustly. If it's true, our anger is justified, but very often it's just our *perception* that what's happening is unfair.

Keep in mind that anger is often a *secondary* emotion. What this means is that other emotions trigger it. Some of the most common ones are as follows:

Frustration: When we are trying to get a task done and something or someone is in the way, our frustration will probably make us mad. For example, you are working on an important report with a looming deadline, and your computer dies, or the people responsible for getting you needed information are dragging their heels. Or maybe you are flying to an important meeting, and the plane is late getting off the ground so that you miss your connecting flight. Frustration is a major reason for getting angry.

Unmet expectations: Another trigger for anger is when things don't turn out the way we anticipated. It can be a little thing, like your favorite team losing a game they were *supposed* to win, or something bigger, like raining the whole week of your vacation. Or, even more important, losing a promotion or contract you were sure you were best suited for, because somebody else had connections you were lacking.

Anxiety or fear: When we feel a threat to our own well-being or those we love, we react in anger. That threat could be physical, in the form of an illness, accident, or a dangerous situation. It could be financial, like an unjustified lawsuit (it happened to me), or the loss of a job or business. It could be parental, as in the case of having a child in trouble with the law, involved in drugs, running with the wrong crowd, or simply not at home hours after their curfew. Fear often triggers anger.

Feeling devalued: When other people don't take us seriously, when our values, convictions, or ideas are disrespected, when we are kept waiting needlessly, when our generosity is taken advantage of, when people don't call or show up to an appointment they were scheduled for, or when people fail to thank us for favors done—the list goes on and on. We all like to feel that our time, our ideas, and our contributions should be respected, and when they're not, it makes us angry. Personally, nothing makes me angrier than when I feel I'm being taken advantage of by someone. Perhaps you can relate.

Regardless of what may trigger your anger, it's always wise to stop and examine the situation. Because it isn't circumstances that make us angry; it's our *interpretation* of the circumstances. For example, when the so-called "housing bubble" burst a few years ago, those who were sitting on a large mortgage were unhappy to say the least, because their house was now worth a lot less than what they paid for it. On the other hand, those buying real estate were delighted, because now they could get a lot more bang for their buck. Different perceptions of the same event elicited different feelings. So, when you are feeling angry, ask yourself, "What's behind these feelings? Am I frustrated, anxious, disrespected, disappointed, or what?"

Once you understand *why* you are angry, the next step is to determine *what* to do about it, how to respond. There are really just four options. One is to explode, let it all out: yell, scream, or throw things. If you do this at home, you'll probably scare the dog, send your kids running for cover, and have your wife not speak to you for a week. At work, your staff may begin putting out resumes. Not a good option.

A second way of dealing with your anger is to stuff it. Don't say anything, don't do anything, just let that feeling sit in your gut and eat you up inside—a sure recipe for a number of stress-related illnesses. It will also tend to leak out in the form of nagging, sarcasm, emotional coldness, revenge, and numerous other ways that are sure to lose friends and irritate people.

A third and healthier way to handle anger is to calmly talk about what happened with the person who upset you. Don't accuse them. Don't tell them *they* made you angry (because no one can *make* us angry; it's our choice). Instead, recall what was said or done, and explain why it angered you. That way, you own the problem, and they have the freedom to respond (or not) to that information, however they may choose. But you get it off your chest in a non-offensive way. In Ephesians 4:26-27, we are encouraged not to let our anger turn to sin, but to deal with it quickly.

Sometimes, for any number of reasons, it may not be wise to confront the other person, even in a respectful way. Which brings us to a fourth option: just let it go. This is different than stuffing it. You're acknowledging the problem or offense and are fully aware of your feelings. But you are also *choosing* to do something positive in response. Maybe you simply give that person the benefit of the doubt, making allowances for what they may be dealing with in their lives at the time.

Whatever your reasoning process, this response is called *forgiveness*. It's not judging, or getting even, or even letting the other person off the hook by denying your hurt or relieving them of responsibility. It's simply extending undeserved grace, like God does with us, and not holding it against them any longer. (Ephesians 4:31-32)

Guilt

Guilt is the opposite of anger. If anger is triggered by hurtful things done to us, guilt is our emotional response to pain we have inflicted on others. Living with a guilty conscience is a difficult existence. We all have regrets: things we said or did we wish had never happened, or could be done over. Some of those things may even make us feel ashamed, as well as guilty.

The good news is, we don't have to live with guilt. The Bible is very clear about what we need to do with it. First of all, like anger, we have to face it. This is not always easy, because our pride gets in the way. We can find a hundred ways to justify our words or actions, or turn the situation around so that the other person looks guilty. Psalm 36:2 observes this about the wicked person: "In his own eyes he flatters himself too much to detect or hate his sin." And 1 John 1:8 says, "If we claim to be without sin, we deceive ourselves and the truth is not in us." Thus, pride and self-deception have to be eliminated, before we can really see ourselves as God sees us.

Once we have admitted our guilt, the next step is to confess it to God. The good news in 1 John 1:9 is, "If we confess our sins, he (God) is faithful and just and will forgive us our sins and purify us from all unrighteousness." John goes on to tell us in chapter 2:1-2 that God is able to do this, because we have someone speaking to him on our behalf: Jesus Christ, who sacrificed himself for our sins. This is the good news of the gospel that continues to apply in our lives, even after we have begun a relationship with Christ.

Knowing we have been forgiven, that God has let our offenses go, can give us a tremendous sense of inner peace. But there is usually another issue to be dealt with: other people who have been offended or hurt by our sinful words or actions. We rarely sin in a vacuum. It usually affects others. So, we need to deal with that part of the equation as well.

If our pride gets in the way of our acknowledging our sins to God, who loves us and wants to forgive us, it really does a number on us when we think about asking forgiveness from another person. How often have we wrestled internally when realizing that we owe our wife or children an apology? And they're easy! How much more difficult is it when we have to admit our failure to a friend or business colleague? We worry about losing face. Yet the reality is, we probably *gain* their respect by taking full responsibility for our actions.

The other person may or may not forgive you. That's their choice, and their responsibility. But at least you have done your part. Romans 12:18 says, "If it is possible, as far as it depends on you, live at peace with everyone." You can only do what you need to do, and then leave the rest to God.

What we have been discussing above is *real guilt*, doing or saying something that is wrong in the eyes of God. But there is also something called *false guilt*, which is the guilt we feel when we have failed to live up to our own or others' expectations. While it emotionally *feels* the same, it isn't something we need to confess as sin.

When we *feel* guilty, it's good to examine that guilt to make sure it's the real thing. If it's false guilt, we need to ask ourselves some key questions: Why am I trying to live up to others' expectations? Is it to be respected, accepted, or loved? Or, what was I expecting from myself in this situation? Given the circumstances, were my expectations realistic: who I am and what I'm capable of? Ruminating about what we *should* have done is a dead-end street, leading us to beat ourselves up, and to possible depression.

Questions for Personal Reflection or Group Discussion

1. Honestly speaking, how much do you react to situations based on your emotions?

2. What are the kind of situations that make you angry? How do you usually express your anger? What's the usual result?

3. Think or talk about what might be a better way of handling your anger.

4. Looking at your past, are there things that you feel guilty about? What are they? Have you successfully resolved them, asked for forgiveness?

Anxiety

Another common emotion we men struggle with at times is anxiety. Life is full of situations that give us reason to worry: waiting for a biopsy report on our wife or parent, our child's failing grades at school, a downturn in the economy, the political and racial divisions in our society giving us concern about our children's future, or a global nuclear threat. At times, we identify it as simple concern. But at other times, a situation grabs our gut, dominates our thinking, and keeps us awake at night. As Christians, how do we handle these situations? A longer answer is given in Chapter Eleven, "Integrity Under Fire," but here are a few brief thoughts that might help.

If you think about anxious situations, keep in mind they have two primary characteristics: (1) They involve the *future*. We don't worry about the past; that's behind us and unchangeable. And the only things we worry about in the present are those that have future ramifications. (2) They are things over which we have *no control*. If we thought we could manage the outcome, we wouldn't be worried about them.

The ironic thing is, generally speaking, most of the things we worry about never come to pass. So, why do we still worry? The easy answer is we *do* feel threatened, and that's scary. But I think there is also an unconscious and more subtle reason. Because most of what we worry about *doesn't* happen, a part of our brain tells us that our worrying keeps it from happening! Or if it *does* happen, at least we won't be caught off guard. Also, *not* to worry would send a message to others that we really don't care, which, of course, isn't true.

So, how do we deal with anxiety? One practical way is to ask yourself, "What's the worst possible outcome in this situation, and could I handle that?" It's scary to go there, but it's a way to face a *possible* reality. Your answer might be painful to think about, but in many situations, it may quiet your anxious heart.

From a Christian perspective, the best way to deal with anxiety is to follow the teaching of Scripture. I begin with the words of Jesus in the Sermon on the Mount:

> "So, do not worry, saying, 'What shall we eat?' or 'What shall we drink?' or 'What shall we wear?' For the pagans run after all these things, and your Heavenly Father knows that you need them. But seek first his kingdom and his righteousness, and all these things will be given you as well." *Matthew 7:31-33*

Basically, Jesus is reminding us that God knows what we need, and as a loving heavenly Father who cares about us, we can trust him with our concerns. We may not get what we *want*, but he'll give us what we *need*. Since anxiety involves the unknown future and things we can't control, how wise and comforting it is to give our worry to God, who both *knows* the future and has everything under *his* control. It's a matter of trust, which is why Jesus addresses his audience of worriers in v. 30 as, "O you of little faith."

In their letters, both Paul and Peter give the same advice for dealing with worry. In Philippians 4:6-7 Paul writes, "Do not be anxious about anything, but in everything, by prayer and petition, *with thanksgiving*, present your requests to God. And the peace of God, which transcends all understanding, will guard your hearts and your minds in Christ Jesus." And Peter adds, "Humble yourselves, therefore, under God's mighty hand, that he may lift you up in due time. Cast all your anxiety on him, because he cares for you."

Prayer is the key. Give it to God. I know that's easier said than done. When we're worried, we tend to give it to God and then *take it back* again, because it's still on our minds. But *keep giving it* to him and *thanking him* that he has it in his hands (as Paul says, "with thanksgiving"). Ask him to help you let go of it and to grant you his peace.

Loneliness

While highly sought by many people, positions of leadership have their own set of difficulties and challenges. One of them is loneliness. Someone has well said, "It's lonely at the top." This is true for many reasons. One is that it's hard to develop friendships with people who work for you, or to maintain the ones you had before you reached the top. Others will think you are playing favorites. Another reason is that there are things you can't share with those who report to you, which you have to wrestle with alone. Then, there is the problem of whom you can trust. Are people being nice to you because of your position, or just because they like you? And if you are at the very top of your organization, "the buck stops with you" as they say. Bearing that burden can be lonely.

Two of the groups I meet with on a regular basis are made up of clergy who are lead pastors in their churches. We get together every other week for lunch and discuss a current book chosen by the group (something related to ministry or their personal lives). The value of these groups is threefold: First, they get to meet with other men who understand the struggles of their work, and with whom they can vent freely. Second, they can share their personal needs and pray for one another. Third, the book they study together gives them ideas they can talk about, benefitting from the different theological perspectives and experiences of each person in the group. Perhaps a group like that would work for you.

Besides the loneliness that may come with the job, there is the loneliness that is the result of not taking the time and effort to develop deep relationships outside of your work: with friends (Chapter One), or your wife (Chapter Four). We all need close relationships. If you are an introvert, you don't need as many, but you still do need some. Perhaps you came from a family that was dysfunctional to the degree that you never learned how to effectively connect with others, or maybe you have problems trusting anyone. If so, you may need to work that through with a counselor or a spiritual mentor.

Loneliness can also make you vulnerable to a number of temptations. People who are seeking intimacy often engage in pornography, and settle for its pseudo-intimacy. Loneliness may also drive the excessive time many spend on social media websites. And it's possible to find ourselves getting emotionally involved in unhealthy relationships, the most harmful of which are extramarital affairs (see Chapter Five).

Of course, the most common reason for loneliness is separation from those we love, whether permanently through death or divorce, or temporarily. If either you or your spouse is away on business, or caring for a needy relative, you will naturally feel some loneliness. We are attached and dependent on those closest to us, and we naturally miss them when separated. We also feel this when a son or daughter goes away to college, or moves to another state.

How do we deal with loneliness? Begin by deepening the relationships you already have. This starts with spending time with them; one on one is best. Show an interest in them as persons, and also in their lives and activities. Keep in touch; don't allow long time lapses between contacts. If you have to be away on business, call home frequently. Talk to your kids as well as your spouse. Take family photos with you.

If you lack relationships, go out of your way to develop them with people you have things in common, whether spiritually, businesswise, recreationally, or intellectually. As mentioned in Chapter One, be intentional about meeting versus just saying, "Let's get together sometime." Join organizations, leagues, clubs, etc., where you have a chance to come in contact with those whose interests you share.

Spiritually, your most important relationship is with the Lord. Developing more intimacy with him is also a great way to overcome loneliness. Ways to work on this is also covered in Chapter One.

Depression

We all get depressed at times. It's a normal reaction when things are going badly in our lives, especially when dealing with loss or failure.

Depression is well named, for when we are depressed, everything gets pushed down: our mood, our energy, our outlook, our self-esteem. We may even lose our appetite, our ability to sleep, and our sex drive. We become discouraged and despondent. The light goes out of our eyes, and the spring disappears from our step. The world feels like a negative, even dark, place. It's not a pleasant state to be in.

There is a difference between *being* depressed and *having* depression. The first is what we all experience at difficult times (as described above). The latter is a more serious form called clinical depression. This is the most common form of emotional illness, and those who have a family history of depression are more susceptible to it. Clinical depression is deeper. It affects our ability to function. It isn't related to a specific issue or problem, but is a general, overall mood, and it gives the feeling that one is seeing the world through dark glasses. In its most serious form, the sufferer has thoughts of hurting oneself, even taking one's life. It needs to be treated with therapy, and possibly medication, at its worst.

When struggling with ordinary depressed moods, it's good to reflect (as with all negative emotions) on why you are feeling this way. When did it begin, and what were the events that triggered it? Do you fully understand what happened and the consequences of the event? Are you angry? Anger is often a component of depression, especially if it has been stuffed rather than expressed (see above). Who are you angry with, and why? If you are keeping it inside instead of talking to the person(s) about it, what is your reason or motive? Did you help create the situation, and are you angry at yourself?

Once you have looked within, it's good to look up. God is the source of peace and joy. Psalm 42:5 says, "Why are you downcast, O my soul? Why so disturbed within me? Put your hope in God, for I will yet praise him, my Savior and my God." Notice the Psalmist is talking to himself, reminding himself that God is the one he should be looking to. When going through difficulties, there are three places we can focus: (1) on our circumstances, which are scary and the reason we're depressed in the first place, (2) on our ability to deal with those circumstances, which is not functioning well or we *would be* handling it, and (3) on our heavenly Father, who is bigger than our circumstances.

Sometimes it's hard to pray when we're depressed. In our negative mood, we may feel like he doesn't hear us, or that he doesn't care. Satan would love to convince us that both are true, but they're not. God does hear the prayers of his children, whether we feel like he does or not. And he does care.

There are many examples in Scripture of men who had bouts of depression, from Moses to David to Elijah to Jonah to Peter and Paul. But the most obvious one was Job, recorded in the book bearing his name. Job had lost everything: ten children, vast wealth, and his health. He was deep in grief leading to depression, wishing he could die, or better still, that he had never been born. And to top it off, the three friends who came to "comfort" Job spent their time insisting that his troubles were due to sin. They believed that bad things only happen to bad people. In times of distress, nobody needs friends like that.

Throughout his long ordeal, Job keeps defending himself against his accusers and pleading with God to tell him why. To his credit (for even his wife had told him to curse God and die), Job never took his eyes off of God. At the end of the book, the Lord finally responds to Job, but not in the way he expected. Instead of telling him why, God simply reminds Job of his awesome greatness, as displayed in creation. And Job learns a valuable lesson: it's not our place to *question* God (although he does hear our questions). Our place is to *submit* to his sovereign rule in our lives, and to *trust* him.

And when we see the bigger picture, like Job did, it helps put things in perspective for us as well. The world doesn't revolve around us and our needs. God is working out his purposes in the world, and in our lives, sometimes painfully so. I personally went through a depressive period in my mid-thirties. It lasted eighteen months. I was a pastor at the time and was able to function only because I was convinced that God's word was true, whether I felt it or not. Emotionally, it was one of the worst periods of my life, complete with panic attacks. But God taught me so many important lessons about himself, and about myself, that I can look back and be thankful for the experience.

There are the usual practical things you can do for yourself while going through a bout of depression: regular exercise, eating right, trying to get enough sleep (lack of sleep by itself can depress us), doing things you enjoy, finding people who make you laugh, etc. It's really good to talk to someone as well. It may be a counselor, your pastor, or a good friend who is also wise; you need someone to give you a different perspective than your own. But especially, don't stop talking to God, for no one has more wisdom or cares more than he does.

Questions for Personal Reflection or Group Discussion

1. What makes you anxious? Can talk about your concern(s) with your spouse or a friend? If not, why not?

2. How do you deal with anxious feelings?

3. Are you ever lonely? Under what circumstances?

4. Are you tempted to handle your lonely feelings in an unhelpful way? What do you do that *is* beneficial?

5. What events or situations make you depressed?

6. Have you ever struggled with an ongoing period of depression? What triggered it? Did you pull out of it, and what or who helped you do that?

GoingFurther: Meditate on, or discuss, the following passages: on anger, (Ephesians 4:26-27, 31-32) on guilt, (1 John 1:9-2:2) on anxiety, (Philippians 4:6-9) on loneliness, (Psalm 1:39:1-10) and on depression. (Psalm 42)

Bottom Line

The attitudes we have toward others and the circumstances of life reflect on our character and, even more importantly, our Christian witness. The same is true with how we handle our emotions. We can't help how we feel, but we can't let our feelings control us, or be expressed in ways that affect our relationships with others in a negative way. Being careful with our actions is important, but it's also important to monitor our inner life, for as Proverbs 4:23 says, "Above all else, guard your heart, for everything you do flows from it."

Additional Resources

On Attitudes

John Ortberg, *Faith & Doubt*. Zondervan, 2008.

Art Lindsley, *Love, The Ultimate Apologetic: The Heart of Christian Witness*. InterVarsity Press, 2008.

Ken Blanchard & S. Truett Cathy, *The Generosity Factor: The Joy of Discovering Your Time, Talent and Treasure*. Zondervan, 2002.

Nancy L. DeMoss, *Choosing Gratitude: Your Journey to Joy*. Moody Press, 2011. C. J. Mahanney, *Humility: True Greatness*. Multnomah, 2005.

Richard A. Swenson, *Contentment: The Secret to a Lasting Calm.* NavPress, 2013.

On Emotions

Dan B. Allender & Tremper Longman III, *Cry of the Soul: How Our Emotions Reveal Our Deepest Questions About God.* NavPress, 1994.

Don Colbert, *Deadly Emotions: Understand the Mind-Body-Spirit Connection That Can Heal or Destroy You.* Thomas Nelson, 2003.

Gary J. Oliver, *Real Men Have Emotions Too.* Moody Press, 1993.

"The measure of everyman's virtue is best revealed in time of adversity—adversity that does not weaken a man but rather shows what he is."

—*Thomas à Kempis*

Chapter Eleven: Integrity Under Fire

"Who you are when no one is looking" is said to be the best test of a person's character. There's a lot of truth in that statement. What we do when no one is around to keep us accountable *is* a good indication of the kind of people we are. But I think there's an even more accurate test, and that is, *who you are under fire,* whether anyone is looking or not. Integrity, in the sense of Christ-like behavior, is much easier to maintain when things are going well in our lives. When we're enjoying good health and success, our family life is satisfying, bills are paid, and stress level is minimal, it is relatively easy to be a man of God (although good times do have their own set of temptations). But how do we respond in the face of adversity? That question exposes the core of who we are. That's when godly character really can't be faked.

In life we face many kinds of trials. It's the reality (and curse) of living in a fallen world. Job 5:7 says, "Man is born to trouble as surely as sparks fly upward." And Jesus warns, "In this world you will have trouble. But take heart! I have overcome the world." Wouldn't it be nice if God would arrange for believers to float through life in some sort of protective bubble? Unfortunately, it doesn't work that way. Though, to my amazement, there *are* sincere believers who do believe that bad things *shouldn't* happen to them, simply because they're God's children. And when adversity comes, they question his goodness, or reject their faith altogether.

The fact is, Christians may have *more* adversity in life than others, *because* of our faith! Persecuted believers all over the world can testify to this. Jesus said, "If the world hates you, keep in mind that it hated me first." (John 15:18) And Peter writes, "Dear friends don't be surprised at the painful trial you are suffering, as though something strange were happening to you." (1 Peter 4:12) Persecution could happen to us, as well. We need to remind ourselves that we *are* people of the cross. The cross *is* the symbol of our faith, not a brass one on a church steeple or a gold one on a chain around one's neck, but a bloody wooden one, where Jesus died for us. And Jesus commands us to take up *our* cross daily and follow him.

Some bad things that happen to us are beyond our control: a natural disaster destroys our home, we have an auto accident that's not our fault, we are struck with a serious illness, a loved one dies, we lose our job (or a whole business) owing to an economic downturn, etc.

We might also be a victim of slander because of someone's envy, anger, or downright hatred. It's a fallen world of broken people that we live in (ourselves not excluded). A coworker could resent your promotion. A business competitor may feel he should have been given the contract that your company received. Some people might be envious of your success. Or, as mentioned above, you could be victimized because of your Christian faith, held back in your career, or the target of unfounded accusations, costing you your reputation and/or your position.

Then there are those problems we bring on ourselves owing to sin, negligence, being careless, or foolish. How many things do we regret, things we'd do differently if we had the chance? How many men have derailed their lives because of an addiction, an extramarital affair, financial indiscretion, failing to take of their health, or neglecting their responsibilities as a husband and father? "In this world you will have trouble" indeed.

So again, the question is not, "Will we have trouble?" But, "How will we handle the trouble that's certain to come?" Our response to that question will determine the strength of our Christian faith, *and* the character we've developed as a result. It will also either hinder or accelerate our spiritual growth, depending on our response. And this, in turn, will impact those around us: our family members, Christian friends, and the unbelievers who are watching, to see if our faith is real or not.

Typical Reactions to Adversity

I have found, in working with people in crisis (especially those dealing with the loss of a loved one), that there are three burning questions asked over and over again. The first is, "Why?" Why me? Why my loved one? Unfortunately, there's usually not a satisfactory answer to this question, if one at all. Job (whose name is synonymous with adversity) asked this question no less than fourteen times in the book that bears his name. To cite one example, "If I have sinned, what have I done to you O watcher of men? *Why* have you made me your target? Have I become a burden to you?" (Job 7:20)

A second burning question people ask is, "How long?" When in pain, whether physical or mental, we want to know when it is going to be over. And again, there is usually no clear answer, especially for people who are grieving. The Psalmist had this struggle. Psalm 6:3

says, "My soul is in anguish. How long, O Lord, *how long*?" When life is good, we want the good times to last forever, but when things are going bad, we'd like to put them behind us as quickly as possible.

A third question posed by people in pain is, "What now?" Quoting from the Psalms again, "When the foundations are being destroyed, *what* can the righteous do?" (Psalm 11:3, italics mine) We want to know what we can do to make it better; how do we make the pain go away? That's why people seek professional counsel—to figure out how to fix it. Men, in particular, have this urge, to fix problems, built into our DNA. Thus, trying to find a way out of adversity is our knee-jerk reaction.

But for the follower of Christ, the bigger issue (and challenge) is not how to escape our pain, but how do we handle it in a way that honors God? Doing that requires, first of all, having God's perspective on times of pain and difficulty in our lives.

How God Uses Adversity in Our Lives

To begin with, it's good to keep in mind that our suffering is not meaningless. There is a purpose behind our pain, and God uses adversity in a number of ways in his relationship with us.

To Get Our Attention: One can't read the Bible without noticing how often the Israelites strayed from her commitment to God, broke his laws, mistreated each other, and worshiped other deities. Time and time again, he issued warnings through his prophets, which were mostly ignored. When that failed, God used various kinds of trouble to get their attention. See what he said through Isaiah: "I am the Lord your God, who teaches you what is best for you, who directs you in the way you should go. If only you had paid attention to my commands, your peace would have been like a river, your righteousness like the waves of the sea." (Isa. 48:17-18) If only they had listened, they would have been spared a lot of trouble.

How many of us came into a living relationship with Christ *after* he got our attention through pain? Or, as believers, how often does he use it when we begin to drift spiritually? C. S. Lewis writes, "God whispers to us in our pleasures, speaks in our conscience, but shouts in our pain. It is his megaphone to rouse a deaf world." God also uses pain to wake us up to problems in our marriages, with our children, in our businesses, or involving our health. Have you ever made changes in your diet or lifestyle after a negative diagnosis from your doctor? I have.

To Test Our Faith: Job says, "He (God) knows the way I take; when he has *tested* me, I will come forth as gold." (Job 23:10) The writer of Hebrews says, "By faith, Abraham, when God *tested* him, offered Isaac as a sacrifice." (Heb. 11:17) And Matthew begins his account of Jesus ministry with these words: "Then Jesus was led by the Spirit into the desert to be *tempted* by the devil." (Matt. 4:1) Note that tempted, tried, and tested use the same underlying Greek term. Evidently, the Father even required his Son to be battle-tested right from the start of his ongoing, lifelong war with Satan. Military leaders and athletic coaches know the importance of putting their men through hardship, so they won't fold in the heat of battle. God is no less concerned about us.

I think it can be safely said that an untested faith isn't genuine. The Apostle Peter, who had his own faith tested many times, writes about suffering through trials and their purpose: "These have come so that your faith[—]of greater worth than gold, which perishes even though refined by fire[—]may be proved *genuine* and may result in praise, glory and honor when Jesus Christ is revealed." (1 Pet. 1:7) Gold is refined by melting it down until the impurities float to the surface, where they can be skimmed off. So too, when the heat of adversity is applied to our lives and faith, God skims off some of the impurities that keep us from being more like his Son and accomplishing what he desires for us.

To be sure, the testing that God directed in the lives of Job, Abraham, and Jesus was special and for unique purposes. I don't believe that most of the trials we endure in life are the result of God's direct intervention. We have a sinful nature, and live in a broken world with a tendency to create our own messes. God has plenty of material to use for faith-testing, without having to initiate trials. But, as with the men mentioned above, God *does* test our ability to trust him, so that we can be prepared for our own service and battles.

To Teach Us Obedience: The only way we learn obedience is through experience, i.e., by actually obeying. Hebrews 5:8-9 tells us that Jesus "learned obedience from what he suffered and, once made perfect, he became the source of eternal salvation for all who obey him." Jesus *always* obeyed his Father; he said so himself. (John 15:10) But the *full maturing* (the meaning of "made perfect") of that obedience came through his willingness to go to the cross. Paul also points out that Jesus "humbled himself and became *obedient* to death[—]even death on a cross." (Phil. 2:5-8, italics mine) From his agonizing prayer in Gethsemane, it's clear that facing crucifixion was *the* test of obedience for our Lord, and understandably so. The same is true for us. While we'll never face a challenge as daunting as the cross, we still have to learn how to obey God, no matter what the circumstances or the cost.

To Remind Us We're *Not* in Control: Throughout the Book of Job, he continually asks, "Why?" but is never given an answer. However, at the end of the book, God breaks his silence. He says, "Who is this that darkens my counsel with words without knowledge? Brace yourself like a man; I will question you, and you will answer me. Where were you when I laid the earth's foundation? Tell me if you understand." And for the next four chapters, God point outs to Job the wonders of his creation. (Job 38:2-41:34) When he is finished, Job responds by saying, "I know you can do all things; no plan of yours can be thwarted ... Surely, I spoke of things I did not understand, things too wonderful for me to know ... My ears had heard of you but now my eyes have seen you. Therefore, I despise myself and respond in dust and ashes." (42:2-6)

Job learned what we all need to remember: it's God's world, and not our place to question but simply to submit. When things are going well for us, we tend to think that we have everything under control. This is really a false sense of security. In fact, we don't control anything, including the length of our lives. Just observe the effects of a blizzard, hurricane, or tornado, and remember that the weather is one way God reminds us we're not *really* in control.

To Discipline Us for Our Good: In Hebrews 12, we read, "Endure hardship as discipline; God is treating you as sons. For what son is not disciplined by his father? ... Our fathers disciplined us for a little while as they thought best; but God disciplines us for our good, that we may share in his holiness." (vs. 7, 10) We tend to think of discipline as punishment, but they are two different things. Punishment is used to even a score or correct an injustice. But the purpose of discipline is to change bad behavior and to teach us how to do things right. While it may feel painful at the time, (v. 11) it is always for our good: to make us holy, which is God's ultimate plan for us.

To Grow and Mature Us: James 1:2-4 tells us to "consider it pure joy, my brothers, whenever you face trials of many kinds, because you know that the testing of your faith develops perseverance. Perseverance must finish its work so that you may be mature and complete, not lacking anything." Children who are overly protected by their parents never fully mature. Growing up requires a few hard knocks in life. As parents, it's hard to watch our children struggle with problems, but we know it's a necessary part of their becoming responsible adults, so also, for us, in the spiritual realm. Faith needs to be combined with perseverance in order for us to mature.

Jesus used the analogy of the vinedresser and his pruning process to illustrate the same thing. He refers to himself as the vine and his followers as branches, with the Father as the gardener who prunes the branches to make them more fruitful. (Jn 15:1-2) Have you ever observed an orchard in early spring after the farmer has trimmed the branches of the trees? Or if you have flowering bushes, have you thought about how you cut them back so drastically each year? In each case, the goal is to get bigger fruit or blooms, versus the nutrients going into fruitless branches and leaves. In the same way, God needs to cut out of our lives things that hinder the spiritual fruit he wants to produce in and through us. Adversity often serves that purpose.

To build godly character: Paul writes in Romans 5:2-4, "We rejoice in the hope of the glory of God. Not only so, but we also rejoice in our sufferings, because we know that suffering produces perseverance; perseverance, character; and character hope." Notice that perseverance in the face of suffering produces character. And when the pressure is on, when we are under fire, it's character that will make the crucial difference in our response and how we come out on the other side. Character is the key, and (as stated earlier) *you can't fake character*. Either you have it or you don't. God uses adversity to build it into us, so we can do the what pleases him in every situation.

To train us for future ministry: One of the more intriguing passages of Scripture is 2 Corinthians 1:3-4. There Paul writes, "Praise be to the God and Father of our Lord Jesus Christ, the Father of compassion and the God of all comfort, who comforts us in all our troubles, so that we can comfort those in any trouble with the comfort we ourselves have received from God." The underlying Greek word for "comfort" here has the sense of coming alongside to give encouragement or aid.

There are two things of note in these verses: First, God is there for us during adversity. We never have to go it alone. This is also stressed in another context where God says, "Never will I leave you; never will I forsake you." (Hebrews 13:5; The "nevers" in this verse are both double negatives in Greek, giving a strong emphasis to God's faithfulness in trouble) Second, what God does for us empowers us to do for others. Over and over I have observed, in others' lives, as well as my own, how God uses trials to prepare us to help others in similar situations. Think of Charles Colson, whose time in prison led him to found Prison Fellowship, or the woman who started Mothers Against Drunk Drivers after her own child was killed in that way. The best addiction counselors are former addicts, and the most effective grief counselors are those who have experienced major losses themselves.

Questions for Personal Reflection or Group Discussion

1. Have you ever thought about how God may be using adversity in your life?

2. Looking at the eight items listed above, which ones specifically has he used with you?

3. What difference has it made in your perspective and behavior?

How Should We Respond to Adversity?

Since problems in life are unavoidable, and they do have a place in God's plans, the question remains: how are we going to handle them when they come? Or, more specifically, how should we, as Christian men, respond to the trials we encounter, in a way that is honoring to God? To that question, I would recommend the following:

First, we remember that God is sovereign and Jesus is Lord. Paul in Colossians 1:16-17 reminds us, "For by him (Christ) all things were created . . . created by him and for him. He is before all things, and in him all things hold together." When in crisis, our perspective tends to narrow. We get stuck in thinking there are only one or two ways of looking at the situation or working our way out of it. When I'm counseling people in crisis, part of my job is to *broaden* their perspective so they can explore all the options available to them, which they may not see at first.

As followers of Christ, our thinking should be wide enough to also include *God's perspective* on our situation. It's good to know, whatever we are going through, that God hasn't been caught off guard. He not only knows what's going on, he also knew it was *going* to happen. And he's not anxiously wringing his hands, wondering what he should do about it or how it's all going to turn out. God is still in control, whether we want to recognize it or not.

Second, we set aside our egos and agendas. When in pain, we tend to turn inward and focus on our feelings—a normal reaction. But as Christians, we also need to remember, like Job, that *it's not about us.* Paul writes, "You are not your own, you are bought at a price." (1 Cor. 6:19-20) In his second letter to the Corinthians, he adds, "And he died for all, that those who live should no longer live for themselves but for him who died for them and was raised again." (5:15) We *are* God's sons, but we're *also* his servants. It's all about him: his kingdom, his purposes! We are expendable.

Paul suffered more than most Christians ever will: lashings, imprisonment, stoning, an extremely painful "thorn in the flesh," etc. And yet, he saw his pain as the privilege of participating in the sufferings of Christ, declaring "our light and momentary troubles are achieving for us an eternal glory that far outweighs them all." And he delighted in his weakness "so that Christ's power may rest on me." (Rom. 8:17, 2 Cor. 4:17, 2 Cor 12:9) Paul knew he was expendable, and that God had a higher purpose for his life. And he has a purpose for us as well. The suffering we go through may well be a part of that purpose.

Third, we keep in mind that God is doing something good. When we are in the midst of pain and trouble, it's easy to begin to doubt, to feel like God has forgotten us, that nothing good can come from our suffering. In fact, Satan, who loves to attack us when we're down, will whisper those very things in our ears. None of it is true. Again, Paul says, "And we know that in *all things* God works for the *good* of those who love him . . . Who shall separate us from the love of Christ? . . . Trouble? . . . Hardship? . . . Persecution? . . . Famine? . . . Nakedness? . . . Danger? . . . Sword? No . . . *nothing* will be able to separate us from the love of God." (Rom. 8:28, 35-39, italics mine)

Because God loves us, his ultimate aim is to do us good. Think of Joseph, who could have gotten even with his brothers for the years of hardship they put him through. When they feared for their lives, Joseph said to them, "Don't be afraid. Am I in the place of God? You intended to harm me, but God intended it for good; to accomplish what is now being done, the saving of many lives." (Gen. 50:19-20) Or consider Russian author Aleksandr Solzhenitsyn's first words, on being released after eight years in a communist labor camp, "I bless you prison[.] I bless you for being in my life[,] for there, lying in rotting prison straw, I learned the object of life is not prosperity, as I had grown up believing, but the maturing of the soul." (source unknown) Those were hard times for both men, but ultimately, in God's plans, for good.

Fourth, we work past our anger and fears. Two common emotional responses to pain and trouble are anger and fear. This is understandable. In the middle of a crisis, fear grips us with questions like, "How will this turn out?" "Will we survive this illness, this financial setback, this family problem, this loss?" "How will it affect us, and the lives of those we love?" And fear sometimes triggers anger. We may get angry because this is happening to us, and usually not at a convenient time (is any time convenient for a crisis?). If someone is responsible for our pain, we direct our anger at them. If we are responsible, we get angry at ourselves. And if no one else is to blame, we can always be mad at God for allowing this to happen. Sometimes we take our anger out on those around us who don't deserve it, simply because they're easy targets.

A wise person has said, "We can't prevent thoughts, or their accompanying emotions, from popping into our heads, but we don't have to let them control us." And the way to prevent their control is to focus on our values and goals: What's most important here? And what am I trying to accomplish? As sons of God, the most important thing in our lives should be to love God and our neighbor. And our primary goal, like Jesus and Paul, should be to please him in everything we do. Recognize your feelings; don't stuff them (they'll only surface someplace else). Try to understand what's behind them, and then move toward your goals, doing what you need to do.

Fifth, we hold on to God in faith. As indicated earlier, it's easy to trust God when everything is going well, more difficult when things are bad. Again, our faith is being tested. Can we hang in there by hanging on to God? When Job was in the middle of his anguish and grief, he declared, "Though he (God) slay me, yet will I hope in him." (13:15) And immediately after Job lost everything, "he fell to the ground in worship." (1:20) Instead of turning *to* God, like Job, some people react by turning *against* God. They say, "If this is the way God treats his children, then I don't believe in him anymore." And that choice is one we must make: do we turn away from God in anger, or do we lean into him in trust? The Bible and history are full of stories about people who did both.

Consider two of Jesus disciples, who both failed their Lord. Judas betrayed Jesus; Peter denied knowing him. Both were filled with guilt and remorse. Judas turned away and hung himself. Peter turned back, found forgiveness and restoration, becoming a respected, spirit-filled leader of the early church. Those are our choices too.

Sixth, we grieve our losses. Every loss we experience involves grief. Whether we lose a loved one, our health, our home, our business, our job, or even a beloved pet, we are going to grieve those losses, some more than others. It's healthy to grieve, to get in touch with our feelings and express them, and to make the necessary changes involved with any loss. As men, many of us have a tendency in the face of grief to suck it up and try to be brave. We see it as a test of our manhood. Speaking from experience, I can tell you it doesn't work. Buried grief tends to resurrect itself in other forms, harmful to one's physical and mental health, not to mention relationships.

The best way is to simply embrace the pain, shed all the tears you need to shed, and work it through (with help if you need it). During a major loss, men also have a tendency to try to lose themselves in their jobs, hobbies, recreational activities, or through alcohol and drugs. This doesn't work either. Nor is the pain of losing a wife through death or divorce relieved by rushing into a new relationship (which many men also do). You need to give yourself time to heal, to feel like a whole person again. Then you'll be in a frame of mind to make wise, not impulsive, decisions about your future.

Seventh, we learn from our adversity. There are always things to be learned from painful situations. If we fail to learn them, we will not only miss taking something positive from the experience, but (depending on how we got there) we might end up needing to go through it all over again. Examples of things we learn are, we learn that God is faithful, if we trust him; we learn who our true friends are; we may also gain new friends or a fresh appreciation for life, for health, for our church or company, etc.

I personally learned several important lessons when my first wife died. I came to understand what the Bible means when it refers to the marriage bond as "two becoming one flesh." I felt like half a person. I learned humility, that I have no control over my life or my relationships. Anyone can be taken from me at any time. I should value and enjoy them, but not be too dependent on them while they are here. I also learned that the only relationship I can *always* count on is my relationship with God. He is the one who has been with me from the beginning, and who will be with me to the end . . . and beyond. I also learned to be grateful for the years that I had with my wife and for the many good things I *still had* in my life, in spite of my pain. Valuable lessons all.

Eighth, we develop an eternal perspective. A great example of this is the comment on Jesus' suffering in Hebrews 12:2: "Let us fix our eyes on Jesus, the author and perfecter of our faith, who for the joy set before him endured the cross, scorning its shame, and sat down at the right hand of the throne of God." In the midst of his suffering, Jesus looked ahead to being with his heavenly Father and the joy that was waiting for him there. And every martyr of the church since Christ has had that same perspective—they were willing to give up their lives *here*, because they knew something better was waiting for them *there*.

While few of us will ever have to lay down our lives for the sake of Christ, it's important for us to see the problems and pains of life as temporary. This world is not our final home. In the end, we leave it all behind. This can help us put things in proper perspective when we are tempted to place too much value on the things of this life. As Paul instructs us in Colossians 3:2-4, "Set your hearts on things above, not on earthly things. For you died, and your life is now hidden with

Christ in God. When Christ, who is your life, appears, then you also will appear with him in glory."

Questions for Personal Reflection or Group Discussion

1. Of the responses listed above, which would you find the most difficult to use during adversity?

2. Which have you *actually* used, and how did it benefit you?

3. Think about (or discuss) difficult times you have experienced, and how you wish you had responded differently.

Adversity and Decision-Making

In the midst of a deep trial, there are always decisions to be made. Some kind of response is necessary. Where nothing can be done to change a situation, like grieving a major loss, there are only two choices (as mentioned): do I trust God, or turn away from him? As Christian men, the answer should be obvious. Other situations, however, require more difficult choices for maintaining our integrity.

One of those is the pressure to give in to temptation. If you are battling an addiction, you sometimes have a hard, lonely struggle to resist. Under financial stress, there is the temptation to cheat or lie a little to dig our way out. Then there are the subtle temptations where people pressure us to do something appealing or that would make our lives easier. Examples that come to mind are, William Wilberforce, who probably could have been England's prime minister if he hadn't fought so hard to end slave trading; or Jackie Robinson, who took abuse resisting the efforts of racist ball players and fans to make him quit; or Dietrich Bonhoeffer, who could have stayed safely in the Unites States during World War II instead of returning to Germany and eventual execution. Christians all.

A second kind of pressure is the pressure to succeed. Christopher Lasch, in his book *Culture of Narcissism*, said, "Men would rather be envied for their material success than respected for their character." Even Christian men are not exempt from feeling this pressure as well.

But we can do better than that. As followers of Jesus, we must continually face two issues. The first is the issue of identity: *who am I?* Am I a man because I am successful by the world's standards and rewarded for it? Or do I measure my manhood by how well I reflect the character of Christ in all my dealings and relationships? The second is the issue of authority: *whose am I?* Do I ultimately belong to this world (a product of my culture), owned by public opinion, or by the evaluation of my boss or peers? Or am I a child of God, determined to please my heavenly Father (and real master) no matter what? Until we settle those issues, we will live an unstable, double-minded life that James warns us about. (James 1:8 & 4:8)

How Good Decisions Are Made

In their book, *Character, Choices and Community*, theology professors Russell Connors and Patrick McCormick demonstrate the triangular relationship between the three components listed in their title. Basically, it can be summarized like this:

Choices and Community: Our choices are influenced by the communities of which we are a part. We call this social pressure, and it affects us all, more than we'd like to admit. On the other hand, we also choose (to some extent) the communities to which we belong. We can't control the families or the neighborhoods we grew up in, but as adults, we do get to choose where we live, work, worship, socialize, etc.

And our choices also influence our communities; how much we decide to be involved and what we choose to do affects that particular group. If you're in a leadership position, your decisions will have even more impact. Think of how people who steal, or make promises they don't keep, influence the groups that they lead. And even good people can make bad choices that dramatically impact a community, such as a business owner who makes a deal costing people their jobs, or a minister who gets involved in an extramarital affair.

Character and Community: The character we bring to the communities of our choice also impacts them, either positively or negatively. Corruption in our government, business, or academic sectors are the result of individuals lacking moral character. And their behavior affects us all. Trust, as we indicated in an earlier chapter, is built on truth and honesty. Where those qualities are lacking, the impact is far-reaching.

Our character, in turn, is influenced by our community. Thus, belonging to the right groups is very important. What our parents told us is true: we *are* influenced by the company we keep. This is why we monitor our children's friends closely, and why we also need to be careful about the groups of which *we* are a part. As a university freshman, I was rushed by a fraternity, with a reputation as "the drinking fraternity." Not being my lifestyle, I declined. However, I was active in the InterVarsity group, which gave me both fellowship and a support system for my Christian values on a secular campus.

This is why church involvement and fellowship (especially in a small group) are so crucial for us in maintaining a Christ-like character. The Bible urges us to admonish, (Col. 3:16) encourage, (1 Thess. 5:11) and "spur one another on toward love and good deeds." (Heb. 10:24) We need to be "salt and light" for our non-Christian neighbors and coworkers as well, but to maintain integrity in our society, especially during times of adversity, we need those who will support and pray for us on a regular basis.

Character and Choices: Good people make good choices and bad people make bad decisions. Jesus said this pointedly in Matthew 7:17 where he declared, "A good tree cannot bear bad fruit, and a bad tree cannot bear good fruit," referring to the fruit of human behavior. On the other hand, as indicated above, our choices also contribute to our character. How does one acquire a reputation for honesty and integrity except by consistently doing the right thing in every situation? And even if we occasionally blow it (as we all do), and are honest enough to admit our mistakes, apologize, and make amends, it only enhances a good reputation.

I don't think non-believers expect Christians to be perfect. Yes, they notice when we act in a way that is inconsistent with what we say we believe. But they typically don't come down hard on us if we own up to our failures. It's hypocrisy they hate, and frankly it's what Jesus also hated about the Pharisees he encountered in his day.

Choices influence our character layer upon layer. Every time we make a good ethical decision, it builds that part of our moral character until it becomes a habit. Habits are developed and reinforced by repeated actions. Ultimately, our goal should be to develop such habits of honesty and integrity that we do the right thing automatically, without giving it much thought. If we have to constantly wrestle with every choice we make, it's clear we really haven't settled the primary issue of *who* we belong to and *how* we are going to live out our relationship with Christ.

Questions for Personal Reflection or Group Discussion

1. What temptations or pressures to you typically face when having to make decisions?

2. How much does your community (church or otherwise) influence your character and decisions?

3. Do you see any changes that should be made?

The Importance of Prayer

Assuming, then, that we have a community giving us positive reinforcement, and that we are developing Christ-like character, another key element in decision-making for the man of God is prayer. The examples in Scripture of leaders seeking God under pressure are numerous:

Moses faced trial after trial leading his people out of Egypt and through forty years of survival in the wilderness, continually having his leadership challenged. He turned to God in prayer over and over again.

Gideon prayed to God several times before going out to face the powerful Midianite army with his rag-tag group of men.

David fought the Philistines numerous times, spent years running from a mad king determined to destroy him, and faced many enemies when he was king, including his own son, who was determined to kill him. Many of his prayers are recorded for us in the book of Psalms.

Solomon, David's son, felt the weight of following his father as king at a young age, and earnestly sought God's help in the process.

Nehemiah prayed time and time again while facing brutal opposition as he worked to rebuild the walls of Jerusalem.

Paul prayed and worshipped in a Philippian jail, and during a storm on a boat that was facing certain shipwreck.

As in everything, our prime example is Jesus himself. It's clear that our Lord faced more than his share of adversity. He had opposition from Satan, the religious leaders, and even from his home town and members of his own family. He was betrayed by Judas, denied by Peter, and deserted by the rest of his disciples. Arrested, falsely accused, and wrongly convicted, he was sentenced to death by a judge who declared him innocent. Jesus was turned away by the people he came to help and save, brutally beaten by soldiers, and nailed naked to a cross in public view, mocked and jeered by a crowd. There, he died a most horrible death, carrying the sins of the world (including yours and mine), and feeling abandoned by his heavenly Father.

And how did Jesus handle all this? With prayer and grace. The gospels tell us that time and time again, he would get alone to pray, gaining direction for future ministry, (Mark 2:35-39) getting clarity on who should be in his inner circle of twelve, (Luke 6:12-16) retreating to a quiet place to rest and mourn, (Matt. 14:13, Mark 6:31, 46) or praying for little children who were brought to him. (Matt. 19:13-15) We have several examples in the Bible of prayers he actually said, but the most moving one was uttered in Gethsemane. There, before his anticipated arrest and crucifixion, Jesus wrestled in agonizing prayer with his Father. And there, on his knees, he submitted to carry out his Father's will, as excruciatingly painful as it was. Once it was settled, he moved forward with a sense of confidence and calm that rattled even Pilot, the Roman governor who tried and sentenced him.

It's important for us as well, especially on the horns of a dilemma or under the pull of a strong temptation, to have settled in our mind the direction we should take. The minute we begin to question our Christian values, or rationalize what we know in our gut to be right, we're on the downward path to a bad choice. Our feelings, especially desires, anger, and fears, are not a reliable basis for making good decisions. More often than not, they get us in trouble and leave us with regrets. Firm convictions, rooted in Scripture, reinforced by fellow believers, and practiced regularly, are the best way to build the kind of character that responds appropriately in the heat of spiritual conflict.

Remember the man with the drinking problem in a quandary about how he would handle the situation when everyone in his group would drink a lot after working all day? (Chapter 5) The end result was, all of the drinkers, including the boss, consumed a lot less alcohol that week, and my client stayed dry. This is a good illustration of the triangular effect discussed above. His courage (character) influenced his choice not to drink, which in turn influenced the group (community) that formally had influenced him. It also shows the importance of having a plan for maintaining one's integrity in situations where you know it will be challenged.

That being said, there are times when we encounter situations where the line between right and wrong isn't clearly defined. Those "gray areas" are especially challenging if we are determined to do the right thing. And under the pressure of time commitments and/or social pressure, we might be tempted to take the easy way out (i.e., the one that seems to benefit us most). So how do we handle such times? While there are no simple formulas for the many kinds of situations we face, there are some well thought-out, proven principles that can guide us.

Principles for Decision-Making

1. Make sure you see the whole picture. In times of crisis, as mentioned, there is a tendency for one's focus to be narrow, to only see one or maybe two solutions to the problem you are facing. You need to broaden your perspective. How well do you understand the situation? Do you have all the necessary information to make an informed and wise decision? And are you aware of all the options or alternatives available to you? These are good questions to ask yourself.

2. Seek out God's perspective. Start with the Scriptures, your own understanding of what God's word may say about the problem at hand, or with help from people (like your pastor) who may have a better grasp than you. Seek godly counsel from people who are spiritually mature, who know you well, and who will tell you what you *need* to hear, even if it's unpleasant. (Prov. 27:6) And of course, as discussed earlier, pray. Pray at the beginning, throughout the decision-making process, and even after a decision is reached. Fasting helps too. Lay the situation out before God, and ask him to make you sensitive to his voice. (Caution: It's too easy to confuse your voice for God's voice.) What he says will always be consistent with Scripture, and will be recognized as such by those whose godly counsel you seek. (Prov. 15:22)

3. Don't rush the decision. There will be situations where you won't have the luxury of much time to think about it. That's when you have to trust your character and godly instincts to guide you. But most major and/or complex problems allow you space to give them serious consideration. You may want to get away (like Jesus did) for a couple of days, while you pray and think it through. I have found that to be helpful with major decisions I've had to make.

4. Consider the long-term consequences. Under pressure, it's tempting to come up with a quick solution that provides temporary relief, but in the long run, it wouldn't be wise. Wise decisions are always forward looking. And be sure to keep in mind the impact your decision will have on others, not just yourself. If it's a business decision, what repercussions is it going to have for others in your organization or business community? On a personal level, how will your decision affect your wife, your children, your church, or your friends? Will it be good for everyone impacted by it? Check your motives. It's too easy to give in to our own desires and self-deception, as the Bible clearly points out. (Jer. 17:9)

5. Double-check your decision with others. After you have come to a decision, it's good to run it by several people, especially those who will be most affected by it. Encourage them to honestly critique it, rather than simply agree with you. They may see things you overlooked. This will also give you a chance to explain your decision (without getting defensive) and detect any flaws in your decision-making process. The more input and affirmation you can have, the more confidence you will gain in your own thinking and conclusion.

Even after reaching your decision, talk it over with God in prayer to make sure you are on the right track. This will provide an opportunity for him to steer you in the right direction, if you have missed something in the process. As in all things, God needs to have the final word.

Questions for Personal Reflection or Group Discussion

1. How much do you pray about the decisions you make regarding your work, your family, other activities or commitments?

2. Of the five principles for decision-making, which ones do you commonly use? Which ones should you use more often?

3. Have you ever taken a brief retreat when wrestling with an important decision? What was the outcome? If in a group, share your experience.

Going Further: Read 2 Corinthians 4:8-18, 11:23-30, and 12:1-10. How did Paul handle the adversity he went through while serving God? What were the keys to the positive attitude he maintained? How can you apply that to your life?

Bottom Line

Times of adversity are challenging for anyone, but in some ways, even more so for followers of Jesus. It's comforting to know God is in control, and that we have a spiritual family to comfort and support during the difficulties life offers. But, on the other hand, it may cause us to question our faith in the goodness of God, whom we serve. Plus, we can count on Satan attacking us at that point. He did it with Jesus, who taught us that we should expect it also. This is where faith is tested and grows. For when we trust God during those times, we find that he is indeed faithful, will provide whatever we need, and will bring us out on the other side the better for it.

For Further Reading

Os Guinness, *Character Counts: Leadership Qualities in Washington, Wilberforce, Lincoln, and Solzhenitsyn.* Baker Books, 1999.

Michael S. Horton, *A Place for Weakness: Preparing Yourself for Suffering.* Zondervan, 2006.

Timothy Keller, *Walking with God through Pain and Suffering.* Dutton, 2013.

John Maxwell, *Failing Forward: Turning Mistakes into Stepping Stones for Success.* Nelson, 2000.

Haddon W. Robinson, *Decision Making by the Book: How to Choose Wisely in an Age of Options.* Discovery House, 1998.

Richard E. Simmons III, *The True Measure of a Man: How Perceptions of Success, Achievement & Recognition Fail Men in Difficult Times.* Evergreen, 2011.

Joni Eareckson Tada & Steven Estes, *When God Weeps: Why Our Sufferings Matter to the Almighty.* Zondervan, 1997.

"As we grow older, we become like an old car—more and more repairs and replacements are necessary. We must look forward to the fine new machines (the latest Resurrection model) which are waiting for us, we hope, in the Divine garage!"

—*C. S. Lewis*

Chapter Twelve: Finishing with Integrity

Passing middle age and entering our senior years, we face a whole new set of challenges. Typically, the child-rearing days are behind us, our children are launched, and we are now, as they say, "empty-nesters." Ahead of us looms retirement (unless it has already arrived) and the prospect of our so-called "declining years," or to state it more positively, our *reclining years*.

In this latter stage of life, several questions and decisions call for our attention, to name just a few: How long should we keep working before retiring? Will we have enough income to retire? When and if we do retire, where shall we live? Can we afford to stay where we are, and do we want to? And how will we use the extra time we will have on our hands?

Then there are family issues to consider. If you or your spouse have aging parents still living, what will your responsibility be for their end-of-life care? If adult children need your help, it raises similar concerns. And what about the grandchildren (if you are fortunate enough to have them). How much involvement in their lives do you desire, or do they *require* from you?

In addition, we all face health concerns as we grow older. Realistically, none of us is going to live forever (at least in this life), and with advancing age comes a gradual slowing down and a collection of doctors treating various parts of our bodies. While in my seventies and in very good health, I still have, in addition to my dentist, an internist, a pediatrist, a dermatologist, and two eye doctors looking after my well-being.

Thoughts about the end of life cross our minds more often now than when we were younger. And if our parents have passed away, the age at which they died sticks in our brain as a marker to either shoot for or exceed. The fact is, regardless of our genes, there are no guarantees as to how long any of us can expect to be around. That's in God's hands. I know this isn't exactly a news flash, but it's amazing how little thought many people give to an event we will all face someday.

In this chapter, we will be discussing the above subjects and more, looking at them, as always, from a Christian perspective. And even if you're not close to retirement age yet, it's always good to look ahead and prepare as much as possible, for those years will creep up on you sooner than you expect.

Giving Up Our Livelihood

Probably the biggest challenge men face when approaching retirement age is letting go of something that has dominated most of our lives: our professions. In our North American culture, we tend to get most of our identity and self-esteem from our work. The first question we typically ask when meeting another man is, "What do you do (i.e., for a living)?" Then we quickly size them up, based on their answer. Not every culture is like this. In Australia, for instance, if you ask a man what he does, he will talk about his leisure activities, rather than his job. But in America, working is what we do best, which is why many of us have a problem with overwork.

But even if you are not a workaholic, the transition from businessman, teacher, engineer, doctor, pastor, etc. to virtually no professional identity at all is a major one. You suddenly have time on your hands you didn't have before, and the structure of your days and weeks is gone. It feels like you are on vacation, and that's what many men expect retirement to be: time to travel, play golf, visit kids and grandkids, or pursue a hobby, which looks really good after many years of working with all of its pressures.

But there are also fears connected with retirement. There's the natural fear of change (we're all more comfortable with what's familiar) and the aging process. Unless retiring quite young, we can't escape the idea that retirement is the period between our productive work years and the end of life. In reality, retirement is a mixed bag: not as ideal as you dreamed, nor (I'm told) as bad as you feared. Frankly, adult life is full of transitions, and this is just one more. As the writer of Ecclesiastes observed, "There is a time for everything, and a season for every activity under heaven." (3:1)

Keys to Successful Retirement

There appear to be three keys to a successful retirement transition. The first key is to know yourself and be aware of your feelings. At first, you will probably experience a period of grieving, especially if you enjoyed what you did for a living. Some men are glad to leave their vocation behind because it has become a source of too much stress, or even pain. But for those of us who truly enjoy our work, giving it up (for any number of reasons) will bring a sense of loss. So, don't be surprised if you initially feel some sadness, if for no other reason than having to leave important work relationships, along with the loss of your identity.

Self-awareness also means knowing what you like and dislike, knowing your dreams and interests, knowing what's important to you and what isn't. If you have a good sense of who you are and what you want to do, retirement will be that much easier.

Which brings us to the second key: preparation. Before you retire, it's good to have a plan. We tend to think mostly of retiring *from* our work. But those who have the most fulfilling retirements also retire *to* something they want to do. The retired people I know all talk about how busy they are, wondering how they were able to handle their home and family activities while still working. What most have done is fill that time with things they put off while working or with a whole list of projects their wives have been saving up for them to do.

The important thing is not to wait until you retire and then hope everything will work out. I have found that, if you don't plan your time and activities, someone else will plan them for you. Before you know it, you'll be providing daycare for your grandchildren while their parents work, doing handyman projects for your neighbors, and an expanded "honey do" list for your wife. That may not be what you want.

Some guys avoid that trap by spending the first couple months of retirement like a vacation: golfing, fishing, traveling . . . whatever. Then they discover that many of those things are too expensive on a fixed income. And to top it off, many come to the realization they are also somewhat bored. Recreation is more enjoyable when it's a welcome *change* from your normal routine, not as much when it *becomes* your normal routine. We'll expand on this later.

The third key to a successful retirement is attitude. One of the challenges of the retirement years is that our culture tends to look at aging in a negative way. Even in the media, with few exceptions, older people are looked at as falling apart: dependent and decrepit, unproductive, boring and monotonous, having no sex life, and less important in a culture that values youth. While the above may be true for some seniors, it doesn't have to be for you. If you have a positive attitude, can look at your retirement years as an adventure, and if you are open to experiencing new things and having new goals, it can be one of the best periods of your life.

A Biblical example of this attitude is Caleb. He was one of the twelve men sent to spy out the land of Canaan before Moses tried to lead Israel in to conquer it. Ten of the spies came back reporting that it would be impossible, but Caleb and Joshua were confident they could take the land with God's help. Unfortunately, the people listened to the ten and rebelled against Moses, refusing to go in. For the next forty years, they wandered in the wilderness until that generation died off. Then Joshua led the next generation in, and Caleb with him. What's noteworthy and admirable is that Caleb never lost his confidence in God, and at the age of eighty-five, he was just as ready to do battle and take what God had promised him forty years before. (Joshua 14:6-13) You've got to love his spirit!

Biblically, it's difficult to find passages that deal directly with the subject of retirement, because retirement was unheard of in ancient times. People pretty much worked until they were no longer able, and then were taken care of by their children until they died. One passage that *can* be directly related is Luke 12:16-21, where Jesus tells the parable of the rich farmer, who had such a big crop he figured it was time to sit back and enjoy life. He said to himself, "You have plenty of good things laid up for many years. Take life easy; eat, drink and be merry." (v. 19) Basically, he was living the American dream. But Jesus called him a fool, for two reasons: he didn't consider the untimeliness of his death, and he left God out of his equation.

Jesus told this parable as a warning against greed, and a reminder that life is more than the amount of stuff we own, (v. 15) but a secondary application could certainly be made concerning the *need to prepare* ourselves for the future, whatever it may hold, *and* especially to consider what God might expect of us for those retirement years. With that in mind, let's consider the kind of plans we need to make for this phase of our lives.

Questions for Personal Reflection or Group Discussion

1. How much thought have you given to your retirement? Does it make you feel excited or anxious? Why?

2. Have you done any planning in preparation? What specifically have you done?

3. How do you view the aging process? Some people are afraid of growing old. Does that describe you? If so, what are your fears?

Factors That Affect Adjusting to Retirement

There are several factors that will make your transition more or less difficult. First, is your retirement forced by age, health, etc., or is it your choice? Naturally, it is easier to handle if *you* made the decision versus having it made for you. Second, do you have adequate financial resources in pension and/or social security, savings, and investments? Third, how's your health? If you enjoy good health, are active and vital, you will be able to handle retirement much better.

Fourth, your marital status and strength are also factors. Single people take more of a social hit when they retire, and those with bad marriages now have to deal with each other 24/7! Fifth is your support system. It always helps having extended family and friends who know you well to help you through any major transition. **Sixth** is the extent of your involvement in your work. If your job consumed a lot of your time, energy, and thinking, your adjustment to retirement will be greater. This is especially true if you were a business owner, an executive, or a professional.

Finally, as mentioned previously, how much thought and planning have you done in preparation for retirement? Those who haven't given it much attention tend to struggle more than those who do. Those who adjust well to retirement have an accurate idea of what it will be like, through reading or talking to others who have retired. They accept the necessary changes as a challenge rather than a burden. They see the potential and possibilities of retirement in a positive way. And, *most* importantly, they stay focused on the present and future, rather than simply reliving "the good old days" of the past.

Physical Aspects of Retirement

The first thing to consider is your health. Former President Jimmy Carter has said, "It is better to be [seventy] years young than [forty] years old," and he is a walking example of someone whose activity level in retirement has been truly admirable. For many reasons, older people are living longer, more active lives than ever. While good genes are part of the reason, how well you take care of yourself after the age of sixty is essential. This starts with your attitude. If you see yourself as over the hill and not needing to look good in the workplace any longer, you'll probably go to pot. But if you want to look and feel your best, you'll need to work at it. This includes maintaining a healthy weight by eating right, getting regular, not-too-strenuous exercise, learning how to relax, getting plenty of sleep, and not taking on too many activities that will raise your stress level.

A second consideration is finances. You should have some idea of what your retirement income will be and if it is adequate for the lifestyle you desire. This is where good financial advisors can be worth their weight in gold. You really can't begin soon enough to start putting away for those later years. Many guys wait until they pay off mortgages and college loans before thinking about retirement. As you well know, social security is not enough! Here's an example of starting early that has been around for years:

Steve and Tom are two men the same age, fresh out of college, and into their careers. At age twenty-five, Steve decides to start saving for retirement, so he invests $100 per month in a retirement vehicle. His friend Tom thinks he's crazy to be worrying about retirement so soon. Ten years later, at age thirty-five, Tom has second thoughts, and begins to also invest $100 per month toward retirement, and does so until age sixty-five. Meanwhile, Steve stops investing at age thirty-five and just lets his initial ten years of savings grow. At age sixty-five, Tom's savings still won't catch up to Steve's, even though he has invested twenty years longer. That's the multiplying effect of investments. The sooner you start, the better returns you'll get.

Your finances also factor into the next consideration, which is retirement housing. Do you stay in the house where you raised your kids so you'll have room when they return home for holidays and vacations (if they live out of town)? Or do you downsize to a place that is adequate for you and your spouse, requiring less expense, yard work, and maintenance? And do you want one-level living for that time when climbing stairs will be too much effort? Maybe an over-fifty-five retirement community appeals to you.

Related is the issue of location. Many retired people living in the north move south for their senior years, where the weather is more appealing, especially during the winter months. Some folks from the northeast, where I live, are called "halfbacks." They moved to Florida, only to find the summer heat was too much to take. So, they settled in North Carolina, *halfway back* to where they originally started. Location is important, but there is more to be considered than just cheaper housing and nicer weather.

I believe that the most important thing in life, aside from our relationship with God, is our relationships with family and friends. When my parents retired, they moved from Michigan to Florida, far from their children and grandchildren, who lived in New Jersey, Virginia, and Michigan. My siblings and I felt they made a mistake, because it limited their contact with our families. As a result, my brothers, who are now retired, chose to stay near their kids and grandkids, and I will do the same. We all want our grandchildren to grow up knowing their grandparents. In addition, we would like to have our children close when we reach the age where they have to come to us.

In addition to family considerations, it's important to think about the cost of leaving long-term friendships and a church home that has been an important part of your life, especially if you are engaged in ministries in your local fellowship. There's something to be said for growing old with people who share a long history together.

Finally, there are the decisions related to transportation. How much traveling do you anticipate doing, how often, and how far? It's wise to get your big trips in while you are still young enough to enjoy them. And do you anticipate needing one car or two for your local jaunts? Some couples scale down to one car to save on expenses, but this decision will also largely be determined by your lifestyle and activities.

Retirement Occupation

Another big issue you will need to consider is, how to use the time, energy, and abilities you devoted to your vocation? You will have spent forty to sixty hours (or more) a week expending a lot of energy and developing many skills over thirty-five to forty years. Now what? Do you just set that aside and do nothing? While most men find that appealing at first, after a while the thrill is gone. With the term "retirement occupation," I mean more than simply a job. An occupation is whatever *occupies* your time, energy, and interest. Here are some of the possible options:

1. Work part-time at your old profession, or do consulting in your field.

2. Train for a new profession before or after retirement. I have a friend who was a business manager and realized his company was going to be bought out. So, he went back to school to take courses in non-profit management. When he got his "golden parachute," he went to work for a Christian organization, using the skills he had honed in business over those many years. He's having the time of his life.

3. Use your leadership skills to serve on a board, run for office, or head up a charitable organization.

4. Use your talents to work as a volunteer in a service organization. Whether it's organizing, training, marketing, or whatever, many organizations can use the talents you have.

5. Use your spiritual gifts for an expanded ministry in your church. A businessman who was an elder in our church transferred to another state. He eventually took an early retirement and returned to New Jersey and our congregation, using his organizational and spiritual gifts to get a thriving men's ministry going.

6. Pursue learning opportunities, adventures, or new experiences. You may want to finish your degree, earn another one, audit courses just for personal enrichment, or study on your own. Or maybe you'd like to visit new places, take up a sport or hobby, join a singing group—whatever piques your interest.

7. Pursue activities for self-expression or personal development. You could take up painting, sculpting, or woodworking; writing poetry or short stories; learning to play an instrument; or to speak a foreign language. The options are endless.

8. Use your time for more social activities with family and friends.

9. Perhaps you would prefer recreational activities like golf, tennis, fishing, etc. I have an acquaintance who loves salt water fishing. He had a place at the Jersey shore and a boat that he took chartered groups out on weekends after he got his captain's license. On retirement from his school administrator's position, he moved to the shore and continued to charter on a more regular basis.

The point is this: your retirement will be much more enjoyable and vital if you have some stimulation in your life. There's a difference between the stimulation you had at work, where *others* were making demands on you, and the stimulation *you choose*, doing what *you* enjoy.

Besides social stimulation, three others kinds are helpful. The first is exercise, where you can even challenge yourself physically. You can be in shape comparable to men twenty years younger. Research with nursing home residents has shown that getting in shape actually enabled residents using walkers not need them anymore.

The second kind of stimulation is intellectual. As we age, our brains slow down some and our retrieval isn't as fast. The good news is that you can still learn new things, challenge your brain, and stay mentally sharp.

Finally, there is creative stimulation. Anytime you can get your creative juices flowing, it's good for you. It breaks you out of your rut and keeps you vitalized. I love the following quote by Garrison Keillor, best known for his program on Public Radio called, "The Prairie Home Companion": "You're supposed to get reckless as you grow older. That way you keep   saying 'yes' to life. And perhaps saying 'yes,' not playing it safe, is the real point to life."

All of the above require motivation. It's easy to get fat and lazy when we retire and demands aren't being made on our time and energy. But a successful retirement requires some thoughtful planning and execution. Whatever you choose, the following criteria should be used: It should be interesting—life is too short to waste your time on things that don't interest you. It should be worthwhile—stimulating, challenging, and making a contribution. And, above all else, it should be honoring to God. Retiring from a job does *not* mean retiring spiritually. More on that later.

Questions for Personal Reflection or Group Discussion

1. How's your health? Are you taking good care of your body? What areas could use improvement?

2. Have you put aside savings for retirement? Do you have a good idea of the amount you'll need?

3. Have you and your wife talked about where you'll live, and how big/small a house you'll need when you (both?) retire?

4. Do you have interesting things you want to do after you leave your work? What are they? Do you need to prepare for them now?

Your Marriage

There are various retirement combinations of which you should be aware. If you are retiring and your wife has been a full-time wife and mother, there are certain adjustments you will face. The home has been her domain; you will be invading her turf and messing with her routine. Some women complain that their retired husbands follow them around all day, trying to organize their work for them. On the other hand, your wife may expect you to *do more* around the house now that you "have nothing to do." This points to the previously discussed need for a game plan.

Another combination that is becoming more frequent is the still-working husband and the retiring career wife. When both of you were working, responsibilities at home were (hopefully) divided between you. Now that she's retired, you might assume that she is going to do it all. Of course, she may have other ideas. This will need to be negotiated.

A third possible scenario is if *both* you and your wife are retiring from your careers. Previously having very little quality time together (between jobs and household chores), you now have *a lot* of time together, maybe for the first time in your married life. This too can put a strain on the marriage, and will require working out how much time you want to spend together and what you will do apart.

The final combination is if you are retiring and your wife continues to work at her career. This is also happening more these days and seems to be the hardest of all the adjustments to make. If you have been comfortable being the primary breadwinner (which is more often the case), it may be difficult for you to accept this role reversal and become a full-time "house husband."

Someone has identified the four Ts of marital adjustment during retirement: tasks, turf, time, and temperament. Under "tasks," you will have to work out who's going to do what, along with when and how things are to be done. With "turf," it comes down to negotiating a new routine and sharing space you didn't have to share before. "Time" is another area of adjustment. How do you handle each partner's social needs, and the balance between doing things together and apart? Finally, there is "temperament." If one of you is an extravert, needing more social interaction, while the other is more of an introvert, requiring more time to him or herself, you'll need to iron that out. Plus, work has provided a buffer from having to deal with certain of each other's personality traits, and now that's gone. You may be an organizer who is now trying to organize your wife, or she may be more of a talker than you, which was easier to handle when you could "escape" to your job.

Sex

Yes, there is sexual activity in the retirement years, regardless of what your adult children may think. You'll have more time and freedom: no work-related schedules, stress, or tiredness; no children around; and the ability to act when you're in the mood. Research shows that 70 percent of couples over sixty have sex at least once a week. The key is to stay in shape. It's all about blood getting to the right places. If your circulation is good, you can have a fulfilling sex life into your later years. You either "use it or lose it."

There are many benefits to this. It keeps a spark in your marriage, helps relieve anxiety and stress, and makes you feel good about yourself. You will need to anticipate certain changes as you age. Owing to hormonal shifts, you may require direct stimulation, and your wife some artificial lubrication. Thus, it may take longer to reach an orgasm, but that only extends the pleasure. Or neither of you may feel a need to reach an orgasm and just enjoy the closeness and affection more than the passion. Of course, as always with things sexual, the nature of your relationship, past experiences, and the depth of intimacy you enjoy at other levels will be large factors in determining the satisfaction derived in this area (see Chapter Five).

Family

When it comes to dealing with adult children and grandchildren, you will also need to do some planning. How close or distant do you want live? If you choose to live at more of a distance, they may expect you to visit them rather than coming your way. They will still have work and child-rearing responsibilities. On the other hand, if you live nearby, they may expect your assistance with babysitting and home chores, etc.

How much time you spend with the grandkids may be another issue you have to negotiate, not only with your children, but with your wife, if her desires are different than yours. Living close by will also mean expected attendance at various activities your grandchildren are involved in: sports, concerts, recitals, etc., which is great, depending on your energy and interests. It's good to keep in mind that grandparents have a tremendous influence in the lives of children, second only to their parents. You have the opportunity to impact another generation for Christ. Take advantage of it.

Here are some basic principles to keep in mind in this area: Set your priorities. Make clear to your family when and how much you will be available, barring special needs, emergencies, etc. As a rule, it's good to wait until your kids, parents, or whoever ask for help. If you jump in quickly and volunteer, they may think you have too much time on your hands and take advantage of your good nature. Like with any rule, there are, of course, exceptions.

Retirement is also a good time to take care of any unresolved issues you may have with your children, siblings, or friends, before either you or they die. This is also a good time to let people know, in various ways, how much they have meant to you. Too many things go unspoken between people, leaving many regrets after someone has passed.

Friends

Unlike family, you can choose your friends, and friendship is important. Friends meet our need for social interaction, sharing, support, practical assistance, belonging, and just plain fun. Friends run the gamut, from casual to very close. Women build their friendships around disclosure and emotional support. They tend to have more friends and more depth to their friendships. As men, we tend to have friends we can do things with and for discussing intellectual issues. On a personal level, men often view their wife as their best friend.

A woman's friendships will generally continue into retirement. Your friends at work will be left behind, and you'll need to make new ones. You may try to keep in contact with your work buddies, but it's not the same; you're not part of the inner circle anymore. That's why it's good to be developing friendships outside of work, for which (as mentioned in Chapter One) you'll need to be more intentional. Also, if your wife is socially more active, you may feel neglected when she maintains her usual social schedule, instead of paying more attention to you.

Questions for Personal Reflection or Group Discussion

1. Think about what life will be like with your wife when you, or both of you, are retired. Can you see areas of major adjustment and/or negotiation?

2. Do you look forward to those years, or feel that your marriage may need a tune-up before then?

3. Have you thought about the demands or expectations that your children or extended family might put on you?

4. Have you developed the kind of friendships that can enhance those years for you? Work on developing them now, if they are lacking.

Spiritual Aspects of Retirement

As followers of Christ, we need to integrate our faith into our retirement years as well as our working and child-rearing ones. Because of the radical changes in our time use and routines, we may become lax when it comes to our spiritual lives and activities. There are a number of things to consider as you deal with this important part of life.

A Christian Perspective

Michael Cassidy has said, "If we do not live under the aspect of eternity, we will be corrupted into thinking that earth is our home." As Christians, we are naturally forward-looking, or at least we *should* be. This is true, because we know this world is *not* our final home. But we also live with a sense of purpose: living lives of service to God here, right to the end.

Along with looking forward, retirement is a time to reflect back on our life as well. With that reflection, there will probably be regrets for past failures, opportunities missed, or not reaching our full potential. The good news is that God's grace covers that. We can forgive ourselves, because we have been forgiven. On the positive side, it's a time to reflect, as well, on the many blessings we have received from God and others during our life, and a time to give thanks, not only to God but also to people who have blessed us, perhaps with a note or letter.

As we look to the future, there are certain things we wonder about: What will it be like? Will we retain our health? How many years will we have left? How will we die? Those thoughts can be anxious ones, but here again, our Christian faith should give us perspective. We know that whatever the future holds, the same God, who has been a constant companion in our lives by his holy spirit, will be there then, and we can trust him to handle every situation that comes our way.

What we really need is a new vision for whatever time we may have left, whether it's five years or thirty-five. We should see these as "bonus years" to serve God, and they can be the most exciting time of our lives. Think of people you know, or have read about, who have accomplished a great deal later in life.

From Work Ethic to Worth Ethic

In the world of our work, we are measured by our performance: what we do and how well we do it. As mentioned, so much of our self-esteem and social status tends to come through our jobs. Men often feel useless and worthless when they retire. We need to find a better way to look at ourselves. A lot of men with questionable morals and values have had so-called "successful" professional careers.

It's far better to see ourselves as God sees us. He doesn't measure us by our performance. Certainly, we all want to hear, "Well done, good and faithful servant," but ultimately, God is far more interested in *who we are* than in *what we do*. He's not at all impressed by our talents and skills. After all, he's the one who gave them to us! He's far more interested in *our character*. His goal is to make us like Christ. Does he desire our service? Of course. But the effectiveness of our service is directly related to our maturity and dependence on him. Your worth to God is far more than what you do or have done. And, as Christians, *he* is our primary source of identity. You may lose your vocational identity when you retire, but your identity as a child of God remains intact.

Deepening our Relationship with God

Our Lord wants us to be good stewards of the resources he gives us, including our time. In retirement, you'll have more time to work on your relationship with God as well as to serve him. I once heard Charles Swindoll comment on his colleagues in the ministry who had retired, "Where in the Bible is it written that we get to retire from serving God?" The answer, of course, is, "It's not!" And he hasn't.

One of the benefits of the retirement years is being able to spend more time on your devotional life. Most men, including pastors, find that the demands of work often crowd out the kind of quality time they would like to have with the Lord. This doesn't come automatically, even if you do have more time. Having the desire and establishing of a new set of priorities is necessary, so it's good to work on cultivating that habit now.

Retirement will also afford you more time for spiritual reflection—a lost art in our society. Reflecting on Scriptures, rather than simply reading them, will take your understanding to new depths. You can also spend time really taking in God's creation, something that often happens only when we're on vacation, if then. Listening to God's voice and thinking about his goodness will also feed your soul.

Then too, your retirement years will be the final stage of life, where you will strive to complete what the Lord has been trying to make you all along—a mature child of God, reflecting the character of his Divine Son. It's never too late to grow up spiritually, as the

Scriptures encourage us to do. (Eph. 4:15, 1 Pet. 2:2) C. S. Lewis has commented: "Yes, autumn is really the best of all seasons; and I'm not sure that old age isn't the best part of life. But, of course, like autumn, it doesn't last."

Finding New Avenues of Service for God

The Bible talks a lot about stewardship, using the resources we have been blessed with to serve God and others. In our later years, we may not have the same energy and financial resources as when we were younger, but the energy we do have can be expended in service rather than work. In addition, our talents are more fully developed and our wisdom is greater (hopefully) than in earlier years. All of this can be used for God's kingdom.

For example, some retired physicians use their medical skills in free clinics or on short-term mission trips, retired contractors ply their building skills with Habitat for Humanity, businessmen serve as administrators for churches, Christian schools, and mission organizations. I have a friend who was forced, because of age, to retire from his career as a commercial airline pilot. He spent the next several years working in various parts of the world, doing three-month stints relieving pilots with Missionary Aviation Fellowship. The possibilities are only limited by your willingness and imagination.

During your working years, the responsibilities of your vocation may be so consuming that you haven't given much time or thought to discovering and using your spiritual gifts. In retirement, you can follow your interests, or a burden God has placed on your heart, and find a whole new avenue of service. Don't volunteer for a job in your church simply because there is a need. Be sure that you have an interest in, are gifted for, and have prayed about the situation. Serving in a place that doesn't fit you will leave you both unfulfilled and not very effective.

This is not dissimilar to employees you may have let go because they were ill suited to their particular task.

You may also sense God leading you to start a particular kind of ministry that you've never attempted before. Friends of mine tragically lost their only child in an accident. After working through their grief, they began to think about others who may have had similar losses. By reading the local obituaries, they would reach out in compassionate friendship to other parents in their situation. This was the start of a ministry that now every week reaches over hundred people who have experienced all kinds of losses, including suicides and drug overdoses. Sometimes all we need to do is look around and ask ourselves, "Where are the needs? Who is hurting? How can I help?"

Another thing you can do with the added time available in retirement is to cultivate friendships with neighbors or others you meet, pursuing common interests or activities. God can use those relationships to draw people to himself through you. A retired pastor friend was looking for a new ministry. He liked to stay in shape at a local gym playing racket ball. As he's gotten to know some of the guys he plays with, he has discovered they have spiritual questions and needs they are willing to talk about with him. Rick has discovered his new "congregation."

Be careful that you don't form friendships *just* for purposes of evangelism. You need to be a friend, regardless of how responsive they may or may not be to the gospel. Besides, you don't know God's timetable in any person's life and the role he may be having you play. Your job is just to reach out to them in love.

Preparing for Eternity

Retirement, as we have seen, involves far more than just sitting around, waiting to die. However, we *are* going to die, and we need to give this reality some thought and prepare for this final step. God has a place ready for us. (John 14:2-3) He's waiting to meet us and transform us. And we will share in the inheritance of Christ. (Rom. 8:17) It's good to reflect on those truths and allow them to sink deep into our thinking.

Besides the people we love, we'll all be leaving a lot of "stuff" behind when we die, things that have accumulated over the years. Some of it we have been saving for our children, most of which, realistically, they'll probably not keep. It's now a disposable society. The years of retirement are a good time to trim down and give things away, making it easier on those we leave behind. You may not want to wait until retirement, especially if you are going to "downsize" as part of your plan. You'll also find that there is a freedom that comes with living leaner.

Your final act of stewardship will be your will. You may not want to leave it all to your children or other relatives. Designating part of it for the work of God's kingdom is something that many people do. In some cases, where their children are financially well fixed, they may leave most or virtually all of it to their church or mission work. That's certainly something to be considered.

Finally, it's good to give some thought to what you will leave behind as a spiritual legacy. Are there things you want to share with your children or grandchildren about your life with God, and what you have learned during your time here on earth? Maybe you'll want to write lengthy letters or a journal or even a book to be left behind (which is something I'm hoping to do). Or maybe you want to designate some part of your estate to provide an ongoing spiritual lesson after you are gone. I have a retired friend whom God has blessed financially to the point where he has been able to set up a foundation to provide funds for various ministries to children. His daughter and son administer this foundation with him and will run it after he is gone—a legacy for them to continue, and a blessing to those on the receiving end.

Questions for Personal Reflection or Group Discussion

1. Are there areas of your devotional life with God you would like to focus on during a more relaxed schedule in retirement?

2. What areas of service to the church or God's kingdom would you like to explore/be involved in?

3. What legacy, especially spiritually, would you like to leave for your children and grandchildren? What are you doing now to build that legacy?

Going Further: Read Ecclesiastes 12:1-8, Psalm 78:1-7, Psalm 90:1-12, and Luke 12:13-21. Think about (or discuss) the principles found in these passages concerning the last years of life. How can you apply them to your life, and what difference do you think it would make if you took them seriously?

Bottom Line

Whether you are close to retirement or not, it's good to keep in mind that the senior years are just another phase of life, with its own unique set of challenges and adjustments. It can be the best one of your life, especially if you anticipate and plan well. But it *is* the last phase, and one that normally includes a decline in energy and health as we move toward the end. For me, personally, I want to be productive, in the best sense of that word, right up to the end. I want to finish well, to make sure that I am not leaving any loose ends behind for my children to clean up. And I want to leave behind a legacy of love and service to God, and to those he has brought into my life over the years. I want people to say about me when I'm gone, "He lived a life of Christian integrity. He was who he appeared to be." But most of all, I want them to be able to say, "He loved his Lord, his family, and his friends." I pray that for you as well.

For Further Reading

Joshua Becker, *The More of Less*. WaterBrook Press, 2016.

Ted W. Engstrom, *The Most Important Thing a Man Needs to Know About the Rest of His Life*. Revell, 1981.

Harold G. Koenig, *Purpose and Power in Retirement*. Templeton Foundation Press, 2002.

Greg McKeown, *Essentialism: The Disciplined Pursuit of Less*. Currency Books, 2014.

J. I. Packer, *Finishing Our Course with Joy*. Crossway, 2014.

Dwight H. Small, *When Christians Retire*. Beacon Hill Press, 2000.

Sara Yogev, *For Better or for Worse . . . But Not for Lunch*. McGraw-Hill, 2002.